# KHAKI MISCHIEF

*CLASSIC CRIME SERIES*

# KHAKI MISCHIEF
## The Agra Murder Case

*Molly Whittington-Egan*

*SOUVENIR PRESS*

For my mother and my husband

First published 1990 by Souvenir Press Ltd,
43 Great Russell Street, London WCIB 3PA
and simultaneously in Canada

ISBN 0 285 62988 3

Photoset, printed and bound
in Great Britain by
WBC Ltd, Bridgend, Mid Glamorgan

# Acknowledgements

My gratitude to the family of the late Henry Hope, who have helped and encouraged me by the gift of the results of their research into their background, and by their interest and enthusiasm.

My gratitude to Jonathan Goodman, whose generous gift of an introduction to that family, after they had contacted him on reading his *Posts-Mortem*, so greatly enriched my own work.

Special thanks to Mary Neilson, Brigadier R. B. Scott, D.S.O., and David Ward, for conversations about British India.

I am indebted also to
Hilary Bailey;
I. A. Baxter, India Office Records, The British Library;
Annabel Carey;
Ealing Public Library, Mattock Lane;
The Editor, *Standard Twentieth Century Dictionary: Urdu into English*;
J. H. H. Gaute;
Paul Guy, British Library Document Supply Centre;
Malvern Library;
Jerry Mullaney, for photographic expertise;
Rajkeeya Public Library, Allahabad;
Records Branch, Department of Social Security, Newcastle;
Reverend Mother, Loreto House, Calcutta;
John Sinkins, Wildy's, Lincoln's Inn;
Alison West, Suffolk Record Office;
Christian Wright, National Library of Scotland;
D. Wyn Evans, The University Library, Exeter;

and to my husband, Richard Whittington-Egan, *éminence grise* of matters criminous, whose experience, and library, were always at my disposal.

# Contents

# List of Illustrations

# Chapter One

# The Pilot's Daughter

It was a hot evening in Agra, and the little girl, aged nine, lay awake in the sweltering bungalow at 9 Metcalfe Road. Outside, in the compound, undergrowth rustled and shapes slithered, while the fever-bird called in a rising crescendo, 'Are you ill? Are you ill? Brain fever! *Brain fever!*'

Kathleen was suspicious, and she was watching. Her father had been sick—again—and had gone to bed. Through the open doorway of her bedroom, she had an oblique, partial view of the dining-room. Two grown-up figures were passing back and forth: her mother and her mother's friend, a doctor.

She saw the doctor's hand take a red box from a shelf. Then—let Kathleen speak; her voice is small and innocent, but precise, deadly—'He opened the box and brought out a glass needle and opened a paper which he also took from the shelf. He poured out some white powder in a wine-glass and poured some water in it. He put the needle into the glass and then pulled it up.'

Next—and the witness who had been underestimated, discounted, could still see through the doorway—'He took the glass needle into my father's room, and poked it into his heart and his arm and his shoulder. I thought it was a very cruel thing to do.'

The doctor went back into the dining-room, and her father was left alone. After about a minute, he began to make a funny, gargling noise.

The little girl stole out of bed in her long, white nightdress and stood beside her father as he lay on his back, gargling, until he was quiet. But she did not know death when she saw it, even though she had lived all her short life in India, where death lurks in varied guise around any corner.

9

Back to her bed she crept, and kept watch. Presently, the doctor returned to the stilled man and felt his hand. It was only then, when he said one word—'*Gone*'—that Kathleen understood. There was no sound of crying from her mother.

\* \*

Agra\* was a black time, but once—before Agra, before the doctor came—there had been bright, white days in Meerut, where, in 1908, when the drama begins, Edward and Augusta Fullam lived with their three children.

Meerut was a museum of bad memories for the British. Lest they should forget the Indian Mutiny of 1857, which began there during Sunday morning service, certain bungalows bore a plaque inscribed with the chilling message that 'Here Mrs Smith-Smith and her four children were killed and thrown down a well.'† Not surprisingly, some of these marked bungalows were reputed to be haunted. Sensitive English dogs howled and shunned them.

Buried not too deeply in the collective memory lay the nice detail that the Mrs Smith-Smiths had been ravished with batons of burning tow. On Sunday mornings, in weekly commemoration of a time of fatal British unpreparedness, troops filed into church equipped with their sidearms and rifles, and deposited them into special slots designed for that purpose.

None of these associations disturbed the Fullams, snug in their spacious bungalow at 33 Warwick Row. Augusta loved Meerut. Every day, Edward cycled off to his office and she was deliciously free to indulge in the trivial pursuits of the minor memsahib who was not burdened with a social conscience.

Augusta ran her household in the style that was expected of her. The entire story that follows is set against the listening, muttering background of white-robed native servants. Somehow, the bashful British managed to cope with the lack of privacy—often, as Mrs Montgomery in J. R. Ackerley's *Hindoo Holiday* would advise, by pretending that the Indians did not exist.

\* Pronounced Áfgră.
† *Plain Tales from the Raj*, Charles Allen (André Deutsch, 1975).

Shuffling, bare-footed figures—far too many of them—whisked round corners unexpectedly and were fond of crouching on the back verandah, within hearing of the matrimonial bed. In some homes, during the dreaded Hot Weather, the man who pulled the string of the punkah fan suspended over the bed was stationed actually inside the bedroom.

Each separate bungalow, exposed and baking in its own compound, was as open as a film-set. The servants were linked by threads in the web of caste and kin to the shadow households of servants which backed up all the other British establishments. It was impossible to opt out of the grapevine of gossip, and anyone who chose to behave in a manner that would cause comment was obliged to balance the value of the indulgence against the consequences of its broadcasting.

The modest Fullam *ménage*, an unpretentious set-up, as befitted their social position, was quite imposing enough: bearer, cook, *ayah* for the children, gardener, water-carrier, part-time washerman, and lowly sweeper, who saw to the thunder-box. A *syce* tended the one horse kept to draw the light *fitton*, or phaeton, which was Augusta's main form of transport. She was no rider; her heritage was far from that of the full-blown memsahib who rode to hounds, side-saddle, on jackal hunts, or set off on jungle safari. Mick was the family dog. It was the done thing to keep an English dog, especially a smooth-coated fox-terrier or a bull-terrier, even though the most cherished pet was very likely to catch rabies from some starved pye-dog.

India was not a bad way of life, as long as your health lasted. Wife and children of some classes* could be packed off to the Hills for the worst of the Hot Weather, and the husband, if he were so placed, could join them for periods of leave.

But outside the whitewashed walls of the compound, the wild Plains were waiting to invade the watered lawns and the tubs of nostalgic country-garden flowers. Unless the vegetation was constantly cut back, deadly snakes, unseen, would boldly scale the verandah, lurk under rugs and cushions, and pop up through bathroom outlets.

* A point newly made by Eugenie Fraser in *A Home by the Hooghly: A Jute Wallah's Wife* (Mainstream Publishing, 1989).

The mysterious, pungent, jangling, scheming bazaar was never far away. *Thuggee* was over, but dacoits abounded. Death lay in a sunbeam, in a pink sweetmeat—or in a woman's heart.

\* \* \*

Augusta Fairfield Fullam was probably—not certainly—of pure British descent. Sir Cecil Walsh, an Appeal Court Judge of India, the author of the only previous volume on this case, said without qualification that she was 'English'—and he was placed to be particularly sensitive to nuances of class and race. 'She was superior,' he wrote, 'probably in birth, certainly in education and intellect, to the other three actors in this drama.'

However, the author has had sight of a confidential document which describes her as 'Anglo-Indian'. The matter is not straightforward. Before 1900, those of mixed blood in India were called 'Eurasians', and the British were 'Anglo-Indians'. The Eurasians disliked the distinction, and in 1900 it was officially decreed that, thenceforth, Eurasians were to be termed Anglo-Indians. The British of the old school, in their turn, resented this change, and carried on calling themselves 'Anglo-Indian'. The confusion thus caused persists to this day.

The high official who, some years after 1900, completed the form, himself British, might have automatically scrawled in 'Anglo-Indian' without checking the small print, which is actually extremely specific, viz: 'Nationality (i.e., European, Anglo-Indian, Indian, etc. If European, state special country).' There is no doubt that Augusta's father, Leonard Peirson Goodwyn, was English. Born in Suffolk, he was baptised on 4th November, 1836, son of Edmund Goodwyn, gentleman farmer, later High Constable, of Framlingham. Edmund and his wife, Eliza, baptised thirteen other children between the years 1833 and 1851. Leonard was third in line. Perhaps the first-born son, Edmund, was the ultimate heir to the yeoman land. Leonard looked to the Empire for his future. Confirmation of his Englishness—if confirmation were needed—comes from the fact that he became a member of the Bengal Pilot Service, and, at the time when he joined, the pilots were recruited in England. The service was not open to Indians until the 1930s.

Certainly, Augusta's family on both sides had roots in India. On her father's side there was a firm military tradition of commisioned officers in modest regiments.* She was born Augusta Fairfield Goodwyn, on 23rd June, 1875, in Calcutta, and baptised at the Methodist Episcopal Church there on August 12th.

Her mother, Mary Augusta, born in 1840, daughter of William Cox, was married twice. Firstly, in 1855, she married Joseph Burridge, a dealer in musical instruments, and they had one daughter, Catherine Jane, Augusta's half-sister, born in Rangoon on 5th October, 1857. Secondly, after she was widowed, Mary Augusta married Leonard Goodwyn, on 11th September, 1867, at St Thomas Church, Howrah, a large city opposite Calcutta. They had two daughters: Augusta and her younger sister, Dora Olive, born on 26th March, 1879.

Augusta was not out of the top drawer. Indeed, Walsh remarked that her tendency to call herself a 'young lady' was a give-away. When she referred to Edward Fullam as her 'hubby', she was not joking.

A fierce pecking-order, or caste-system, of British devising, ruled the ranks of the Raj. British families permanently domiciled, as opposed to posted, in India, were at the bottom of the pile. At the apex was the élite Indian Civil Service, closely followed by the Military. To be born and educated in India was to be 'country-born' and 'country-bred', and the fact that the native ponies were also so termed was no coincidence.

There were, however, ambiguities of class, and Augusta's father, by the mere nature of his career in the Bengal Pilot Service, had condemned his daughters, from birth, to a position in life that was precarious and lacked precise social definition. The river-pilots were in a box of their own, because they were highly respected for their life-saving skills, and known to be paid accordingly. If they wished, they could live in

---

* Thus, Alfred George Goodwyn, Lieutenant of the Bengal Engineers, on 11th April, 1844, at Simla, married Maria Anne Rofs. His brother, Henry William Goodwyn, Captain of Her Majesty's 75th Foot, on 12th March, 1850, at Umballa, in the Punjab, married Frances Dora Henderson Naylor. These may have been Augusta's great-uncles.

considerable style. That helped.

Their varied backgrounds also fudged the issue. Some were salty old sea-dogs, such as J. B. P. Le Patourel, from Jersey, 'very broad and sturdy and bull-necked, with a blustering and rapid manner of speaking',* but a number of unexpected individuals were attracted to the adventure, and perhaps the autonomy, of the job. One, A. W. Phipson, had been a missionary, and another, in the twentieth century, afterwards became a successful publisher.

They were all characters; brave, eccentric, nonconformist. It used to be said of them that one third went mad, one third ended up as alcoholics, and one third got away with it. At his best, the pilot was a powerful and impressive figure, endowed with the authority of being indispensable. A journalist who had made the risky passage down the River Hooghly in a cargo-steamer contributed a grateful sketch, entitled 'The Bengal Pilot', to the *Pall Mall Gazette* of 19th September, 1911:

> Ships leaving Calcutta anchor off Garden Reach to await the tide. It is here that the pilot arrives on board. Let it be carefully noted that he *arrives*—he does not come, he is too great a man. He arrives in State, accompanied by his leadsman and his servant. For the Bengal Pilot Service is different from other services. Its senior members—Branch Pilots they are called—earn from two to three thousand rupees a month (the latter when trade is good and ships are plentiful), and a man who earns the salary which a civilian does not attain until he becomes a Commissioner of Division is entitled to much respect. He demands this respect, and extracts it from everybody indiscriminately....
>
> [He was arrayed in] all the glory of a beautifully starched white suit, and a resplendently varnished solar topee of imposing dimensions. In appearance he was tall and lanky (wire all through), with a clean-shaven, clear-cut, tanned face, that would have become a naval officer and at once conveyed the impression that its owner was a strong man. He gave his orders in a curt, quiet manner,

---

* *On the Hooghly*, M. H. Beattie (P. Allan, 1935).

and in five minutes we were under way.

He stood under the awning over the bridge with a telescope at his eye, watching intently the various signals which were placed along the banks of the Hooghly to intimate the different depths of water obtaining in the stream. Ever and anon, on the sultry breeze, the voice of his leadsman rose and fell: 'By the mark five.' 'And a half four.' 'By the mark four,' and so on. Ever and anon he rasped out some curt order, which the subservient mate of the watch passed on to the man at the wheel; round went the spokes with many creaks and groans, and the snub nose of the old *Amaryllis* swung off two or three points on to another course.

Gradually, as the day wore on we slipped down the muddy Hooghly, and gradually and by degrees the colour of the flowing waters changed from a dirty, evil-looking brown, to a more refreshing green, showing that slowly but surely our pilot was bringing us out to sea.

Augusta's father had joined the Service in 1863 as one of the earliest Licensed, not Covenanted, Pilots,* who, with their mixed antecedents, did not all make the grade—although he lasted the course to become Branch Pilot. The career climb from Mate Pilot through intermediary grades to Branch Pilot could take at least twenty years.

The sacred Ganges is frighteningly swift, changeable and treacherous. The channels of the Hooghly, the westernmost of its mouths, on which Calcutta stands, some ninety miles from the sea coast, are baited with shifting sandbanks.

Navigation was not the only problem that faced the pilot, lonely in his authority on the bridge. Sudden storms, even cyclones, were sent to try his courage. A waterspout might rear up in 'a huge black column, reaching to and mingling with the dark clouds overhead. As it passed our stern with a roaring sound, the spray from its troubled base fell on us like rain.'†

---

* A mere licence did not carry the prestige or benefits of being 'covenanted'—in the special Indian sense of having entered into a formal agreement of service with the Government.

† M. H. Beattie, *op. cit.*

Grim old wrecks were visible at all points. Defending themselves against a stress that was unreasonable, the pilots tended to become choleric, or tightly obsessional, cultivating complicated hobbies such as compiling an elaborate book of signals for the use of the Service.

But there were rewards other than financial. There was 'the far-off sound of a conch or a tom-tom from the villages at evening as we passed through the upper reaches after a long day's work.'* There was comradeship. The pilot was always hospitably received on incoming vessels and regaled with the fowl which had been saved for him. Christmas was kept up in good style, with the pilot brigs stationed at the Sandheads dressed with all flags, and punch served generously.

French captains provided the comedy. One such ventured ashore and shot a vulture, taking it for a turkey. In triumph, he handed it over to the horrified cook. Another, 'short and stout, was clad in a tartan pyjama suit and carrying a pink parasol'. Yet another jester 'wore wooden sabots, and had painted the right foot green and the left one red, in keeping with the starboard and port navigating lights.'†

Master Pilot S. M. Anderson once boarded an English vessel and was startled to find the decks crawling with foxhound puppies. During the five-month voyage, the captain had allowed the cargo of forty specially line-bred hounds to multiply to over eighty. Airily, he dismissed the suggestion that the indigo-planter who was awaiting their arrival would not be overjoyed.

When Augusta was ten years old, her father was lucky to live through the severe cyclone of 21st September, 1885, which sent storm-waves fifteen feet high rushing twelve miles inland. At that time, he had reached the grade of Master Pilot.

Two days after that Act of God, on 23rd September, the ship *Viscount* suddenly appeared like a battered ghost to the north-west of the watching pilot brig *Cassandra*. Eagerly, the pilot crew

took Mr Goodwyn out of her. She had left Saugor on the

---

* M. H. Beattie, *op. cit.*
† M. H. Beattie, *op. cit.*

21st in tow, but the weather had become so bad while towing down the Eastern Channel that the tug had to cast off. The *Viscount* made sail and stood across the tail of the Eastern Sea Reef. Being a very smart ship she managed to survive, but they had an anxious time beating about in Balasore Bay and had narrowly escaped disaster amongst the sands.*

One feels that the Master Pilot's skill made an unacknowledged contribution to the *Viscount*'s deliverance!

Augusta's home-life, then, was unsettled—an unspoken edge of apprehension to it—with her father forever saying farewell, perhaps for the last time, and leaving in a hurry with his servant and ready-packed impedimenta—a chest, a bag, and a swinging cot laced up in a canvas cover.

There was a glamour in his job, for her to boast of to her schoolfriends, and her imagination must have been affected by the nautical scenes along the palaced waterfront of the great port of Calcutta. Some of the finest sailing ships in the world lay moored four-abreast all the way up-river to Calcutta Reach: wooden ships and barques from America and New-foundland, and Arab ships from Jeddah and Muscat—fine old teak-built vessels with large, square sterns and quarter-galleries reminiscent of Nelson's day. The King of Oudh's Palace at Garden Reach, with its crying peacocks and caged tigers, was a place of pure fantasy for any sheltered English child.

If Augusta had been a boy, the maritime sights would have had deeper significance for her. Sons frequently followed their pilot fathers in a proud service, but there is only one Goodwyn in the Rolls among the recurring names such as Wawn and Lindquist. Marriage was the best option open to her, but first she had to be educated.

The children of the English in post were, fashionably, sent 'Home' to school, exiled for their own good from the age of seven to seventeen. Augusta was not subjected to any such character-forming separation, although, in fact, her family could well have afforded the expense of educating two girls in England.

* M. H. Beattie, *op. cit.*

17

Augusta and Dora probably attended, instead, one of the excellent convent schools of Calcutta, of which the most famous is Loreto House, situated at 7 Middleton Row. Its earliest extant admission book to have survived the white ants begins in January 1845, before the relevant period, but there is no record of a Goodwyn girl. This is sad, because the school was founded precisely for pupils of Augusta's background: in 1841, the nuns went out from Ireland to set up Loreto House for the particular reason that 'there was no school for the girls of the Military or Railways, etc.'* Other enquiries, such as to La Martinière School, have not been well received.

However socially handicapped Augusta might have been by the place of her schooling, the nuns did a good job, and, especially, inculcated an easy familiarity with the plays of Shakespeare—that staple element of the English-medium curriculum in India. But it would not have escaped the notice of the tutelary nuns that she was a frivolous girl, fond of trashy, romantic novels. Naturally, she 'played and sang', but her repertoire was of sentimental songs that tinkled.

As she grew up, what she really enjoyed was the social life of Calcutta, the twirling and glitter of dances and theatres—which she *was* permitted to attend—and the scrutiny of potential husbands. She was denied entry to the most exclusive circles—and very formal they were, too, although Calcutta was observed to be basically provincial—but she made her presence felt.

It would have been a nice compensation for the pilot's daughter to be known as a raving beauty, but, alas, she was short and dumpy, and had to rely on being regarded as vivacious and quite attractive. Springy brown tresses made up for her broad, stubby nose and wide, rather amphibian mouth, but her real triumph was her china-doll complexion. Here, being Indian-reared, she had the advantage over English roses transplanted to the sultry climate of Calcutta, where they quickly lost their bloom. In slightly ambiguous words, she once wrote in a letter,

> Won't I have a jolly fine time this evening, dancing and

* Letter to the author from the Principal of Loreto House, 29th April, 1988.

18

looking as sweet as I can in pale blue, which suits my fair complexion so admirably. My dear mother always used to warn me not to be so boastful and vain about my skin and colour, but just to accept it as a blessing from One above.

A legend has somehow gained credence that Augusta was a dusky, slinky *femme fatale*—'a slim, tall brunette' with skin of 'a rich coffee colour', prone to posing by tall windows, while idly waving her fan.* Let her photograph, with its failed, soulful expression, cabbagy hat, and lacy frippery, scotch this fiction for ever.

And so, then, this small, sociable, mischievous person, equipped with the requisite airs and graces to attract a husband, arrived at nubility. English girls were in demand, the supply not satisfied by the regular batches of hopeful maidens from Home, called the 'Fishing Fleet'. (Those unfortunates who sailed back without a catch were 'Returned Empties'!) But Augusta Goodwyn was no beauty, and she lacked the touch of class that would have netted a young salmon such as a junior officer.

Portia-like, she viewed the available suitors with a shrewd and mocking eye. On a later occasion, after receiving an invitation to a Quadrille Dance, given by the Medical Athletic Club, she showed her contempt for weediness, writing, 'but what I want to know is who are the athletes? Not Gomes or Theodore, surely! As Portia says: "God made them so they pass for men."'

Portia's final choice was not a romantic one. It was safe and prudent, but it did not suit her temperament, and, in fact, as the daughter of an English Branch Pilot, she could have done rather better.

Opting for security, in an environment where people would die for a pension, Augusta, or her parents, settled for a bridegroom who was, in effect, no more than a rising clerk. Edward McKeon Fullam was marred, too, by a physical defect, a withered arm—the left one, thin, but usable. The subject was never mentioned.

The detail that Edward, born in Barrackpore on 22nd

---

* *Such Women are Deadly.* Leonard Gribble, (John Long, 1965).

February, 1867, was eight years older than his bride was neither here nor there. The joining of young girls to frankly middle-aged husbands was a mere commonplace in British India. An old joke referred to the desirability of the 'three hundred a year dead or alive man' in the Indian Civil Service. When he joined, he received a salary of £300 per year, and he was obliged to subscribe to a fund which, after a number of years' service, would guarantee his grieving widow a pension of £300 similarly per year.

Edward's ultimate salary, when he attained the peak of Deputy Examiner in the Military Accounts Department at the important garrison of Meerut, where he was the *burra sahib* or head official of his department, was a hugely respectable 550 rupees per month, which was about £440 a year.

What is much more surprising than his other circumstances in life is Edward Fullam's provenance. He was slightly Indian. This is known, although his photograph shows a fair-skinned, Pooter-like fellow, with a neat moustache. His hair was blondish.

There was no chance of concealing his origins, and when, on 17th June, 1896, Augusta married him, she had (*unless* she, too, were slightly Indian) decidedly broken ranks. The marriage took place at the cantonment church in Barrackpore, situated in pilot territory on the River Hooghly, fifteen miles north of Calcutta, where both were resident. Mary Augusta Goodwyn and Eliza Fullam, two widowed mothers, were witnesses.

Later, on 10th February, 1909, her sister, Dora Olive, married a 28-year-old 'mercantile assistant', who appears to have been a Frenchman. This was Pierre Edgar Langlois, son of Pierre Louis Langlois. A Jesuit father officiated at the marriage in St Teresa's Church, 92 Lower Circular Road, Calcutta.

Edward Fullam belonged, with Augusta, to the inferior stratum of those domiciled, not in post, in India. His mother lived in Calcutta, and his father, William, had been a 'conductor'—not the musical kind, but an administrator, most probably, in his case, with the military.* He had come from

* By Royal Warrant of 11th January, 1879, Conductors of Supplies

20

Ireland, where the Fullams are still very strong in the Dublin area. It was Edward's brother, William Arnold, not his father (as Walsh stated) who was a First Class Assistant-Surgeon in the Indian Subordinate Medical Department*

Like the Goodwyns, the Fullams had a history of residence and service in India, stretching back to the earliest traceable Fullam, Michael, born in Berhampore on 27th September, 1827, the son of Patrick, a private in Her Majesty's 47th Regiment of Foot.

Augusta's 'Eddie' had opted for a tame career in the ruling bureaucracy. He had the reputation of not being particularly strong, and he suffered in the Hot Weather. He was certainly a misfortuned traveller; in 1904, during a rare trip to England, with his brother, William, where coolness and green fields should have soothed him, he had a 'cerebral attack'.

It is hardly necessary to state that Augusta found him a dull stick, and in that expanse of boredom she joined many colonial wives with their older, hidebound husbands. Patiently, he put up with her junketings, and was proud of her when she shone. His likeness shows a mild enough paterfamilias. Nothing to his discredit is known, although a horrible aspersion was subsequently cast against him.

What a shame it is that Augusta adopted the pose that 'My husband has never been in love with me'! What she really meant, of course, was that she felt that he did not appreciate her finer talents and sensibilities. She should have known that the Bovary syndrome leads only to tragedy....

The propagation of offspring ought, theoretically, to have given meaning to the marriage and subdued any flightiness in the sparkling bride. It has not been reported before that there was a first child, Doris Goodwyn, born on 23rd October, 1897. Barrackpore, where the Fullams began their married life, although a favourite resort of Europeans, and the suburban seat of the Viceroy, was not a great deal healthier than nearby, famously muggy and debilitating Calcutta, and on 22nd August, 1900, Doris died of 'malarious fever and spleen, liver

and Conductors of Stores were raised to the rank of Warrant Officers.

* See pp. 25–7.

and dropsy'. She was buried the following day at the General Episcopal Cemeteries, Circular Road, Park Street, Calcutta.

Meanwhile, the elder son, William Leonard Murray, had been born on 10th July, 1899. Apart from the first tragedy, Augusta was exceptionally lucky in being able to rear healthy children. Kathleen Augusta was born on 3rd September, 1902, followed by Frank Edward, born on 4th May, 1906.

Promotion led to the move from Barrackpore to Meerut, at some time in 1908. The change from the city to an up-country station in the United Provinces of Agra and Oudh (now Uttar Pradesh) in the north-west Plains suited Augusta. Not dwarfed by too much grand company, and with her liveliness an asset and found amusing, she became a person of more consequence. It must be said, however, that in the wide whispering-gallery of India, Edward would not have been able to slough off the stigma of his native blood.

His extra-curricular activities indicate a man who was eager to conform and to be respected in the community. He was a keen Mason, a Sunday School teacher (C. of E., of course) and, bravely, considering his weak left arm, a Second Lieutenant in the local Voluntary Force. *Then*, like little Major Armstrong of Hay-on-Wye,* what a dash he could cut in his spick, smart uniform!

Edward's efforts were not in vain, because the Fullams were well accepted into the thriving social life of the station, and Augusta, at least, while not sharing his sense of public duty or, perhaps, his need for acceptance, was able to enjoy the fruits of his spadework.

Nor was she expected to make a wider contribution. The memsahib's beleaguered existence in her bungalow was considered to be sufficient in itself.† Social work among the Indians was regarded as dangerous meddling. A modicum of artistic activity was permissible.

But then, Augusta was no wondering bride, fresh from Home and determined to make the best of her strange new

---

* The only case of a solicitor hanged for murder. Herbert Rowse Armstrong poisoned his wife with arsenic in 1921.
† *The Memsahibs*, Pat Barr (Secker, 1976).
*Women of the Raj*, Margaret MacMillan (Thames and Hudson, 1988).

world. The great canopy of the sky of India was as familiar to her as its shell to a turtle. She did not care to chart the brilliant flora and fauna that surrounded her; butterfly delights of social intercourse and giggly gossiping were her daily excitement.

Maybe she was inured to the colours and scents of the teeming, Technicolor streets, the sensuality that always shimmered in the hot, spicy air, the rich fecundity glimpsed in the bared breast of a woman openly suckling her baby. She was supposed to be, to stride on regardless; above all, British.

Life was a quadrille, to be danced in landlocked Meerut, far from the sands of the coast; but the blood of her father, the taste for adventure, told her:

*What matters it how far we go?...*
*There is another shore, you know, upon the other side.*

## Chapter Two

## A Brother Mason

Because she loved to dance, somehow, as time has passed, a scenario has been created for Augusta that is romantic, and feels right. On some enchanted evening—so it goes—when the crowded room whirled and spun with the pattern of the Lancers, she exchanged glances with the man who was destined to alter her life for ever.

But it was not like that at all.

The encounter took place in her own home, at her own insistence. Edward already knew Henry Lovell William Clark, who enjoyed the reputation of being a dangerous man, with power over women. Indoors, there lurked a smouldering wife, cowed to obey.

Something that she had heard about Clark intrigued Augusta and prompted her to petition Edward for his company, and so, to please her, her husband invited under his safe roof a fierce tiger, who was to roam the rooms and gnaw and savage all that Edward held dear.

Ironically, it was Edward himself, then, who introduced to his wife a handsome, dashing figure, tall and upright in his uniform, with broad shoulders and strong, masterful arms. Walsh's report of Clark as a loathsome monster, a Caliban in aspect, is utterly false. Once he had made the connection, Edward never had a chance.

When first a woman stoops to folly, she carries in her mind, for constant replay, like a favourite record, the image of that primal scene. Later, perhaps when repudiation has soured the sweetness, the memory clouds. By Augusta's own, not entirely specific account, it was at some time towards the end of 1908, or the beginning of 1909, that she and Clark became acquainted, and by the middle of 1909 flirtation had merged into heavy commitment.

Augusta's lover was born in Calcutta on 15th August, 1868, a year and a half later than Edward Fullam. His father, Cornelius Smith Clark, born at Rajeshahye, Calcutta, on 22nd February, 1829, was the son of Thomas Clark, an indigo-planter, and his wife Charlotte. On the day of Henry Lovell William's baptism at the Old Church, Fort William, Calcutta, Cornelius stands out in the register by virtue of being 'unemployed', against the other paternal entries of 'master mariner', 'merchant', and 'accountant'.

Cornelius had two, successive wives. At Berhampore, on 16th November, 1857, his first marriage was to Louisa Delphine Christien, daughter of Eugina Pierre Christien. At that time, Cornelius was an indigo-seed merchant, but when (widowed) on 26th June, 1867, he married Victoria Starling, daughter of Charles Samuel Starling, he was a clerk in the East Indian Railway. Victoria Starling was Henry's mother.

A pleasing mystery became attached to Henry Clark's ancestry. He was said to be a great-grandson of the famous Captain Clark of the East India Company's service, whose grave at Berhampore was kept up by the Bengal Government. There was a story* that if Clark and his brother, a silk-grower at Plassey, could only prove their entitlement, forty thousand pounds lying in Chancery would be theirs. During his courtship of Augusta, Clark sought to impress her with his claim to belong to an old, distinguished family, and she played up to her 'pedigree gentleman'. He was decorated with his family crest, in the shape of a gold signet which depended from his watch-chain.

By a moderate coincidence, he shared with Edward Fullam's brother, William Arnold, the small distinction of being a member of the Indian Subordinate Medical Department, in which he had served since 1889. Henry Clark was a doctor, but not a top-grade one. In British India, it was not a grand station in life, although to some degree respected—retired army men remember the subordinate doctors as perfectly competent, good chaps.

* *Daily Telegraph*, 3rd February, 1913.

There is no English equivalent of the I.S.M.D. Fully accredited European doctors were thin on the ground, and, of necessity, a grade of capable subordinate doctor had evolved, subject to supervision and qualified to perform only minor operations.

From very early times, the East India Company's medical officers had employed indigenous assistants in their hospitals, at first as mere dressers, and native or 'banyan' doctors were also on the establishment. From these small beginnings there sprang the Military Subordinate Medical Department (the precursor of the I.S.M.D.), set up in Bengal and Madras in 1812. Recruits, mainly boys from Orphan Schools and the Free School, were usually locally born of European or Eurasian parentage, but occasionally came from the ranks of the East India Company's European regiments, or from British Army regiments stationed in India.

By a General Order of 25th June, 1847, it was laid down that after two years' service in military hospitals, hospital apprentices should be sent to the Calcutta Medical College, to undergo there a course of two years' professional instruction. Many officers of the I.S.M.D. did go on to obtain commissions in the Indian Medical Service, to whose élite members they were, otherwise, always inferior, and some obtained European qualifications.

By Clark's time, the Service was recruited entirely in India and very few of its officers chose retirement in Britain. It attracted a number of domiciled Englishmen, and some Indians, but its personnel were mainly Eurasian.

And Clark, indeed, was Eurasian—manifestly so, with a yellowish skin. Augusta was now seriously letting the side down. He was not even a totally respectable subordinate doctor: always short of money, he could occasionally be persuaded to terminate a pregnancy.

It is well accepted that the Eurasians were, in fact, the backbone of the British administration in India. In return, they were called 'twelve annas in the rupee', 'half-baked bread', and 'half a pound'. They ran the railway system. The women did the nursing.

Unless they were educated overseas, all the senior and

26

covenanted posts were barred to them.* Often, they clustered together in the railway communities which were, in effect, a kind of ghetto. The beautiful, seductive daughters—'B class girls'—who smelt of garlic and cheap perfume, were readily available at Railway Institute dances.

Becoming a subordinate doctor was going some way towards acceptance. With scarcely a qualm, English women did, of necessity, accept Eurasian doctors at their bedside during illness and childbirth. Qualifying in the I.S.M.D. was undoubtedly an achievement. There were not many such personnel in the whole of India; the Indian Army List of January 1913 shows a strength of 695, of whom 231 were seconded for civil employment.

Academically, Clark had had to struggle, and the examinations had taxed him severely. His difficulties were a bit of a joke with his fellow-students. As a Senior Assistant Surgeon he only just scraped into his honorary commission in 1911. There was a report that he was created a lieutenant for his work during the China War—the Boxer Rising of 1900—and he certainly did serve in China, but, more reliably, his rank refers to his grade in the I.S.M.D.

Advancement was all in India. A sharp goad, too, was Clark's ever-pressing need for the wherewithal to finance his multifarious activities. He did rise to be in sub-medical charge of a hospital. As against Edward Fullam's 500 rupees per month, he drew 360 rupees—and it was never enough.

An active, restless man, not a loner, his hobbies were of the raffish, wagering nature associated with the opportunity to make a quick rupee—card-playing, cock-fighting, duck-fighting... Versatile and bazaar-wise, he would slide off from a polite game of tennis to frequent risky native prostitutes in their questionable hovels. He was not entirely clean in his habits.

Basically he was a loser. It is surprising that a man of such known bad character ever obtained preferment at all. His undoubted success with women fuelled a self-esteem that would otherwise have faltered.

* *Raj: a Scrapbook of British India 1877–1947*, Charles Allen (André Deutsch, 1977).

Even—or especially—rotters seek out a bride, the more innocent and gullible the better. Louisa Amelia Guest, also a Eurasian, was a nurse at the Medical College Hospital in Calcutta when the young Clark was doing his training there. She, ironically, may have been the slender enchantress—then —that Augusta was imagined to be, although later she became stout and matronly. At least two of her sisters also lived in Calcutta.

It did not seem to matter, in those early days, that Louisa was ten years older than Clark: he wanted her as his wife. She hesitated. Twice he proposed to her, and, in the end, she accepted him, on condition that he passed his examinations. Her reward for waiting for him was years of cruelty and adultery. After the marriage, which took place in Calcutta, on 4th March, 1889, at which her father, John Guest, was a witness, Clark soon tired of her.

Life with a rotter is so often endured in private, but cataclysmic events can uncover hidden bruisings and slights inconceivable:

> The privacy of marriage is a shocking thing. We try to present our own, particularly if we are women, in a good light, or, if men, in no light at all. We struggle not to listen to the secrets of other people's marriages. Thus marriages live in isolation, sometimes becoming, for want of compassion and criticism, more bizarre, more cruel, more wild or more eccentric, than any of us can possibly imagine.*

No doubt suave and unctuous as he walked the wards, when, late, Clark lurched into the matrimonial home at night, the mere sight of patient Louisa, the angel at the hearth, surrounded by her apprehensive children, triggered him into a paroxysm of cursing and beating his entire family. He liked to kick them.

Louisa's only defence was a mild 'You too.' She did have a special champion, though—her mettlesome daughter, Maud, whose teenage gift for invective rivalled her father's. There were two other surviving children of the troubled union. John

* *Mrs Mulvaney*, Hilary Bailey (Constable, 1978).

had died as a baby in Calcutta. Henry and Walter, grown boys, had been placed in clerkly positions in Edward Fullam's Military Accounts Office, no less.

Clark's Indian heritage was supposed to account for the primitive, savage part of his mentality, and, indeed, the treatment of wives in ordinary village society was often barbaric. *Suttee* had been just about (not quite) eliminated by an outraged Raj, but murder and mutilation of wives were still commonplace. If he even *suspected* her of infidelity, a man might slice off his wife's nose, or her breast.

The Eurasian households, however, particularly where the husband was a professional man, would adopt English mores. Louisa could have obtained a divorce from the court of the District Judge, both rapidly and cheaply.* The children had grown up. The reasons why a wife with good cause fails to seek a divorce are always murky and not easily accessible to an outsider.

By any standards, Henry Clark was a bad lot, but he, this brutish creature caged inside a front of gallantry, was to be tamed by Augusta Fullam, a tubby temptress with tenacious claws. Both were deeply smitten. He was awed and impressed, and on his best behaviour, with this willing sexual partner who was English, better educated than he was, and had ample financial means. (To be fair to Clark, however, there is no evidence that he ever drew upon those means.) He never kicked her.

She, in her turn, clothed her physical need for him in the trappings of sentiment and romance, and he was happy to play her game—in so far as he had the mental equipment. There was a piquancy in his being a doctor, of course, and he soon became her personal physician.

The satisfaction of the affair took place in the Fullam bungalow. Louisa and Maud Clark guarded the Clark citadel. Edward's office hours were regular. William Leonard, the elder son, went away to the Bishop Cotton School,† at Kalka.

* Walsh, thus airily.
† This good school, for British boys, sons of minor civil servants etc., had one school term, from March to November. Kalka, the depot for Simla, is in the Hills.

Frank was only three years old, and Kathleen a little mouse of seven: both could be kept in the care of the motherly *ayah*, while the memsahib and the doctor-sahib absented themselves in the bedroom.

In the prickly heat of day, in that illicit, shuttered room, Augusta's layers of starched petticoats under high-collared, long-sleeved dresses frustrated—or inflamed—their transports. Half-smothered in all that fret and froth of lace and coils of hair, he rogered her (let's not beat about the bush) while outside, in the sun-baked garden, small monkeys swung and gibbered. Ah! How she sighed and giggled, as odd snatches of poetry popped up in her fluffy head.

Edward Fullam was not denied access to the connubial bed—Augusta was too clever for that. On 26th January, 1910, a further baby, Myrtle Phyllis, a.k.a. 'Carrots' or their 'little mixture of copper and tin', blessed the Fullam family. Clark attended the birth, which was difficult. Perhaps there had been an attempt at an abortion and Clark had bungled it. Anyway, the baby thrived, and was baptised at St John's Church, Meerut, on 20th February, 1910, daughter of Edward and Augusta.

Poor Edward, soundly cuckolded, was gratefully convinced that Clark had saved the lives of both his wife and his daughter. According to Walsh, Augusta and Clark thought that Myrtle was the offspring of their union, but the date of her arrival certainly caused Edward no concern.

All Meerut is supposed to have been whispering about the liaison, although none told Edward Fullam, a ridiculous, horned figure on his bicycle, pedalling the dusty road to and from his dishonoured bungalow.

There is, as it happens, a special reason why Edward trusted Clark. They were brothers. They belonged to the same Masonic lodge in Meerut. Each, in his own way, eager to advance professionally and socially, had calculated that membership of the Brotherhood held its own rewards. There was, too, in Edward, but not in Clark, a genuine philanthropic drive, and he entered as a man of very good report. Clark's character and conduct were tolerated. He was known to be a man of the world, and a busy man of affairs. By the skin of his teeth, he got away with it again, as he did in his career.

## A Brother Mason

Not a lot of people know that Freemasonry was active throughout the Raj, with a lodge powerful in almost every sizeable station.* Village Indians were greatly in awe of these imagined temples of potent magic. Explanations of their functions proved ineffectual: it was the secrecy that so impressed.

Membership was multi-racial, so Freemasonry in India cut a refreshing swathe across distinctions which, in the profane world outside the temple, held firm and hard. When, as he related in *Something of Myself*, Rudyard Kipling was inducted into the Lodge of Hope and Perseverance in Lahore, in 1885, he was 'entered by a member of the Brahmin Somaj, passed by a Mohammedan, and raised by an Englishman. Our tyler was an Indian Jew.'

Fullam and Clark, then, would have felt free from the constraints normally imposed by the minute and complicated differences of their standing in the community. They were sworn together as brothers in trust and confidence, and this fact is of more importance than its mere coincidence. It deepens the relationship between them into a quasi-mystical bond, whose severance has the mark of Judas.

While Edward was possessed of an almost naïve idealism, and clung to the concept of the English gentleman, no such scrupulosities vexed the conscience of worldly Lieutenant Clark.

In November 1910, the uninterrupted idyll was over. Clark was transferred from Meerut Hospital to Delhi. It may be that his superiors judged it better to remove him from Mrs Fullam's influence. Louisa, who knew all, rejoiced. Constancy was not Clark's mode—he might have shrugged and moved on to fresh conquests—but Augusta would not let him go.

She would write to him—letters wise and sweet and witty. Snippets of verse could be slipped in as they occurred to her, to impress, to remind him that she was different from all the rest. She had a brain as well as a body ... Clinging could sever; she would be cool, not possessive, about other women.

A whole, thrilling, new dimension of courtship suddenly opened up. Almost every weekday, she sat down—one can

* *Bound to Exile*, Michael Edwardes (Sidgwick & Jackson, 1969).

31

picture her, plump and flushed, with her hair loose, at a
bureau, perhaps—and wrote terms of endearment in her
distinctive, flowing hand. Not on Sundays—hardly, when
hubby was around.

Other people's love-letters—stale blandishments—usually
wither when the moment has passed. Augusta's copious
effusions are trite and trivial, arch and winsome, parochial,
and in the worst possible taste, but they have a kind of sturdy
vitality—and they are also very informative. They are not at all
cunning, but utterly transparent.

Overwhelmed, out of his depth, Clark struggled to respond.
With no culture to fall back on—what was Shakespeare to
him?—he enlisted the services of a young confidant who
framed phrases, dredged up poetry, and suggested newsy
material for incorporation into Clark's laboured replies. Such
an expedient was natural enough in India, where professional
letter-writers would—and still do—for a modest fee, concoct
any needed document, be it petition, testimonial, or pressing
personal letter.

This confidant was one Alick M. Joseph, a clerkly person,
aged about twenty-one, either a Eurasian or an Indian
Christian. He knew the Clark family well, having been at
school with Walter Clark, the younger son, and, later, he was
actually to live with them. By his own account, he bore the
reputation of being able to write a good letter. Clark—not a
gentleman—showed him Augusta's letters, and there was an
element of sniggering about the whole transaction.

Augusta did not dare to keep Clark's hybrid letters. Not that
they were worth keeping: they were stilted and inky to the end,
tending to sign off with the hope that his Gussie was well 'as it
leaves me at present'. She soon spotted that his words of love
were often plagiarised from her own tendernesses.

Clark kept all her letters, each in its original envelope,
carefully endorsed with the date of his reply—good business
practice. Perhaps he thought they might come in useful, one
day. At first, she marked them *Tear Up*, but, in time, she
abandoned this injunction. She had no idea that, at one stage,
Alick Joseph was the repository of her most private letters:
Clark asked him to hold on to them.

There were other pleasurable possibilities. Delhi was only

The pilot's salty colleagues:
E.F. Hudson (*left*) and
R. Rust, Branch Pilots in the
Bengal Pilot Service with
Augusta's father.

Babu Denoo Nath
Mookerjee: one of the
capable clerks who
administered the Bengal
Pilot Service. A great chess
expert.

The pilot's daughter:
Augusta Fairfield
Fullam.

Edward McKeon
Fullam: unwanted
'hubby'.

forty miles away. Clark could steam into Meerut by train, once
a month or so, for brief encounters in the *dak* bungalow.
Monthly visits to the Fullams' home would make even poor old
Eddie suspicious.

The lovers' new venue was a kind of guest-house. *'Dak'*
means 'post', and originally, before the railways came, there
were *dak* bungalows every forty or fifty miles on a civilised
road; the post-master laid on bearers. It was a recklessly
indiscreet place to meet, but there was nowhere else to go, no
equivalent of an anonymous, modern motel.

Augusta's first letter is dated 30th November, 1910. Clark
initials the envelope, 'Answered H.L.C. 2/12/10.' Setting the
tone, it is launched with a rhyming motto:

Dear Heart of Mine,

I greet you with loving thoughts and true,
And pray that every happiness may be vouchsafed to you.

I am so very glad to know that you will be here in
Meerut tomorrow, Harry darling, and once more we shall
meet and be happy. Oh! darling, I, too, am counting the
hours as they pass, like any school girl. How boyish and
youthful you are my own darling, to act over me just like a
young lover over his first love. I know full well that I am
not your first love, Harry darling, but I also know and
believe that I am the first one you have ever fallen in love
with. Very late in life has true love met you, darling, and
to think that poor I have won your heart, and hold you
spellbound. Why can't you give me up for 'Mabelle'? She
came first in your affections, my sweetheart. You just wait
till I see you tomorrow, darling, and see if I don't talk you
into sound commonsense, and proper reasoning. But
really in your presence I seem to melt and become like
wax, instead of being strong and making you listen to
me. You are just like Harry Middlemore. Do you
remember the book?

Fondest and truest love and kisses, darling. Warmest
love and the sweetest of kisses from your own little loving
and ever devoted little sweetheart and Bucha.

Gussie.

'Mabelle', of course, was their mocking, private name for Louisa Clark. It reminds one irresistibly of Crippen's wife, Belle Elmore. 'Bucha' is Hindustani for 'baby'.

Thus, experimentally, they tested out each other's commitments, as Augusta conjured up the homely cheer of Christmas parties to endorse what she had to lose:

> You must not say, as you do in your letter, that you come after my hubby, and that he is my first love. My precious darling, you come first before anyone else, but of course, as a wife, I must do my duty, and will do it to the end. What say you, Harry darling?
>
> Last evening's Christmas Tree was quite a success, and Eddie made a fine old Father Christmas. He borrowed a white wig and beard from Mr Myers, and a long red cloak from Mr Symonds of the Hotel. So many little ones were made happy, and every one liked and admired our purchases from Delhi.

By 2nd February, 1911, Augusta felt secure enough to state in express terms

> We shall both be rewarded in God's good time and I am quite sure we two shall have a happy home some day.

Even so, 'petty lovers' quarrels' were flaring up. Clark was under stress. In fact, he was *always* under stress at his job, because he was only just up to the theoretical part of it, and his character was so dubious and open to improvement that superiors seemed—to him—to pick on him. His too frequent trips on leave to Meerut had aggravated an always perilous situation. An unfavourable official report on his work was now threatening his chances of getting the commission towards which his whole career had been moving for over two decades. It is extremely unlikely that these words of comfort from Augusta had any power to console him—her flim-flammery was far removed from his real, gritty problems:

> Oh, sweetheart, dearest, I wish I were near to you now in the time of your despondency, to put my loving arms

34

round your dear neck, and kiss all your troubles and fears
away. But although I cannot do this as I wish, take heart
my own love, for my sake, and keep doing your duty, both
at home to wife and family, and also at work with cross-
grained officers.

Sweetheart, I told you yesterday that Myrtle and Mick
are great chums. She plays with him and he is so gentle
and nice with her. We have had Myrtle photographed
twice, but no good results. I am so cross over it.

That was on 3rd February, but by the 22nd she herself was
afflicted by a very weighty problem. It was Edward's forty-
fourth birthday, and he thought he had cause for rejoicing, but
the letter which his wife was writing to another man could, if
seen, have brought on another apoplexy:

This time last year I was laid up with Myrtle. Harry,
darling, my very own precious sweetie, my worst fears are
now realised, and I am quite sure I am caught again. I have
been feeling very sick the past two evenings, but last
evening suddenly, I got so sick and vomited freely. Eddie
had a good laugh, and said, 'Now I hope you are fully
convinced.'

So there is no doubt about the matter now, my Bucha,
and we must simply grin and bear it. We have fought and
struggled against this, but we cannot fight against God's
will, and neither do we wish to. What say you, my own
darling? So now you can think when you are playing
tennis and enjoying yourself of an evening, how your poor
little girl is keeping a rough time, feeling so sick and
miserably wretched.

> Thy way, not mine, O Lord,
> However dark it be;
> Lead me by Thine own Hand,
> Choose out the path for me.
> I dare not choose my lot,
> I would not if I might;
> Choose Thou for me, my God,
> Then shall I walk aright.

These lines are just what my poor sentiments now express,
Harry darling, my very own precious sweetheart, Bucha,
and whatever happens, I leave all to God's Almighty will.

Sweetheart darling, I have shown your confidential
extract to my hubby, and he thought it a very bad one. He
thinks it will be in the way of your getting a commission
soon, as one who can only hold a small charge is
incompetent to hold a commission, darling. However, he
thinks the report is very unfair, in its statement of your
knowledge being superficial. Darling, do not you worry
over it, everything will come right.

Clark did, in fact, receive his commission, and Augusta
congratulated him:

I hope my Lord Lieutenant Henry Lovell William Clark
will lead his second wife up to the hymeneal altar under
arched swords of his brother officers.

Augusta loved her 'pink and white' babies, but she did not
scruple to rid herself of the new pregnancy. European women
were not known commonly to resort to abortion. Indian
methods were lethal: the insertion of a long twig smeared with
ayurvedic* substances caused septic miscarriage. As an orthodox doctor unusually willing to help out, Clark was a godsend
to an Englishwoman in a bit of a fix, and the drugs which he
now supplied to Augusta were successful.

So Edward still did not suspect? It was, then, quite in order
for Augusta to discuss Clark's confidential extract with him:
she was allowed to be in correspondence with their absent
friend. It *is* just feasible that Edward did know, all along, and
quietly hoped that she would repent. Other men have still
regularly visited their wives' beds in such circumstances, but
would he have been so jolly as he diagnosed evening-sickness?

Meanwhile, Clark's Medical Officer took punitive action,
and had him transferred, at short notice, from Delhi to the
Station Hospital at Agra. His family were to follow on later.
Now he was 180 miles away, by rail. But, for as long as trains

* Ayurvedic medicine is the native Indian medical system.

ran the tracks, there was to be no stopping him. On 15th March, he made a farewell visit to Augusta, and, between them, they committed a terrible indiscretion.

My own dearest Lovie,

I am enclosing the letter which I wrote you yesterday, but had not the chance of giving you, my own darling boy.

Sweetheart, darling, my hubby is very angry with me, it appears he was in the verandah this morning at 5 a.m., and saw you talking to me at my bedroom door. He did not see anything beyond our whispering together, but that was enough to make him jealous and angry. He was surprised at me in my nightgown, to be saying the last word to you, my darling. We shall have to be awfully careful now, my very own precious Bucha darling. I think perhaps you had better leave for Agra without seeing me any more, Harry, darling, as it only makes things harder for me, darling love.

Oh, how hard it is for us to struggle against such odds and disadvantages, my own sweetheart, when we love each other so much! God help us. I feel very sorry for you, and pity you, with all my heart, darling, and you know I would gladly help you if I could, but I am helpless and powerless, Bucha darling, and can only ask you to wait for me, till I can come to you free and unfettered, dearest love of mine.

Can you be brave enough to do this, Harry, darling, can I trust you to be a good boy for my sake? God bless and keep you, my own precious treasure.

What can this possibly mean? Not, on balance, even if Augusta did have her own bedroom, that the pair had so far lost caution as to meet by night in a situation where they risked being caught farcically *in flagrante*. Besides, two of her children, Kathleen and Myrtle, customarily slept in her room. Clark must have called surreptitiously to say goodbye before taking an early train back to his duties in Delhi. And he was there in Meerut the very next day, to say goodbye all over again.

Anyway, this is a watershed. The days of innocence are over.

Edward is now on notice. He will not forget the balcony scene, nor cease from wondering what kisses came with the whispers. Augusta will have to use all her kittenish wiles to neutralise an impossibly compromising accident. She wants Clark to think that she has succeeded:

> My darling, you will be glad to hear that the storm has cleared from our horizon, and things are once more bright and clear, my own sweetheart. Oh! How glad I was to see you on Friday, Bucha darling. I firmly believe in mental telepathy after that, for I seemed to *know* you were coming presently in spite of your letters saying you would not come. Are you comfortable, and have you a nice medical officer, dearie? You are better away from the dreadful naggings and scoldings you used to get at home, and yet I know 'it is not good for man to be alone.'
>
> I intend to tell you every single thing that happens here in Meerut, so don't get jealous, Harry darling, if I should mention H. having come over. I mean to choke him off, sweetie, as you told me to do, and have no more of his jokes.
>
> Sweetheart, darling, how did you enjoy the dance you had with Mrs S. the night of the Masonic Dance? You might have told me all about it, Harry dear, and not deceived me. Surely I am not such a dreadful ogre that you are bound to keep things hidden from my knowledge. Does she also write to you, darling? I am not at all angry with you, but I think you might have told me. I would have been better pleased than hearing it from others.

Had the mysterious Mr H. heard that Augusta was an available woman? She added a postscript to this letter of 18th March:

> H. and Eddie have had a most dreadful row. I will write and tell you about it tomorrow. It's nothing about me.

There is a feverish air, now, to the correspondence, with jealousy bartered as the coin of love. The duo of Clark/Joseph contributes a poem which is received with a most disarming, witty derision:

My sweetheart, your poem is awfully pretty, but your fairy has rather a substantial form, don't you think? Now, my dear old humbug, you won't make me believe that you composed this poem. It's very beautiful and well written. Agra air must have inspired you to great deeds. Just imagine calling me, 'A vision sweet of virgin mould'.

Oh! Harry, darling, how *can* you? But I can well believe that 'Your inmost heart with passion's fraught,' for I know my darling's nature and temperament only too well. Now to more mundane affairs, darling, as I suppose you are interested to know how fares your girlie. The old story, I am ill and weak. I have made myself ill these last few days worrying and fretting, and for ever having tears in my eyes, darling.

Augusta was not really ill. She soon recovered, and composed a poem which must have been truly terrible, and which was incomprehensible to Clark. She was offended by his response:

Yes, darling, the poem I sent you was an original one. I am sorry it was so densely written that you failed to grasp the meaning; however, I won't trouble you to read any more.

Harry, sweetheart, my hubby is not well. There is nothing physically wrong with him, but he is suffering from brain fag, and I fear he will get another attack of cerebral apoplexy like he had five years ago when he went to England. This morning he was telling me he wants to take three months' leave, and take us all up to the hills. All this worries me so much, Harry, darling, you know I don't wish to go away anywhere, but will let you know how things go, darling sweetheart, mine.

In all probability, although Augusta will not admit it, ruminating upon the balcony scene has made Edward anxious and depressed, and, above all, insecure. Gone the jovial Father Christmas in his wig and beard, paterfamilias.

With a touch of spite, she prattles on:

Plague is still very bad here in Meerut, and I suppose the Nauchandi will help to spread it. Mrs F. has had another little son, up at Sukkur in the Maternity Home there, so darling, you see your old friend of other days did not join her husband for nothing. You have changed from F. to Fairfield; what an old loving flirt you are my Bucha darling. Now I must not chaff you, for you do not like jokes, I know, but still from your Bucha you can stand anything, can't you, darling? Mrs M., too, has had a son, just the day after her baby completed one year old, and Mr D. of course looks after her.

Plague was real plague: it was not just a term for a more expected illness such as cholera or typhoid. Augusta's reference acts as a reminder of the daily peril of living in a place like Meerut. Wilder parties and spicier gossip could not dull the pain of the ranks of British headstones in the graveyards. The Nauchandi was the Fair of the New Moon, of ancient origin, which took place in Meerut every year, towards the end of the Cold Weather. It lasted for days, and attracted large numbers of traders from all over India.

Augusta concluded with observations which are nothing less than prophetic, but then there was a quality about her—at this stage in her life—that drew events to her. A magnet is passive; it has no choice about what it attracts, but must draw or reject according to its own properties—and those of what is put to it:

Oh, Harry darling, my own true, loving sweetheart, you are nothing but an old coaxer to argue with me, and declare you wish to keep up direct communication with me; be it as you will, my Bucha darling. I must own that I cannot give you up, your letters are food and drink to me, darling sweet, and I will abide patiently and do whatever you tell me. So let this comfort your tired soul my own pet, and let us await the unfolding of events, my own precious darling.

## Chapter Three

## Tonic Powders

What Augusta did not know, then, was that Clark had already elected wickedness. Dark things in his past were still hidden from her, but she was beginning to realise that the pussy-cat in her bedroom was an altogether more formidable creature of the night than he had at first pretended:

> 15th April, 1911
> In your every letter lately, darling, you hint that the way will soon be smooth and clear for us. Are you going to decoy me away in a match-box? Or, how, Harry darling? I am beginning to feel quite afraid of you, my big broad-shouldered love, so bold and brave. You remind me, Harry Bucha, of those brave Knight errants of olden days who used to dare and die for their lady love!

Exiled in Agra, alone at night (well, notionally alone at night!), Clark had been up to no good. His disposition was not improved by a vituperative correspondence with his family. Using their failure to send on to him a treasured leather case of hairbrushes—a present from Augusta—as a focus for his discontent, he made a lukewarm attempt to divest himself of his dependants:

> If you cannot read and understand English please let me know, for then I can write to you either in Hindu or Bengali, as the case may be. If you will take my advice you will either remain in Delhi, or proceed to Meerut, but please do not come here, for the day you place your foot in Agra, you may be quite sure I will promptly resign the service, as I am fed up with your low, disgusting ways, for

41

I am quite sure you don't care a damn what becomes of me, so long as you draw Rs.200 a month. You can go wherever you like, but don't attempt to come near me, otherwise you will know the consequences immediately.

Trusting this will find you all quite well, as it leaves me the same, with fond love and kisses to self, and the rest at home.

I remain, Your affectionate Husband,
H. L. Clark.

Assuming that this *is* Clark's own, unaided composition, it is obvious that abuse was more his *métier* than expressions of love. His own authentic voice can be heard. And yet the tone is petulant, almost childish. The bathetic surprise-ending bears a reek of young Alick Joseph. The offensive references to Louisa's Indian heritage are typical Eurasian insults. How Louisa's 'chee-chee' accent must have grated on Clark's treacherous ears, in comparison with Augusta's refined, or possibly, 'refeened', pronunciation!

Such a monstrous letter drew from Maud Clark a picturesque reply of superior sarcasm:

Station Hospital,
Fort Delhi,
8th April, 1911.

My Own Dearest Father,

Thanks very much for your letter, which was not very pleasant to read, but of course we must excuse you, as you must have been told to write like that. But never mind, God will be good to us. He only knows how we four have been treated in the house by you. I am simply shocked at you writing in such a way to mother, over those brushes that wonderful Mrs Fullam gave you. They are not worth two pice\* to us, and you may rest assured that we all know English, and we are not natives as you imagine us to be. Mother is too quiet for you. You require someone to answer you back in the same way. As for you saying that

---

\* Two Indian pice equal one farthing.

we worry and annoy you, that's the case with you. Hardly
a day passes that you don't row and abuse. If you knew
that mother wouldn't look after you, you shouldn't have
married her. You proposed to her twice, and then she
accepted of you on conditions that you passed your exam.
If she only knew that you were going to treat her like a dog
in after years, she would have married someone better
than you, who would have prized her, and treated her like
his queen. As for you imagining that mother does not care
a damn for you, I really don't know how you can say that.
If she didn't care a button for you or the house, she
wouldn't have stood all the kicking and thumping all
these years. To my knowledge she is treated very badly,
and she has borne it up very patiently.

    With fond love and kisses for dearest self,
      I am,
    Ever your affectionate daughter,
    Maud.

Clark was a bleak pragmatist. Misunderstood husband,
banished lover, he now concocted a two-headed plot, drawing,
for its execution, upon practical experiment of the most sinister
nature. Better not to put it in a letter. At their next meeting, he
would try it out on Augusta, see how she reacted.

Thursday, 20th April, 1911, was to be the day after which
nothing would ever be the same for Augusta Fullam. Reality
would be tilted, or come only in flashes.

Wary, now, of Edward's silent suspicion—for how *can* she
have explained the whispers at dawn?—she plans the reunion
which she half-senses will be out of the ordinary:

Now, darling, let me explain what I want you to say on
the 20th. Of course, you must come straight from the
station and will just arrive here in time for breakfast. I will
be very surprised to see you, and you say that you have
obtained a couple of days' leave to take your family back
to Agra. I think this excuse will do nicely, Bucha, darling,
and you can say you just ran into Meerut to see us all,
while your people were getting ready. Then I think you
had better ask me for an early dinner, saying you will take

43

the 8 p.m. train back to Delhi, so that my hubby won't be jealous, and when going to Lodge—my darling—do you quite understand?

Harry darling, I wish to tell you that on the 20th, when you come, please make the excuse that you have some business to go and see to after breakfast, and that you will be back to tea, so that my hubby will not be jealous. He will be away at the office, and we shall have it all to ourselves when you return, till tea time, lovie, darling. But don't allow him to think that you were closeted here with me all day.

Now ultimatums and show-downs invade the air; ambivalence and confusion. First Augusta tempts Clark, leads him on, then she denies him, and finally she makes an affirmation. It does not augur well for her future conduct, her accuracy of judgement:

19th April, 1911

You are a full-blooded man, and need a nice, good wife constantly near you, and, moreover, one who will look after you, not nagging and worrying you for ever, but a true help-mate and companion in every sense of the word. Am I not right, my own precious darling sweet?

Now I have a statement to make, which I know will upset and worry you, Harry darling, but I cannot help it, Bucha, and it also grieves me more than I can say—but God help us both in this extremity. This is the last letter I can write to you, my heart's own love. There is a crisis impending in both our lives, which I will explain fully on our meeting, darling; but I am not free to do as I please, sweetie. You know I explained this to you before. So I am going to cease all future correspondence, darling, as I shall tell you everything when we meet. Writing is too inadequate to properly express all I have to tell you. Oh, darling, darling, my sweetheart, how can I give you up? I never, never will, but oh, what am I to do?

Augusta had arrived at one of J. B. Priestley's classic 'dangerous corners'. She was poised at the turning to criminality, free to reject, or adopt, Clark's basic proposition, or to adapt it in any way she thought fit. Once he had succeeded in his role of inciter, then a conspiracy of two would be formed.

According to both parties, the plan which he put to her was that he would supply poison, which she would stealthily administer to Edward Fullam, with the sole intention of making him so ill that he would be forced to retire to England, leaving Augusta in India, free for Clark.

On that Thursday, 20th April, 1911, Augusta Fullam chose the criminal path and agreed to poison her husband. But what exactly did she agree to?

The evidence indicates that, quite soon, the plan was to harden into an intent to murder, *or*, that such was always the design. The possibilities are: both always intended to kill; or, neither intended, at first, to kill; or, Clark intended, from the outset, to murder Edward, but persuaded Augusta that the poison would merely make him ill. On the facts, the possibility that Augusta alone intended to kill is not tenable.

Strongly suggestive of Clark's primary intent to kill is the lively suspicion that *he had already attempted to poison his wife.*

It had all happened in another part of the Plain, and it was, characteristically, botched, but it was, even so, a foreshadowing. For years, he had schemed to rid himself of burdensome Mabelle.

At some stage in his relationship with Augusta, presumably after the unveiling of his master-plan, he revealed to her (according to Augusta herself) an early attempt at elimination. While they were still living as a family in Calcutta, he had given Louisa enough arsenic to kill ten men, but she had vomited copiously and recovered. This *may* be a lie of Augusta's, but it fits all round, especially since Louisa is known to have had a lucky knack of vomiting freely at the right time.

There is more: on the Clarks' next posting, to Agra (in the past, before Meerut), Louisa nearly died of poisoning, instigated by her husband, she believed, through the agency of their cook.

Clark had a kind of Indian 'excuse' for his conduct. In Dinapore, round about 1903, when Louisa was in her mid-forties, she had behaved improperly—such was Clark's complaint—with an engine-driver by the name of Shaw. There might have been a pregnancy.

The idea of a liaison with an engine-driver is not so outlandish and fanciful as it first appears, when it is remembered that impressive Eurasians traditionally drove all the trains, and that Louisa came from the same background. However, Clark's slander was not believed then, and there is no reason now to reinstate it.

In all this ominous area, hearsay though it is, there is no sign that the poison for Louisa was meant only to incapacitate her. If Clark risked telling Augusta about Louisa's close call *at the Thursday meeting*, then it is the more likely that a fatal poisoning was planned *ab initio*.

Clark must have been confident, because he came to the meeting fully armed, with a pocketful of deadly arsenic, masquerading as 'tonic powders'.

As he ponders the choice of poison, and the choice of medium for its administration, the poisoner brings into consideration the health and disposition of his victim. Tonics were popular palliatives for ailing, wilting European residents in India. Edward Fullam had been off-colour and sorry for himself, and might well have jumped at the chance of being dosed by a wife who seemed, after all, to care about him.

Over and over again, the onlooker wonders at the credulity of the poison victim, but there it is! Even though Edward had good reason to fear that there was something between his wife and his doctor, it is not beyond the bounds of possibility that he would have trustingly gulped down the powders of destruction. It is a nice point if he would have taken them if Augusta told him that Clark had prescribed them. He certainly thought that Clark was a clever doctor.

However, Clark did not dare to risk such open administration. He was only experimenting, and might require to vary the dose. Common sense told him that Edward might connect the tonic with the resultant symptoms, and refuse to continue taking it. Augusta would have to conceal the arsenic in food or drink. She was a good housekeeper and, no doubt (unlike some Englishwomen, who preferred not to know), entered and supervised her kitchen.

Clark had lived all his life in the atmosphere of India, where arsenic was naturally the poisoner's first choice. It appears to have been as freely available in the bazaars as curry or cardamon. In hole-and-corner booths, there was no signing of registers. As is well known, it is tasteless, or, if anything, slightly sweetish. Its particular uses in India were the destruction of vermin, the preservation of wood, and the preparation of hides and skins. It was regularly ingested as an aphrodisiac.

Concealment was easy, because the gastro-intestinal symptoms produced by the arsenic conveniently mimicked the cholera and acute gastritis endemic in India. The Hindu custom of burning the dead and consigning the ashes to the Sacred River also prevented discovery. The exhumation of a Muslim corpse was far too serious an offence to the religious sentiments of the family for it ever to be ordered, unless the *other* evidence that the deceased had died of poison was overwhelming.

At that time, Clark might have been influenced by a native belief that murder by poisoning was a less heinous crime than murder by the shedding of blood.

Augusta did not even ask if she could sleep on it, because the very next day, Friday, she was writing brightly to Clark:

We now start afresh with a bright hope before us, shining like a beacon: our star of hope and comfort. So to the winds with trouble and care, darling.

My precious sweet, how did you get on with your long journey last night, darling? I am longing to hear of your safe arrival, and that all is well with your work. My hubby returned from Lodge, I believe, at midnight, but I was 'safe in the arms of Morpheus', so I never knew anything till I asked him this morning. He seems very nice and kind, and never referred, by a single word, to your visit, and neither did I. So you see, darling, in some cases 'silence is golden.' How much we enjoyed the day only towards the end that wretched K. A. disturbed our peace of mind, and brought a storm of wrath down upon my ears from you, sweetheart darling. Oh, Harry, darling, please don't think any the worse of me for encouraging and laughing so immoderately with that girl and her jokes. If I fall in your estimation, lovie, what good is there in life?

It would be a misjudgement, as coming events will show, to take Augusta's everyday, insouciant tone as consistent with her having the lesser intent of merely putting Edward out of action. Edward's studied failure to mention the visit at all seems most unnatural. There is a grim comedy in the scene where Clark, glowering, filled with his purpose, slightly paranoid in the presence of (presumably) another young Englishwoman, resented the giggling, and felt excluded.

On Monday, 24th April, after the weekend, Augusta reported:

> I am sorry I was utterly unable, darling, to send you even a few lines on Saturday and Sunday, as I explained to you, Bucha dearest, that I would have no chance my hubby being at home. You are anxious to know about the 'tonic'. Well, sweetheart, darling, I have given it regularly since I last saw you, and I must say it is a good tonic, in very truth, darling. My hubby is quite well and strong, and it really seems to have done him good. I shall certainly continue it, lovie, and let you know later. How is Mrs Clark, your lawful wife?

At this stage, she is cautious in case her letters should fall into the wrong hands. On 26th April, her bulletin would seem to endorse the aphrodisiac properties of arsenic. The matrimonial mockery of Edward's virility is amusing:

> Sweetheart mine, my hubby seems quite unaffected by the tonic powders. In fact, he is stronger and better than before, and more passionate, if such can be the case, in his case, my own darling. Some days I give him two, or even three powders, my Bucha dearest, but never less than one. I want you to let me know in return what you think of it, my own precious sweetie, and tell me how to go on?

Now that the mischief has begun, one would think that there would be a consolidation, a close drawing together, but, instead, there is a strange episode in which sexual jealousy overrides the importance of the plot. Perhaps, in this way, Augusta unconsciously displaced her guilt and fright on to a more acceptable, if equally intense, emotion.

The cause of her distress was the inopportune flaring up of an old flame of Clark's—importunate Miss W. When Clark received a letter from her, his mind was elsewhere, and he was under far too much pressure for multiple affairs. He sent the letter straight on to Augusta, but her reaction was out of all proportion, unreasonable. That evening, still upset by the letter, and with no confidant, she went out and danced wildly, recklessly, until she collapsed—nearly fainted—and had to be revived with port wine and wrapped in a warm coat. At home, she had a quarrel with Edward—possibly over her behaviour at the dance, or perhaps she attacked and reviled him about his short-comings—and it lasted until two o'clock in the morning. Stresses and strains were showing.

She conjures up her own Mr H., who, sadly, is leaving Meerut, and 'would be a kind and useful friend in case I needed one'. The bantering has changed to hectoring:

Do you know, my very own precious Bucha darling, you have made me very jealous by Miss W.'s enclosure. These I consider are incipient beginnings, and it is only an excuse about the cook. She really wishes to make friends with you again, and this is the 'thin end of the wedge'. Oh, how silly men-folk are, it's only we women who understand one another's tactics.

Surely in the whole of Calcutta there is a cook to be had? Oh, no, she just wanted an excuse to re-open the old correspondence. Well, Harry darling, my own precious sweetie, you must now choose between us. Are you an honourable man, or are you not, my darling? Because you cannot correspond with both her and me. If you are going to open up fresh communication, in however friendly a way, Bucha darling, then I cease at once. You know, sweetheart darling, how very jealous and proud your little girlie is, she will have none or all. Anyhow, as I have put my hand to the plough, I will not turn back whatever happens. I can always work, and I may yet live to see Mabelle and self very happy with your ten children. Oh, sweetheart, darling Harry, my Bucha, my heart is aching to-day. The choice lies with you, and you alone must make it, darling.

This lamentable ultimatum has a modern tone, and is a model of how to lose your man! The cryptic reference to the plough *must* mean that she is determined to ship—or see—Edward off, even if she has to go it alone. She cannot have thought this through; trips to the local bazaar, on her own, for arsenic whose dosage she is unsure of, are not a feasible proposition.

Desperately, wishing that he had not done the honourable thing in the first place, Clark sends her a copy of his reply to Miss W., but Augusta is not appeased:

> I read your reply to your old friend, Miss W., which is couched in the most friendly and favourable terms, and I see, darling, with much regret that you are willing, nay, too eager, to do her bidding in every way, and that at once. I am glad you have got her back, Bucha darling. No! I am not glad. It is only my proud spirit makes me write that. Never mind, you decide quick. You are a doctor, and a surgeon, and you must know how the operation hurts, to have one's limb cut off, darling. So my own, my darling love, use the keen sharp knife of separation quickly, and pray do not torture me like this, longer than you can help.

Paradoxically, this is Augusta's masterpiece, her most deeply felt and genuine love-letter, written red-hot, with no pretty posturings. Allowing for her talents and education, the language and rhythms are poetic, with the force and savagery of Webster's

> *I had a limb corrupted to an ulcer,*
> *But I have cut it off; and now I'll go*
> *Weeping to Heaven on crutches.*

A very determined woman is revealed, but Clark is not repelled, and does his best to repair a rift which is dangerous, artificial, and not of his making. The exchanges which follow are like a play within a play—or a trial within a trial:

> Harry, darling, my own precious, dearest Bucha, I am glad to hear you have decided a choice between me and

Miss W. But still that does not satisfy me. You must prove to me, darling, that there has ceased all correspondence between you. You say you are surprised at my jealousy, but put yourself in my place, darling, and then think how you would feel if I wrote to a gentleman friend. I know she will surely reply to your letter about the cook, and then if you send him down, she will write and thank you, through mere courtesy, and so on, the beginning will be established! You say, darling, that I cannot blame you, if she chooses to write to you. No, but I do certainly blame you for so eagerly replying and deferring to her every wish—cook, tatling,* pillows and all! You could have made heaps of excuses, my Bucha. Lots of work in a large hospital, no time, or better still, need not have replied at all, but darling, I don't want to lecture you on the subject, for you must please yourself. You know my wishes on the subject, you know my jealous disposition, and, sweetie darling, if you love me, as you say you do, then very easily you can prove to me that your love is mine alone.

Oh, this is not imagination on my part, my own darling, as you so lightly pronounce it. How can you say so? Harry, darling, how plausible you are! Just imagine telling me not to worry over trifles, do you call this a trifle, to write loving letters to one girl, and nice friendly ones to another. As for promising on your honour, I am afraid men's honour fails, when a woman tempts. Now I dare say you are very cross and angry with me, darling, but the fault is yours, not mine. However, let this only draw us closer together (if you will).

*

Harry, darling, I have read and destroyed your 'copy' of Miss W.'s letter, which you say you have written. Did you only write it, to please me, lovie darling, or have you sent it?

You do not mention that. Never mind, darling, I must accept your word of honour as a gentleman (and a pedigree one at that). But surely she must have replied ere

* *Sic.* Either 'tatting' or 'tattling': both fit!

this, considering the cook is wanted sharp. Please let me
see the reply, if you don't mind.

\*

My sweetheart darling I have not yet made up my mind
to administer those powders. You have set me a very hard
task, Bucha, and I feel afraid, Harry darling. You blame
me for compelling you to be rude to Miss W., and treat her
in an ungentlemanly way, but what do you ask of your
little girlie? Now why do you wish to see me again,
dearest? Try not to be impatient, my sweetie; you saw me
only ten days ago, and since then you have been
quarrelling with me. Miss W. does not really love you as I
do—no, never, it is only for her own ends to make use of
you, darling. But you are mine, you belong to me by all
the sacred ties that exist between us, both past and
present, my own darling. Now do not let me start afresh,
Bucha darling. You don't realise what a jealous woman
suffers.

\*

Sweetheart, thanks, thanks for so solemnly vowing and
promising to cease all future correspondence with Miss
W. You know that I could not bear you to take her
affection back again. Will you, please, lovie darling, like a
good boy, send me her answer to you regarding the cook,
etc. Please do not be afraid of any more lectures and
jealousies on the subject, but darling, I must know and see
how you are going to act.

\*

So you have quite forgiven your little girlie and taken
me back into your heart again. Oh, Harry darling, I
searched minutely every word of your dear letter, and
each line, for reference to some tone of regret in giving up
Miss W., but I could find none, my very own precious
Bucha sweetheart darling. Do you really mean to tell me
that you love me altogether far more than she, whom you
waited for, so many long years?

\*

Sweetheart, darling, my own precious Bucha, let me know if you truly feel any real regret for giving up Miss W., and snubbing her? Am I quite sufficient to atone, all the remainder of our lives, for what you have lost in her darling? Ponder well, and let me have your answer, darling. What would your Buchee do, without her own precious Bucha darling?

\*

What a nice long newsy letter this is, Harry darling. I am sure Miss W. never sent you such nice long loving letters, did she? What about her cook, love?

Augusta did not give up on Miss W. and her cook until she had stamped them into the ground.

As if he sensed Augusta's alienation from him, Edward himself made a symbolic, distancing move—which she found herself resenting:

My hubby has taken to sleeping out in the back verandah, and Frank's bed is also there at nights, so that his room is empty, and of course I have my own room with Katty and Baby. I told Eddie I feel just like a dried up old maid, or else a widow, without nice loving arms around me; and really I can't sleep for hours every night, darling, just on account of this horrid lonely feeling. My hubby would make a splendid old bachelor or widower, he never wants any love in his life. But I am so different. I can't live without plenty of love and caresses. Eddie says that my second husband will make up for it, so I suppose I must wait for that.

Not the most tactful letter to write to a pining lover! It is true that the Hot Weather will have begun at the beginning of April, but even so, Augusta did not interpret Edward's move as merely practical. Since Augusta's own room was so crowded, it may be that Edward's room had been the place in which he had been more passionate if such could be the case... The final sentence—poor Edward's invocation of a second, replacement

53

husband—shows that bitter, marital discussion had been making a misery of his life.

Although the Miss W. affair appeared to be at the centre of Augusta's mind, in fact she was concurrently persisting with the dosing of Edward, in spite of her threat not so to continue, which was voiced in the letter written ten days after the meeting on Thursday, 20th April.

After one week, her stock of powders brought by Clark was depleted, and he began to send her packets of poison by post, addressed to 'Mrs Clarkson' (a small conceit), to be collected by Augusta at the post office.

On 27th April, there is a bombshell in among the first report of actual gastric symptoms suffered by Edward:

> Now, darling, you are very thoughtful in sending me some more powders. I was going to ask you for some, as I have only two left. Yesterday I gave my hubby three during the day, and he came back from the office at 6 p.m. with pains in his stomach, had a loose motion, and felt weak. He soon pulled up, however, and now seems quite well, darling. I don't think these powders are having any effect, Bucha. What do you think, lovie? You say they must be given regularly, and then *you say you can't administer them to Mrs C. as regularly as you would like to. Then what is the use of them, darling? She will need much more than that, lovie.** However, tell me plainly what you think.

In the light of these extremely sinister observations, the previous, polite enquiry after the health of Louisa—'How is Mrs Clark, your lawful wife?'—which was incorporated in the letter of Monday, 24th April, *only three days after the Thursday meeting*, takes on a decidedly suspicious tinge, and throws a darker light on what was actually decided at that meeting.

* Author's italics

54

## Chapter Four

# The Cook's Tale

Bibu was a cook: an honest cook, and a young one. He also waited at the Clarks' table. He was scared stiff of the doctor-sahib, who had a nasty temper, and he was homesick for Delhi and his mother.

The six months working for the Clarks in Delhi had not been too bad, but he did not like Agra at all. There was plague about, and he could not find the food that he was used to in the bazaar.

Life was dangerous and perplexing. He scented trouble in the hot, heavy, diseased air. Trouble for Bibu.

\* \* \*

Clark was a lonely bachelor in Agra for only one month. Unforgivable things had been said, but his family still looked to him as an ill-treated animal waits for its master. On a day between 20th and 24th April, he moved them from Delhi to his new bungalow at 135 Cantonments. Bibu came too. He stayed for only two weeks.

Louisa trusted her cook and refused to let him go when, almost immediately, Bibu asked for leave. He was miserable, and worse was to come. Soon afterwards, Clark summoned him into his bedroom for a private word. (The Clarks, too, had separate bedrooms. One would think that sexual congress had long ceased between them, and that mutual revulsion was extreme, but that might be a rash assumption. As a matter of fact, Clark's bull-terrier bitch, Julie, slept on his bed—a very important dog.)

Bibu kept his distance in the shady, unfamiliar room. Clark's manner was menacing, his face set and cruel. He produced three small, paper packets. '*Don't tell anyone,*' he said, '*but I want you to put these powders in the memsahib's supper tea.*' The dose was one a day, for three days, although if Bibu could not manage to slip in the third one, it did not matter too much.

'What is the powder, sahib?'

'Don't be afraid. It's only a purgative.'

There was no need to worry: the powders were tasteless, and no one would ever know. Fifty rupees was to be Bibu's very sizeable reward, and then he could go home to Delhi.

If, however, Bibu talked, then Clark would throttle him to death.

Bibu cringed, and believed him. He waited until tea-time, when Clark had gone out (to the hospital, the bazaar, or the post office?), and then he took the packets straight to Louisa. Young Harry, on leave from Meerut, watched as she unwrapped the paper. The powder inside was white, and looked like flour.

'I must go home, now,' said Bibu. 'My mother will die of a broken heart if I am hanged.'

'Don't go,' Louisa begged him. 'You can sleep on the verandah, where the sahib *can't* strangle you in your sleep.'

But it was no use; Bibu left there and then, with his small wages, an honest cook.

That evening, while Clark was still out and about, his family had a timely visitor—Assistant-Surgeon Linton, also of the Indian Subordinate Medical Department. Harry showed him the powder—enough to cover an eight-anna bit—and asked him to examine it. Harry probably did not state, in terms, how the powder had come into his hands, but the implication was plain to all concerned.

Linton was on the spot. He formed the immediate and uncomfortable opinion that it was a powerful poison, but fervently wished that he had stayed at home. So he hedged, and took the powder—two or three grains—away with him for analysis. He heated it with a blowpipe—not the most sophisticated test known to man at that time, but then he was no expert in toxicology—and concluded from the garlicky smell thus produced what he already knew: that it was one of the compounds of arsenic. He thought that its effect would be fatal in about twenty minutes.

Now, Linton was junior to Clark in the Department. He was afraid of Clark. His job was at stake. It was all too vague. Where was the legal proof?

Next day, he told young Harry Clark that it was a *slow* poison. He did not specify arsenic. And there the matter rested. Nothing was done.

Clark was lucky, of course, but, even so, he had made a hash of things once again. Louisa was now more on her guard than ever. Any concurrent regimen of arsenic in Meerut *and* Agra was, for the moment, out of the question. Augusta would have to go it alone.

Anyway, what exactly did Clark think he was doing? It is not by any means clear exactly how much powder Linton took away for analysis. Louisa kept some of it, understandably not wishing all the evidence to go out of her hands.

Linton estimated the powder presented to him to weigh two to three grains. Let us suppose that this was pure white arsenic, for it was designed to dissolve in tea without taste or gritty texture. If Linton's portion was, say, only one packet—one third of the total—then Clark was proposing to give Louisa at least six grains of arsenic, spread over three days. As he well knew, two to three grains is quite sufficient to kill an adult.

Susceptibility to arsenic notoriously varies with the individual. Clark had to allow for Louisa's tendency to react to noxious substances with rapid vomiting. He had tried her before, and failed. She was bulky, presumably ate well, and was in fair enough health. On the other hand, she was worn down by the tribulations of her marriage; at 54, she was probably menopausal; and she had just endured a major move, in the heat, from Delhi to Agra.

Whereas the intention was to break Edward Fullam down slowly, it does look as if, to put it bluntly, Clark had decided to finish Louisa off, once and for all. He might have thought that the time was right, and to be seized, because, just after the move, the family was little known in Agra. (It is true that he had been stationed there previously, but that was some years before.) The death from gastro-intestinal disease of an unimportant, stay-at-home, Eurasian woman—such would have been his delightful calculation—was likely to pass without undue comment.

There was now, as Louisa saw it, a frightening gap where once had been a trusty cook who trotted straight to her side with her husband's packets of poison. But not for long. Budhu, Bibu's replacement, was not Louisa's choice—nor Clark's. He was the choice of one Abdul Latif. Louisa sent off to the station hospital (Clark's place of employment) for a new servant, and it was Abdul Latif, a head orderly, or some such, who picked out Budhu for secondment to the doctor's home.

Although, therefore, Budhu was not actually Clark's choice (unless he had instructed Abdul Latif), in fact he might as well have been. At 42, he was more mature than Bibu, and less likely to panic, and he was of diplomatic character, malleable, and resourceful for his own ends. He could walk any tight-rope. And he also had more to lose—his greatly valued post at the hospital.

Budhu's salary was six rupees a month, but there was a bonus—Louisa, as an insurance policy, gave him another six rupees a month, out of her own pocket. So, quite happily, he served two masters, and all was quiet and above-board for some twelve months. Louisa stayed alert, but she had a temporary breathing-space.

Another newcomer in the Clark household that May, 1911, was Alick Joseph, the letter-writer in person, who came to lodge with them for one year. He was very much Clark's man, and Louisa and Maud both loathed him. Maud had once written to her father, 'Please tell Alick Joseph that we don't want his dirty smelling wishes or remembrances. Tell him please to keep them in his dirty pockets as we don't want them.' However, he was not really a bad fellow; there was no wickedness in him, just failings and frailties.

Clark dominated him, and engaged him in disturbing conversations which he would have preferred to avoid. On one occasion, Clark read out a newspaper report about a begum who had poisoned her lover with arsenic. Joseph, an innocent in these matters, remarked that arsenic, surely, could not kill a man, or else why would doctors prescribe it for virility? Not at all, was Clark's chilling reply: it all depended on the dose.

Clark's manner became more confidential, and he told the young man something that shocked him profoundly: Mrs

Clark had been given more than one dose of arsenic, but she had proved to be 'poison proof'.

Around the middle of May, Clark went to Joseph, looking 'rather serious', and, in an extraordinary outburst, informed him that he was sick and tired of Louisa and would get rid of her by poison at the first opportunity. He said, further to appal his young henchman, that he had tried to poison her when she was sick, but had failed because she was too quick for him.

No braver than Assistant-Surgeon Linton before him, Joseph stayed put at the bungalow and kept quiet, mentally overpowered by the older man. He worried, though, and somehow, unimaginably, persuaded Clark and Louisa to go with him to a Roman Catholic priest, in the hope that, through conversion, they would find each other again. Roman Catholics must not be Freemasons, and, while in Agra, Clark *did* resign from his Lodge, but his reason for so doing is a mystery.

\* \* \*

Meanwhile, up in Meerut, Augusta is persevering. Her letters still retain a veiled ambiguity over the exact nature of the much desired end towards which she is working, but only a very charitable reading can soften her actions. She is more impatient than Clark, and keeps pressing him for results. By 4th May, 1911, the dose has been increased, with the wrong effect:

> You will undoubtedly be glad to hear that I screwed up my courage to give one powder yesterday, Harry darling, but no effect so far, except as a very good tonic. I make my husband very amorous, Bucha darling, and I don't want this, please. Today another one will be administered, my sweetheart darling, and you will know results.

\*

> Harry sweetheart, my hubby since yesterday has had slight stomach trouble, and nausea, which he attributes to an attack of indigestion, to which he is subject, darling. The powders are going on being administered steadily, darling, but there is little or no difference, except that my

59

hubby feels the heat very much, and complains of being tired. But that's an old story. I wish to know, darling please, in reply to this, how long I am to continue this treatment, and when should desired results appear, Bucha?

*

Harry, darling, sweetheart mine, and mine alone, those powders are proving themselves a most excellent tonic, and that is about all, darling. My hubby has never looked so well, nor felt so well in all his life, Bucha love. How long am I to continue in this way? I think it would be much nicer to bring about a crisis, soon.

Augusta's letter of 8th May is coarser, more shrill, and less covert:

Now about the powders, Harry darling, I gave two on Saturday, in two cups of tea, you know, as I send his tiffin. But on Sundays only I never get a chance, Bucha. How many hundreds of years will they take? I must say I don't approve of your powders at all, darling. Meanwhile, we are constantly running fearful risks, my own darling. However, if it pleases you, then I am happy.

Her letter of 9th May contains internal evidence of the constituents of the 'tonic powders':

Of course, I have not yet received the tonic powders you mention having sent, lovie, as I did not know anything about them until I read your letter, so I did not inquire about the tiny parcel at the P.O., but I suppose I shall get it tomorrow, and will let you know, Harry darling, sweetheart mine. My hubby is improving greatly on two of the old powders daily (you remember five grains each). His complexion has changed to a lovely pink. I have never seen him look better.

Ten grains of arsenic per day would have been a fatal dose indeed, and therefore Clark must have been mixing some harmless substance such as sugar with the poison. No fatal dose was intended at that time. Clark was still relying on a cumulative effect. Probably, in case of any challenge, he was supplying a compound which *could*, at a pinch, on analysis, pass as a *bona fide* tonic.

There must have been times when Augusta told herself that it was not too late to draw back, that everything could be safe and normal again. Her apparently insensitive ability to sustain a chatty correspondence, in which she demonstrates her own charms and thriftiness, is part of her attempt to keep a grasp on reality, to distance herself from the terror of the project:

> It was most amusing to note how careful my hubby was in handing out Miss Kitty from the phaeton! At any other time, I would have become very jealous, Harry darling, but I only thought if my own Harry were here, I should never be allowed to shift for myself. Anyhow, I would rather wait for you, my darling, than let other hands touch mine, even if they are my hubby's. It was a nice moonlight evening, and we all sat on the *chabootra\** darling, when suddenly Miss G. asked me to take off my white silk gloves. I laughed and said, 'I have on no gloves,' and then they all remarked that my hands and arms were so lily-white in the moonlight, they thought I had gloves. Now darling, I do not mention this for boasting's sake, no never, but just to show you my very own precious love, what a sweet little Buchee darling you have.

*

> Katty is going away to Mussoorie, darling. I am sending her up with Mrs A., and two daughters, who leave on Friday, the 12th, my very own precious darling. The child suffers very much in this heat, and her heart seems weak and run down. So I am sure the hills will improve her, and then I will only pay a little towards her keep, darling, and in that, she will get her tuition and music from the two girls. It's a good chance, and I am not going to let it slip. What do you think of this plan, Bucha

---

\* A raised, bench-like platform outside a building, for taking the air.

dearest? I would like to know your dear opinion because I always like to do what you approve of. I remember you once said to me the hills would not suit Katty's heart, but the child seems so run down and upset by the heat, darling, that I am risking it, and sending her for a change.

A dramatic warning to beware of Louisa Clark reads very oddly at this time:

Glad am I to hear that you are well again, my own darling, and your throat better. I was feeling anxious and worried, darling, as I know that your wife is not to be trusted, and she may do anything, at any time, to you, Harry darling.

It is not like Augusta to swallow all of Clark's propaganda, and she still does not lose sight of his basic—or base—character:

Sweetheart mine, I missed your letter on Sunday so much. I spent a most wretched and miserable day, and in the evening, although we attended church as usual, I must confess my heart was hot and rebellious, and my thoughts had left Meerut and were far away in Agra wondering what my own sweetheart was doing! Do you remember how I used to tease you on Sundays, by asking if you were going to the city to look for black hens, darling?

She may have heard about his thumpings and kickings in the bosom of his family, because she betrays some anxiety about the future of her own, vulnerable children:

I think we will get on A.1 together, dearest love, only I don't know how your grown-up family will tolerate me. I know you will be good and kind to my little ones for my sake, won't you, Bucha?

**Romance** is the engine that drives Augusta on. If she could only switch it off, none of this would be happening:

We dined outside on the lawn last evening, my Bucha, after returning from the Club. It was so enjoyable and romantic, dining under the moon and on the grass, and it reminded me of your 90 days' leave last year, my very own precious darling, and of how we used to enjoy each other's company at all times, darling. Meerut is so full of you, at every turn, Bucha love. But as you say, darling, brighter days, we hope, are in store for us, which will eclipse past records, sweetie.

*

Oh, Harry, my own precious darling, your letter today is one long, yearning cry for your little love. Be good and calm, darling, we will have a nice, long chat on Thursday and talk things over, and see how we can expedite matters that will bring us nearer together, Bucha darling.

In spite of his dodgy stomach (and lively libido) Edward continued to tolerate Clark's visits to Meerut on every third Thursday of the month. These were Thursday meetings because on that day Edward could be relied upon to don his Masonic apron and leave the lovers alone.

There was a special urgency about the Thursday visit of 18th May. Some powders had been lost in the post, and, at Augusta's pressing request, Clark brought replacements. The following day, she wrote a bland and ingenuous letter:

It is now just after breakfast, and I sit down to reply to your most loving and lengthy letter, brought to me yourself yesterday, sweetheart. It is so dull here today, and I miss you so much, lovie darling. Would that I were always near you, darling, or at least had some hopes of seeing you every day. Oh, what a powerful thing is this love, that has the power to make glad or sad according to circumstances?

How did you reach home, my sweetheart? I hope safe and well. My hubby came home at 12 from Lodge, and I had had a good sleep and just woke, lovie. He asked what time you left, and I said the *tonga** came for you after

* Two-wheeled horse-drawn carriage

dinner, and you went to see your son, which was quite true, was it not, Bucha darling? Did you visit your son? My hubby has not referred to your visit, by another word, sweetie, and so I have been perfectly silent too.

Well, now, did you have a nice, enjoyable day, Harry darling? I did all I could to make you happy and comfortable, my sweetest broad-shouldered Bucha Harry, and so it's not my fault if you did not thoroughly enjoy your holiday and outing, my darling, as I gave you the best I had, viz., myself.

Yet, the very next day, down to business:

Yesterday I administered the powder you left with me, viz., the half-dose, my very own precious darling Bucha, with the result, nil. Not so much as the change of a hair's breadth, Harry darling, so I intend to let today and Sunday go by with no further administration. But I shall begin in earnest on Monday, and shall keep you informed of results.

On Monday, 22nd May, Augusta tipped a dollop of jalapin into Edward's tea, sent, in the Indian way, to his office. It may or may not have been in admixture with arsenic. Jalapin, a drastic purgative, whose prolonged effects can kill, would have been familiar to Clark in his trade as occasional abortionist. He did not, however, allow for the new powders' being 'too tasty',* and the experiment was a disaster:

Harry darling, my own precious Bucha, I have news for you, and you must tell me how to act. I administered the full dose in tea yesterday, but my hubby returned the whole jug of tea, untasted, from the office, saying it was bad. When he came home at six, I asked him why he had returned his tea, and he said, 'There was some bad medicine in it,' so Harry darling, I dare not continue with these powders. He also said, 'This is the second time the tea has

---

* Counsel later contended that jalapin was not an objectionable thing to take, and that there must have been an admixture.

Kathleen, the Fullams'
daughter: the watcher in
the wings.

Lieutenant Henry Lovell
William Clark, Indian
Subordinate Medical
Department.

Henry Clark: brother Mason, and a busy man of affairs.

tasted bad,' which shows that the jalapin is readily tasted.

My Bucha darling, Fate is against us, and all our plans are utterly frustrated and have failed. What is to be done, darling? I feel so very disappointed and down-hearted, not so much on my own account as on account of you, for I know darling you want me so much, and the best prime years of your life are being wasted, without love, care, and comfort, darling.

Now I want you to let me know two things in your reply, please, Harry Bucha. Tell me what to do with the powders I have by me, as I cannot give any more, for he can taste them, darling. (2) What is your opinion or best plan of operation for the future, my darling? It is an old saying, 'Love will ever find a way,' or 'Where there's a will there's a way,' Harry darling, so let me know exactly what you think. The first powders were tasteless and un-suspected, but not strong enough, but these jalapin ones do not suit at all, darling.

Now Edward suspects. Separate and apart, in gloomy bungalows in Agra and Meerut, there are *two* tragic, watchful figures. It is worse for Edward. Before Clark, he had thought that Augusta loved him, and he has become a broken man. Louisa, who has long lost all illusions about her husband, is gutsy, defiant, living from day to day, and buttressed by her grown children.

Edward could still break free, and the store of arsenic lying heavily inside his bones and tissues would be gradually eliminated. There is much that he could do, but, like Louisa, he digs in and defends himself as best he can. On 16th June, Augusta will complain:

> The powders I find very hard to administer, as he does not take any food prepared from my hand, makes his own cocoa,* etc. Still I am doing my best.

---

* No Pierre Emile L'Angelier! (A classic 'Not Proven' case of 1857. The Prosecution contended that Madeleine Smith handed out cocoa laced with arsenic through the bars of her basement window in Glasgow to L'Angelier, her redundant lover, *and he drank it*.)

An impasse. And a hiccup in the relationship, too. Augusta plays with Indian fire, and sends off a vicious, disenchanted letter:

My very own precious lovie, don't you think our correspondence rather risky, in case we may be discovered any day? Besides, I do really think you are growing tired, and finding it irksome, for you give me no news whatever, Bucha, darling, but just imitate my letter in return. There seems to be a decided change in you, my own sweetheart, and for the last two days I have been so miserable and unhappy, thinking it all over, darling, I have made myself ill, and so today have treated myself to a big dose of oil, which has weakened me. Please don't think I need to be 'pacified'. Oh, no, just leave me to myself; your conversation on Thursday last, Harry darling, has led me to believe that the so-called ladies (God help them to bear the name), you are at present associating with in Agra, are of a very low order. But I will not dictate to you, my Bucha darling, choose for yourself, you must surely agree with me, lovie darling, when one fair dame wishes to go and marry you as she stands? There is lots of news going in Meerut (dear old Meerut, I love it so). But as you refrain from news-telling, so must I refrain, Harry darling. Perhaps the oil has stirred up my liver and made me 'moody'.

When next she writes, it is by way of an apology, and an encouragement:

Poor old G. is very ill with acute pains in his stomach, Harry darling. He has three doctors attending, enough to kill anyone, I should say, one says gout in the stomach, another says gall-stones, and the third declares it's appendicitis; so let us see between them what they manage to do with the poor man's life, darling. Now this is written with all apologies to my dearest, sweetest darling old Dr. sahib, for, of course, there is none other so clever in my eyes, sweetheart. Harry, darling, as you are so clever, my darling pet, do consider and hit upon a plan that will soon

66

achieve our most desired and longed-for results; and darling, if there is anything you wish to send me in a small parcel, please register it.

Back to the drawing-board. Pachydermatous, unmoved by Augusta's attack on his skills and character, Clark probably continued to supply his arsenic tonic powders (since Edward's symptoms began to multiply), while at the same time poring over his forensic-medicine books, turning down corners with brutish fingers and underlining promising passages.

The next prescription from his researches was, theoretically, a brilliant notion: croton oil, which is highly toxic, was to be given to Edward 'by mistake' for castor oil. The seeds of *Croton tiglium*, which are sometimes called 'purging nuts', resemble castor seeds in both size and shape, although they are somewhat larger, and striated rather than mottled. Their purgative effect is so drastic that croton oil was removed from the British Pharmacopoeia. During the Fascist regime in Italy, the oil was alleged to have been used as a method of extracting 'confessions'. Mistakes *have* occurred. Once, even a druggist mistook croton oil for castor oil, swallowed half an ounce of it, and was seriously ill for a fortnight. In another case, a man died four hours after swallowing, by mistake, two and a half drachms of croton oil.

There was, however, a flaw in Clark's reasoning:

Sweetheart, darling, I think your plan about the croton oil won't do, Bucha, because my hubby seldom or ever takes a dose of castor oil—he hates it. But I don't clearly understand you, my sweetie; you once say you are studying to take\* some other stuff, and then you say you can send me some more powders, if I let you know by return post. Darling sweet, have you decided on anything yet? And please do remember it must be tasteless, my Bucha. If my hubby were only in ill health, and I had to dose him at all, things would be very much easier, wouldn't they?

\* Make?

Life goes on. Appearances are kept up. Edward dances to the music of time. News of a wedding at the end of May contrasts incongruously with the croton-oil letter of 26th May:

> The wedding was a big success, my very own precious darling, and I can tell you their purse must be much lighter after all that expenditure. For my part, I prefer a nice quiet little wedding, to all that display and show, darling. The bride looked most charming and E.* looked very happy, but tired. Mr. Fullam gave a nice speech. Fancy, Harry darling, the newly married pair are still here in Meerut. They leave tonight for Simla, and I think E. will be very glad to get his bride to himself after so much confusion.

A second instalment about the wedding, written a few days later, sets the scene which is the creative origin of the mythical first meeting of the lovers:

> Now my Bucha, as you express a desire to know with whom I danced at the wedding, I hasten to inform you. I first had a waltz with young Mr V. (do you know him, darling?) The second dance was a set of Lancers, and my partner was a Mr W., a big broad fellow, who reminded me very much of my absent darling, my own precious loved one. This Mr W. asked my hubby why he didn't tell him all this time that there was a Mrs Fullam, and that she was so young and girlish. So my hubby looked at me rather astonished, and said he thought everyone knew Mrs Fullam. What was your first impression, Harry darling, when you first met me? Did you think I was 'young and girlish', my own Bucha, lovie darling? I remember worrying Eddie to bring you once, and this is the result, Bucha sweetheart mine.

Edward had not invited Clark to a *dance*! There is, in fact, no evidence that Augusta *ever* danced with Clark. Did Edward

* Probably Edward's nephew and namesake, Edward McKeon Fullam, son of William Arnold, born 16th April, 1893.

look quizzically at her, rather than with astonishment? Was there irony in his comment?

Alick Joseph contributes a decoration, a flourish, to one of Clark's holding letters, and Augusta parries with yet another of her prophetic sayings:

> The lines at the head or commencement of your dear letter are very uncommon and fine. Now, my own darling, which disease have you got, in the world of love? I should say, neither measles, nor nettle-rash, my lovie, but a very serious sickness indeed, from which it appears to me, you will not recover my Bucha pet, what say you, darling?

## Chapter Five

## Bad Omens

India is a land of superstition. Divination stops journeys, marriages, and other rash acts. Omens—bad omens—were beginning to brood around the bungalow in Meerut, like sentinel owls.

By now, Edward's eyes were red and sore. Arsenic was leaking and seeping through the tear-ducts. Red tears of arsenic.

Such unaccountable afflictions were part of everyday life on the Plains in summer—the temperature was 115 degrees in the shade—and Edward soldiered on. He might manage to wangle a spot of leave, soon, and there were things to look forward to, such as the Masonic banquet on 15th June. That would be on a Thursday.

Squabbling and fretful, Augusta and Clark were also looking forward to the 15th:

What was wrong with you to grumble all the letter through and scold your little girl in a way that's astonishing after saying you don't wish to go over the ground again, and then filling your dearest letter with the subject? Harry, darling, my very own precious sweetheart mine, I am sorry I caused you a moment's heartache or disappointment in not hearing from me. What would you do, if you were to lose me, darling? I do not mean by death, only but even if in this life you never win me, after all, Bucha, what will you do? Suppose I were taken off to England, or some distant part of India. I dread to think of it, my own Bucha darling. Why do you call me heartless and cruel and bearing animosity, Harry dearest, my own precious. I would give my very life for you my Bucha, you should know that. Then why get angry and abuse me, darling, at the same time calling me gentle, generous, and loving hearted? I see we are not finished quarrelling and fighting as yet, Harry darling; but I shall wait until we meet next Thursday, to renew the attack my own darling. I am going to punish you a little more I will tell you what your punishment is when I am face to face with you, lovie. It won't hurt you very much, dearest love. You know what I mean only too well, my own darling sweetheart.

A little light whipping with a fly-whisk, perhaps? Either before or after the punishment—as incentive or reward (the imagination boggles)—Clark produced a large, potentially fatal concoction of arsenic, to be boiled into a solution. This is the *first time* that he has dared to supply a massive dose—the big one, no messing! They have fallen back on their old friend, arsenic, because it is tasteless; but, in fact, this solution proves to 'scald' both the throat and the stomach.

That night, the first omen came winging into Augusta's bedroom. The swinging *punkah*, which was suspended directly above her bed, suddenly broke and fell on her.* She could have been injured. It was a hard life, but the next day she perked up enough to write twice to Clark:

Well my own loving Bucha sweetheart, how did you get through your long journey? I hope your train ran to time, darling, and you had a comfortable night's journey, reaching Agra all safe and in good time for your work lovie? I have already told you all about the nasty accident of last night, which might have ended seriously for me, Harry darling, and then what would you have done, Bucha dearest, for a nice little pet like me? Today I have a slight headache, and I do miss you so very much, my own precious love. There seems such a blank in my life when you go out of it, darling. The parting was hard and I want

---

* If Augusta had known her Kipling as well as her Shakespeare, she might have been even more worried:

> '... the punkah stops, and falls the night
> For you or Me.'

you so much. How did you enjoy the whole day and the lovely long twilight drive, darling, and then the walk down 'lovers' lane', and all the blissful hours spent together, my own Bucha, dearest? I was in a perfect dream of bliss and happiness, and I yearn for another soon, lovie. Don't reply to my 'business' letter here to the house, Harry darling, in case any jealous fancies are aroused.

I am writing this in the drawing-room, where we have our dining-room table for the sake of the *punkah*. The dining-room is converted into a bedroom for the *punkah* too. And my bedroom is empty save for the broken hanging *punkah*. The excitement of yesterday and the shock last night was too much for me, and the heart attack was dreadful.

Nonetheless, Friday, 16th June, 1911, was the day on which Augusta again doctored Edward's tea. She knew that it was the largest dose of poison yet administered, and likely to have grave effects. Indeed, if Edward had not, like Louisa, vomited repeatedly—thirty times in all—he might never have recovered.

Augusta drew up a medical record-sheet for Clark's attention:

Since 4 p.m.
  Vomited eight times, purged once.
  Vomited ten times at a quarter to nine.
  Vomited twelve times at ten p.m.
  Slept after that.

When Edward came home ill from the office, Augusta deemed it prudent to send for two doctors—a Staff-Surgeon of the Royal Army Medical Corps and, less exaltedly, an 'old duffer' who lived opposite, Captain William Weston, retired from the Indian Subordinate Medical Service.

Poor, lonely, unwanted Edward told them the plain truth, or half of it, but they did not hear him. The surgeon took the bluff, sophisticated view, while the older, more experienced man delved into cobwebby recesses of his mind and saw there a shadow of Edward's enemy within. But it was preposterous. No one would want to harm mild, mannerly Edward. Now if it had been lusty Clark, frequenter of shady alleys and women's boudoirs, *then* there might have been suspicion.

Augusta writes as if she is genuinely upset, and also frightened:

17th June

Harry Darling,

My hubby has been very ill all Friday night, since four o'clock, with symptoms of cholera. I got the Staff-Surgeon, Captain P., to whom he is entitled, to treat him, and also Captain Weston has been kindly giving him help. I have been up all night giving him ice, etc. My hubby declares his last mouthful of tea and tiffin caused a burning sensation, and he started reaching in office. My darling, I can't go to the P.O. this morning for your dearest letter, sweetheart, as I can't leave him, and I expect Captain P. any minute. They all blame the Masonic dinner on Thursday night, but he himself says the tiffin upset him, darling. You and I know how. I cannot bear to see his suffering, Bucha darling. He has fever this morning, and is quite weak and prostrate, kept in bed, and on cornflour, cooked in water.

18th June

He is very weak, Harry darling, and lies for hours with eyes closed, not speaking much or taking any notice of things. The reaching has all stopped, but he complains of a soreness in his stomach, and seems weak, as I tell you. Also rush of blood to the head, and a headache.

*

Sweetheart mine, as you wish to know, I must tell you that the Staff-Surgeon did not exactly state his diagnosis of my hubby's illness last Friday night; the only remark he made was, 'Oh, Lord, you went to a Masonic Banquet last night,' and then he laughed. But Captain Weston, the old duffer opposite, said the cause of such a severe illness was very strange, and when my hubby persistently told him of the scalding in his stomach as soon as he had swallowed the last mouthful of tea and tiffin, then he said, 'If you had any enemies, I should say you were poisoned with arsenic poisoning.' Harry darling, I firmly believe that my hubby suspects me because he said that the tiffin went to the office with some irritant poison in it. The whole thing has subsided and blown over now, Harry lovie, but you can imagine all I have gone through.

Augusta's tone has changed. At last she can stand at Edward's bedside and see him seriously ill. This is what she wanted, isn't it? But does the shock of the reality make her repent? We can only look for clues within the coils of her letters. For safety, she still preserves a guarded, if inconsistent, style, with indiscreet, cryptic remarks such as "You and I know how.'

'I cannot bear to see his suffering' *does* sound like a genuine outburst, and we like her a little more for it, but then, against it, we have to put her outrageous letter of 21st June:

Oh! I have been through such an awful time lately! This week has seemed an eternity, and I have felt so lonely and miserable. My hubby is sick; he does not improve at all since that Friday night. He gets half a tonic powder every day, and his liver seems affected. He takes all sorts of medicine, Harry darling, and seems a different man. He now goes to office in the phaeton, and returns in it again for tiffin, after which he sleeps till five, and then goes for a drive. Sweetheart darling, I am acting on my own account entirely, as I have not received your letter, and do not know what directions you gave me, or anything. Anyhow, my own Bucha lovie, all for your sweet sake! I am not happy, as the whole tone and trend of this letter will show you, darling.

Edward has risen from his sick-bed and tottered back to work. He is still alive. They have failed. Her tears are for herself: he is not ill enough. Heartless and cruel, as Clark himself called her, she goes on giving to her pitifully weakened husband such of the so-called tonic powders as are in her possession, on her own volition, to keep the illness ticking over until Clark's next *coup*. Let us hope that the thin gruel of cornflour and water—a tempting, white mixture so ominously mentioned by Augusta—was sacrosanct.

*Now* is the time entirely to abandon and repudiate Augusta's fiction that they wished only to procure Edward's absence. Anyway, a man barely capable of just putting in an appearance at his office in the mornings would soon have been invalided out; the Raj did not carry passengers lightly. They had only to wait. The chubby, pink figure crouched at her writing-desk takes on an increasingly sinister aspect:

> 22nd June
>
> My hubby still continues ill. I have come here [to the post office] for a bottle of Sanatogen for him, dearie. He has very bad dyspepsia, rush of blood to the head, insomnia and all, and is talking of going up to Mussoorie on a few days' leave till the rains break.

> 28th June
>
> I give half a tonic powder every day in his Sanatogen, lovie darling, because it lays on the top of the white powder quite unsuspiciously, and he mixes it up in his teaspoon. I find, by boiling into a solution as you direct, Harry darling, the symptoms become much more severe as in Friday's case, darling, and there may be suspicion attached, having that scalding feeling down the throat. But this, in the Sanatogen, is a much easier way, don't you think, my Bucha darling? I told you I was doing my best, and you should trust me.

Augusta is becoming more self-reliant in the dangerous enterprise, because, after the failure, the relationship is in slight disarray:

> I thought you were enjoying your dearest self and were not bothering one bit about me. So I suppose, Harry darling, the old jealous feelings got the upper hand of poor little Gussie, and my proud spirit rebelled and took refuge in silence, which was more bitter for me than to you, lovie darling. Also, my own darling, to tell you the truth, I was very much hurt and offended because you

said that the *punkah* falling on my head must have caused me to lose my memory. I suppose so, Harry darling.

\*

Oh, Harry, darling, thank you so very much for all your loving, kind and tender wishes for my birthday. Sweetheart, no one is so loving and tender towards me, as you are, Bucha, and it is this quality in dearest self that I prize and value so much, lovie darling. I am so sorry I worried and grieved you about the letter I tore up, which caused you such disappointment, Bucha darling. I am a very wicked girl, am I not? Never mind, on my next birthday I may be solely yours, and then you can kiss me to your heart's content, my sweetie!

Her depression is evanescent, as it was after the jalapin disaster. On 21st June, she had written miserably:

Do you know, I have a superstition about that *punkah* falling down, and I think it's a very bad sign, darling. It still remains just as it fell, and we sleep in the dining-room, and eat in the sitting-room. The heat is intense.

Harry darling, please don't trouble to send me anything for my birthday, except love and good wishes, I'd rather not, darling, though there is no ill-feeling between us, but why waste money on me, sweetheart? I don't need anything, so that's understood, isn't it, lovie? I am not punishing you. Fondest love and many sweet kisses from your own little sweetheart and Buchee darling.

Mrs Fullam\* sent me a parcel for my birthday this morning. I wish people would leave me alone, I don't want anything, and I don't deserve it.

In spite of that last sentence, which looks like a depressive's feeling of unworthiness, it was only a passing mood, not a classic symptom. Besides, she *didn't* deserve anything, did she?

---

\* Augusta's mother-in-law, Eliza, or, less likely, Rose, the wife of Edward's brother, William.

Her next letter shows Augusta in better spirits. If there were any doubts about the aphrodisiac properties of arsenic, they must now stand against the performance of weak but risen Edward:

> Sweetheart mine, you wish to know if he has 'been near me at all'. Well, yes, darling, we are quite friendly, and have never quarrelled, even after Friday's affair. He has taken me in his arms once or twice, to relieve his feelings, Harry darling. You know exactly how I mean, lovie. But it makes no difference to me because I think of you all the time. I thoroughly enjoy you and have you for my very own, Harry lovie. You can be quite sure when you get me, that you are the only one who really *does* get me properly, and so I am always yours, and only yours, darling.

A nice, dialectic reassurance for the jealous lover! Edward was, in fact, still under medical supervision, attending hospital as an out-patient:

> 27th June
> Sweetheart mine, as my hubby has gone again to the Cantonment General Hospital today, to see Lieut. Monroe, I take the opportunity of writing my letter, Harry darling, not knowing what the day may bring forth, as his eyes are ordered complete rest, and he is going to apply for ten days' leave. Now, Harry darling, please let me know by return post, whether the tonic powder affects the eyes? I have an idea it does, lovie Bucha.

*

> I don't think my hubby regards you as an enemy, but as a friend and Masonic brother, just the same. He has never mentioned your name since you were here last, darling Bucha, and after all, it may be only imagination on my part that he suspected me.

Going up to the coolness of the foothills of the Himalayas, as Edward was talking of, was widely likened to entering into Eden. The air seemed to sparkle, wild red rhododendrons grew along the slopes, streams trickled, doves cooed, and moon and stars by night were brighter by far. There was a sensation of great space and infinity. From time to time, the clouds parted to reveal the snowy peaks high, high above, hanging in the air like icy palaces of the gods.

Mussoorie was the nearest sizeable hill-station for Meerut, and there Edward, leave granted without question, planned to spend ten days, to recuperate and lick his wounds. It was quite normal for husband and wife to go to the Hills separately, for logistical reasons. High jinks sometimes ensued. It was said that a 'separation bell' used to be rung by the manager of the Charleville Hotel in Mussoorie at four o'clock in the morning!

On the way, Edward was to break his journey at Dehra Dun, the railway terminus (a prettier, greener place than it sounds, with mango forests) and spend a day with his brother, William, whom he had not seen since their joint visit to England, six years previously.* It was to be their last meeting.

Augusta sends Clark a promissory trinket—a miniature photograph of 'my sweet smiling face' for his locket—and announces Edward's programme to him:

> Sweetheart mine, you will say 'what a very strange girl this Gussie of mine is,' when you read the P.S. which is longer than my letter, and so full of red-hot sentiments, lovie. Sweetheart darling, if my hubby leaves on Saturday evening, then on Sunday you can address your dearest letter here to me, until his return, Bucha. I may send Frank up with him, not certain yet. So only 'Carrots' and I will be left, my little 'mixture of copper and tin'. She's a sweet little thing. Darling, now goodbye, I love writing to you, lovie, you are the only one who loves me truly and devotedly. God bless and keep you, Harry darling.

Clark, delighted, proposed coming over by the next mail train. Augusta urged caution. Clark lost his temper. Augusta wheedled:

> Sweetheart mine, I am not disappointed that you

---

* So says Walsh, but 'Mr Fullam' had made a nice speech at the wedding of 'Young E.' in May.

cannot come to Meerut just at present, but rather glad, my own Bucha, because I think it will look much better for servants and friends, and all, if you come a few days after and not immediately hubby's back is turned. So 'everything happens for the best,' Harry darling, don't you agree with me, lovie? We will make up for the time lost, won't we, lovie? I am sorry to see such a dash of temper in your dearest letter, when I think you might have been more reasonable, darling, about my coming to the station to meet you, as you must know and realise perfectly well that it is a hard, nay, almost impossible thing to do. I did it once before, I am quite aware, darling, but you know how risky it was, and how I was seen by young E.*

Edward departed northwards on Saturday, 1st July. Clark waited until Wednesday, 5th July, before making his journey up from the south. He lodged probably at the *dak* bungalow and stayed in Meerut for 'four blissful days'.

The Rains had come, so there was no strolling down Lovers' Lane. Instead, the lovers spent much of their time in the Fullams' bungalow, reading aloud to each other—surely Augusta's idea.

Struggling to get better in Mussoorie, Edward staggered along the main street—the Mall—red-eyed like an inebriate, unsteady, his nose streaming, racked with coughs, and bothered by a strange tingling in his hands and feet—in fact, the peripheral neuritis of chronic arsenical poisoning.

His mood was not good. Gossip might have been the spice of life in the high Hills, but there was small pleasure for him in the hints and veiled warnings which people were delivering to him about the character of Henry Clark. As he looked down across the boundless Plains some 8,000 feet below, and, at twilight, saw the twinkling lights of Dehra Dun, his thoughts were angry and confused. The distant railway which had carried him from Meerut signified to him the pattern of Clark's repeated visits and his wife's availability. He would go home determined to have it out with the pair of them, and put a stop to it all. Come

* Probably Edward's namesake nephew again.

to that—dash it!—he would carry on exercising his conjugal rights.

When Clark had left, Augusta missed him sorely:

> Neither of us can ever forget those happy hours and days together, nor do we wish to forget them my own darling.

> 'Thenceforth in dreams must we each other's
>     shadows see,
> Wandering unsatisfied in empty lands;
> Still the desired face
> Fleets from the vain embrace;
> And still the hands evade the longing hands.'

Evidently no new plan of action had been hatched in the rain-drenched bungalow. Clark's was the original plot to poison, she had improvised the methods of application, but now she, and she alone, devised and instigated a new initiative. On 11th July, the day before Edward's return, she communicated her brainwave to Clark:

> Harry, my own precious sweetheart, I must mention to you that Mr N., whom I think you know, got a heat-stroke evening before last, and is seriously ill. He is about my hubby's height and build, with the same florid complexion. Do you think, lovie darling, that the same symptoms could be produced on someone we know? Especially now, coming down from the Hills to Meerut, which is at present very hot. More especially, darling, as he was suffering from cerebral congestion long before he went up. Let me know what you think of this, and if it can be done without suspicion whatever.

By the same token, however, Clark himself was to avoid heat-stroke at all costs:

> There was a death of Col. B. of heat apoplexy in the train at Ghaziabad, darling, so it's always safe for you to travel at night and not in the day, my own Bucha.

Clark welcomed the idea, and began turning down pages and underlining passages with a new enthusiasm. Over at Meerut, however, all was drama and dénouement:

14th July

Harry, darling, my very own precious, dearest love, it is with a very sad heart indeed that I am writing to you today. I told you in yesterday's letter that we were walking as lovers on the verge of a precipice. Well, my darling, the ground has given way beneath our feet, and now we are hurtled into the abyss below. But I am writing in parables, sweetheart darling, and to be more explicit I must tell you plainly that my hubby had a good row with me last evening, and spoke very plainly to me, forbidding me to have anything more to do with you, lovie. He is very angry that you brought me the shoes, Bucha darling, and also that you came to see me while he was away. He has also noticed that you come regularly on the third Thursday of every month, sweetie, and he expects to see you turn up again next week, when he intends to speak plainly to you, darling. So please do not come to Meerut now, I cannot write and tell you, darling, all that took place during the row, but some day perhaps I shall tell you all. Oh! God, when will the day dawn when I shall see dearest self again? I am locking up the shoes, because it's no use making matters worse by wearing them, the very sight of them makes him furious, he says you are making me obligated to you, darling, and trying to win me away from him. He also said that if he thought there was anything between us, he would shoot me first with a revolver, and then shoot himself.

Who would have thought that boring old Eddie had it in him?

So you see, my own Bucha darling, what a state matters have come to, and how we must now decide at once and for ever, whether we will part or whether we will sacrifice everything to be together, dearest love. Can you forget all about me, and turn your thoughts away from your girlie,

Gussie Buchee, or do you think we should try and use the means of the heat-stroke, to be happy once again, darling love? The only thing that keeps me back from doing it, my Bucha darling, is the thought of ways and means, and how to manage afterwards, for you know how proud I am, and would never touch a pice offered from relatives, or any body else, darling. Do you think I could get the Masons to educate, or help me to educate Leonard? All those and many other thoughts keep worrying your dearest little Buchee night and day, lovie, and sometimes I feel very down-hearted and ill. I look stout and well, Bucha darling, but oh, my heart is sick and heavy within me. He has taken me in his arms, lovie, you know how I mean, more than once. He has come back much stronger and better, and this makes it very difficult for your little girlie, Henry darling.

He came back from Dehra evidently prejudiced against you very much, and as I mentioned that you were here last Saturday he became very jealous, and told me you were a very bad man, and warned me to have nothing to do with you in future, sweetheart.

The reference to Dehra rather than to Mussoorie is puzzling. It may be a slip of the pen, but it may be more subtle than that. If 'young E.', who witnessed Augusta's meeting Clark at Meerut railway station, was, in fact, Edward's nephew and namesake, then young Edward could have told his father, William, what he had seen, and William might have confronted Edward with this information, or, indeed, other similar matters, during the meeting at Dehra Dun.

Then, quite frighteningly, even as she wrote, she came to a decision:

I have fully made up my mind about the heat-stroke affair. Even if you never marry me, I can suffer! So please send me the powder one day next week, when convenient to you, darling, under a registered cover, and addressed to Mrs Clarkson, as usual, and please let me know full instructions. Also how long after taking will the effect take place? He does not perspire so freely as you or I do,

Bucha, but still there is slight moisture. His eyes are better, but still bloodshot.

Clark experimented. This time, it would have to be a liquid:

18th July

Before you send me the liquid syrup containing the powder, write and let me know when to expect it. My hubby told me that one of the Hussar men had died of heat-stroke that very afternoon. So I asked him what sort of death it was, and he said: 'Oh, very easy; one of the easiest I know.' So I warned him not to go working in the garden as he does, morning and evening, his face getting quite red. Really, Harry darling, I don't know how he escapes getting heat-stroke. He gets amorous, but is weak. As you say, he is in a very favourable condition for it. His eyes are bloodshot still, as though he drank, and his face at times is almost purple. I do not give any tonic powders, darling, as he does not need them, and I have no chance to administer them. The liquid will be quite enough.

Edward had taken to gardening. That would be the way to regain his strength. He needed to be fit and strong, to fight off bully Clark. Brushing aside his offended gardener, he bent feverishly over flowers and shrubs as if, through their blooming, he might recover the driving green fuse of life.

## Chapter Six

## Heat-stroke

A second omen visited the bungalow in Meerut.

Another accident. The Fullams' horse fell on uneven, rutted roads, cut his knees, and broke one of the shafts of the phaeton. Augusta had a 'fit of hysterics'. The mishap was indeed, as she saw it, a bad portent, but it also restricted her movements in one important particular—her trip to the post office to collect the heat-stroke potion.

Impatiently, she planned ahead:

> Harry, lovie, please let me know by return of post, if in the heat-stroke treatment, the face will become perfectly black and distorted and convulsions set in? Will you please let me know if it will be a very painful death, or will unconsciousness soon intervene? Also, my darling, please let me know if I can administer the liquid at dinner time, or tea time? Which do you think will be the best, darling? You see, it will be so hard for me to get a doctor, or anybody to help me at night, whereas broad daylight is so much easier. I only hope that no suspicion will point to me, Harry darling!

So there we have it. Death, in terms. Edward's death-letter. Clark told her what she wanted to know. The phaeton would be back in service in about one week's time, and on Wednesday, 19th July, she replied:

> Thanks for letting me know in detail about the symptoms, darling. You know I have a very hard task before me. I am now anxious for your dear advice on all these matters, which torture my poor brain, day and

84

night, darling. You can despatch the liquid by next
Wednesday. I can call for the parcel personally, my own
darling, as it will be risky sending it here.

And now, since all pretence is stripped away, *Louisa's* death-
letter:

Why do you want me, lovie darling? There are nicer,
better and more good people than I, in this world, my very
own precious sweetie. Oh, Harry darling, since you went
away I have not had a strong arm round me, or a strong
arm like yours, to lean upon, I am so lonely and heart-
sick, lovie Bucha. Never mind, I will be brave and carry
out this scheme of ours until the end, my own darling, all
for your sake, and because I love you so devotedly and
passionately. You will never know how much I love you,
Bucha—sweetheart mine.

What would you advise me to do? Should I stay in
Meerut, in a cheaper house, or leave it for a smaller and
cheaper station, darling? What about your part of the
business? How would you free your dearest self of Mrs C.?
Surely you would not offer me any less position than that
of wife.

Oh, Harry darling, how much I love you! This proves
my fond, devoted, passionate and earnest love for you, in
trying to please you, darling, in every way. You should
never in all your life forget such love as this, because you
will get no one else to love you so, darling sweetie, my
Bucha. You must not attempt to free yourself so soon as
next month, as it will look very bad in the eyes of the
world, darling, and you have grown-up children, who
might notice your anxiety to become a widower as soon as
Mrs Fullam is alone in the world. No, my sweetheart, I
will wait for you, as I told you, lovie, and will marry no
one else, darling. I will be your future dear, little brown-
haired, blue-eyed wifie darling, and I only mentioned Mr
H., just to worry and make you jealous, my own loving
Bucha.

*Edward* was jealous. Much more jealous than Clark.

85

Thursday, 20th July, was Masonic night. Prevented by
Augusta, Clark had not visited. Instead, she went out for a
lonely, nostalgic walk, and met, by chance, a woman friend—
someone such as giggly K. A., who had irritated Clark—whom
she invited home for company. And so it was that when
Edward, deliberately early, burst in hoping for a show-down
with Clark, all he found was women gossiping. There are not
many touches of black comedy in this story, except, perhaps,
Edward's importunate libido, but this is one of them. Augusta
was not amused.

Nor, at this time when her mind was otherwise engaged, did
she appreciate Clark's singularly inappropriate offer to send
her some *Kama-Sutra* type of literature. It was coarse of Clark,
and it does suggest that he was tiring of the affair and felt that
some variations might add taste and savour to the ultimate.
After all, the term of passion had lasted now for two and a half
years, during which there had been two pregnancies—one
aborted. To that extent, Augusta's obvious misgivings about
his intentions at this stage appear to be justified. She was not
sure of him:

Saturday, 22nd July

*My ever dearest, very own precious, Harry sweetheart,*
*Bucha darling,*

Your most loving, kind and welcome letter, dated
Friday, 21st, reached my hands quite safely from the P.O.,
through the coachman, my own darling. Thanks many for
the same, Bucha lovie. You request me to be sure and send
you a few pencilled lines, darling, which I cannot promise
to do tomorrow, being Sunday, Bucha, but you know I
will do my best and try and not disappoint you, my very
own precious darling, my own love.

Mrs T. and her two sisters came over this morning and
sat chatting from breakfast time until 12.30, and they
have only just gone, lovie darling. Sweetheart, darling, my
lady friends all say that Mrs Fullam is so nice and
agreeable and kind that they love to stay here with me,
and not go away. We had tea and biscuits and some music
and song.

Harry sweetheart, my very own precious lovie darling,

don't trouble to send me the book of pictures you write and tell me of, I shall see it some day when I am near you, darling, and just now I don't care to see things like that, my mind is filled with other subjects. Why do you keep a book of that description, Harry dear? It only excites the mind and passions, and is not good or wholesome in any way, Bucha. My hubby has read through the *Sexual Science* since his return, sweetheart, but it makes no difference to him. He has his own way and style of doing things. I told him I was a *padmani** woman; not to forget that; and he said I was a little goose, my own darling.

Harry darling, my own precious lovie Bucha, you can send me the heat-stroke liquid, as you say, next week, and I shall see what can be done, dearest love. After I am once free, I shall curtail my expenses, Harry Bucha, perhaps leaving Meerut. Then I shall live very quietly alone, until next March, after I send Leonard and Katty up to school to the Hills, darling. I shall wait for you, my sweetie, until the middle of March, so that you will have ample time to free yourself and get ready, in case you may wish to change your mind, lovie. I daresay both Mr H. and S. may wish to have me, if possible, but if I don't marry you, Harry darling, then I shall marry no one else.

Fondest, warmest, truest and never changing love and many millions of sweetest, loving kisses from your own, true, constant, loving, best-beloved and most devoted little sweetheart and Buchee darling.

Gussie.
Till death.

Try and be a good boy, for my sake, lovie. That book won't help you much!


The idea of a manual compendiously named (the) *Sexual Science* lying around the Fullams' bungalow is quite a shock. In such a way was *Esoteric Anthropology* a well-thumbed volume at the home of Edwin and Adelaide Bartlett† above the

---

\* Spiritually minded.
† In 1886, Adelaide Bartlett was acquitted of administering chloroform by mouth to her grocer husband.

shop in Herne Hill—but that, at least, was a book on birth control. Was it a new acquisition, or had it travelled with them from Calcutta? Did Edward turn to it for inspiration when he came home *redivivus* from the Hills? What *is* the implication of Augusta's words?

On their face-value, the book seems to be a gift from Clark to Augusta herself. Not, surely, to share with Edward to make her happier in the matrimonial bed? Nor, surely, to encourage Augusta to practise with Edward in order to improve her performance with Clark in the envisioned future? But how would Augusta explain to Edward the provenance of the new book? She could not say that it came from Clark. It is incalculable.

Tearing himself away from his picture-book, on 23rd July, Clark marched into a chemist's shop in Agra, where he was exceedingly well known, and bought 30 grains of atropine (belladonna) in powder form.

The repaired phaeton had been promised, and, on 24th July, Augusta pressed on:

> You are impatient to send me the liquid, darling, and so am I—very impatient to get through with this whole business—which is weighing very heavily on my spirits, Bucha lovie, as you may well imagine. But I think you had better wait until Wednesday, the 26th, darling, and then send it to me, so that I can call for it, and I shall disguise my signature, as you so wisely suggest.
>
> Regarding the prescription for drops, I am not going to comply with your dearest wish for once, because I think in your great eagerness to win me, darling, you might injure his eyes and perhaps blind him, and so the last case will be worse than the first. Now, please don't be offended at the above statement, my own darling, for you are the cleverest, dearest, kindest doctor that I know, but I mean in your great love for me, you might only hurt his eyes, and yet not rid ourselves of his presence, darling.

After Edward's death-letter and Louisa's death-letter, all shades of ambiguity have been drained out of ridding themselves of his presence.

Clark warned Augusta that the liquid would be bitter: he could not avoid it. She was equal to the challenge:

25th July

Sweetheart mine, I have fully made up my mind to try and administer the liquid on Thursday night, the 27th, at dinner, and I have ordered the cook to prepare mullighi-tawny* soup, darling, so that we will eat it with rice, and add lime-juice. So my own Bucha lovie, if you disguise the bitter taste with lime-juice, or salt, darling, it will go well with the acid soup, and raise no suspicion, darling. Besides, on Thursday afternoon, I think we will be going to the Berkshire Sports, held in front of your old Section Hospital, Bucha lovie. So, as it is so hot and steamy, without a drop of rain, he will be supposed to have got a touch of the sun that afternoon, darling. So I think Thursday will be the best day to finish off this dreadful business. Don't you agree with me, my darling?

I have no chance to put it in his lime-juice and soda drinks, as he opens the bottle and pours it out himself, lovie. He and I both take Vermouth and lemonade at dinner, and if I had a chance I would mix it up in that, but he mixes it all up himself, so the only thing is the soup. I sincerely hope that no suspicion of any kind will attach itself to me or you, my own sweetie, and then after that, all will be plain sailing.

An admirably composed and argued letter. Mulligatawny soup will never be the same again! In fact, soup, with its heavy taste and blanketing texture has, more than once, been a poisoner's choice. In the Croydon mystery of 1928-9, golf-playing Vera Sidney was finished off by means of a thick brown soup laced with arsenical weed-killer.† But that was a watery concoction of stock, vegetables, and Symington's soup powder—not the thick, fiery, peppery witch's brew that Augusta's cook would create in his mysterious, dark kitchen.

* Her spelling.
† No one was tried for the death by arsenic of Grace Duff's husband, sister and mother.

Even so, Augusta was still worried about camouflaging the bitter taste, and asked for further advice about the addition of lime-juice. In a letter of 26th July—'Send me the liquid after disguising the taste, and trust me to do the rest'—she expresses another anxiety: 'I must confess I do not understand all you mean by raising the thermometer, Bucha, but you will explain all.'

The matter at issue here was that 'heat-stroke' artificially induced by drugs would fail to show the dramatically high temperature—up to 108 degrees—characteristic and diagnostic of true heat-stroke. Augusta's task was therefore to heat up the clinical thermometer by artificial means such as are known to every schoolboy.

Thursday, 27th July, dawned very warm and steamy. 1911 was one of the hottest years within living memory in India, and, in spite of the brief downpours in July, the rains did not break properly until September in Meerut. Four or five people had died there of heat-stroke, and there were a number of cases very ill with it in hospital. Clark occupied himself by going back to the chemist's shop, where he was no stranger, and buying 115 grains of cocaine.

Augusta drove off early in the restored phaeton to collect a special, registered packet from the post office:

Your kind and loving letter dated Wednesday, 26th, together with the small parcel containing the heat-stroke liquid, reached me quite safely at the P.O. this morning. Many thanks, lovie darling, for the same. How very nicely you have packed the box, Harry darling! And I recognised the family seal and crest on the sealing wax. The mixture arrived quite safe and sound with not one drop spilt, lovie, and when I opened the little scent box, I did as you desired, darling, and put one tiny drop on my tongue to taste. Oh, Harry darling, it's very bitter, in spite of your lime-juice and salt! I thought you said it would be a white, colourless liquid, like water, my darling. But it's yellow, thick, sticky and bitter. I suppose the added lime-juice has coloured it yellow? Now, Harry darling, I know you have done your very best. So that if it is God's good will, he will make all our efforts come to a successful issue, and if not, then we must part, sweetie darling, and think no more of each other. We cannot go on very much longer as we are doing, lovie Bucha, as things are getting harder for us.

I am sure when he tastes his plate of soup this evening at dinner, he will remark that it tastes like bad medicine, darling, the same that he complained of the jallap. Anyhow, I shall try unless anything happens to prevent me. If I am successful, I shall send you just a line, letting you know the results. I shall certainly not send you a wire, as you don't wish it. You can't expect much news from me tomorrow, if we are crowned with success, but I shall let you know, lovie darling.

Today is an exceptionally hot day, Harry darling, just the exact weather for heat-stroke. I am very glad to hear that you are quite well again, my lovie, and I pray that God will richly bless you in all your life, even if you may never win me after all, sweetie. This is really a crisis in both our lives, my own Bucha darling, and I only wonder how it will end, sweetheart?

Fondest, warmest, truest and never-changing love, and many millions of sweetest loving kisses, from your own true, constant loving, best-beloved and most devoted, little sweetheart and Buchee darling.

Gussie.

Till death, no matter what happens.

At last, the long, hot, exhausting day drew to its close, and dinner was served. Augusta's blue eyes glinted as Edward's mulligatawny was set in front of him, rich and bubbling. Because she was nervous about the bitterness, she had dripped in *only half the dose* from the scent-bottle, viscid and cloudy like a musky perfume, but she was still apprehensive...
Edward picked up his spoon,

but as soon as he tasted it, he sent for the cook and abused him for making such bad soup, so bitter and so full of mustard oil, as he called it, Bucha darling. Anyhow, he had taken about a couple of spoons, and about gun-fire, when we were seated in the garden, Harry darling, he complained of rush of blood to the head, and asked me to

pour cold water on his neck and hands, which I did. Then
I took his temperature, which was 99.6. So I said, 'Eddie,
dear, you get into bed and I will give you a dose of fever
mixture.' So I mixed half of the remaining half into a full
dose of diaphoretic,* and took it to him in the dark.

He tasted it, and made a very wry face, saying, 'Is that
fever mixture?' I replied, 'Yes! You swallow it quick,' and
I brought the bottle and the lantern, and he sat up and
read the label, and also smelt the contents, after taking the
dose. I then said, 'Now go to sleep, and if you want
anything, you can wake me.' My own precious lovie,
darling, we both fell asleep, but I not very much, and at
2.30 a.m. he woke me up saying he felt very ill, and was
getting paralysed. I called the *ayah*, and she and I sat
chafing his hands and feet, lovie Bucha. But he asked me
to send for Captain Weston, who came and said his heart
was failing. Then by 4.0 a.m. he got worse, my own
darling, so I sent the phaeton, and a line to Captain
Keene. He came, but my husband was quite delirious. So
Captain Keene decided to remove him into hospital at the
first flush of daylight, because he said I would never
manage him. Three orderlies had their work cut out. He
had been very seriously ill, Harry darling, and would have
died had the first whole dose gone down. But it was not
my fault, Bucha pet, the bitter taste was to blame, and not
I, sweetie.

Augusta had bungled it. *Edward was only half dead.* The
addition of a quarter of the dose of poison to the fever mixture
was a clever improvisation, but it was not enough to top up the
couple of spoonfuls of doctored mulligatawny.

However, that last, expressive letter—imagine the scene
where, solicitous, she held the lantern and, by its slant of light
in that dreadful night in Meerut, he peered at the label on the
bottle which she herself had poisoned—was written on the
Saturday, 29th July, when his condition had stabilised. Earlier,
on the day after the deed, death had seemed imminent:

* 'Sweating mixture', consisting of acetate of ammonium, nitrate of
potash, and spirit of nitrous ether.

Friday, 28th July

They have taken away my dear hubby to the Officers' Ward, in the Station Hospital, after a most dreadful night, more like a nightmare. He is raving with delirium, and quite unconscious. I have just been to see him, 11 a.m., but find no improvement. He has three orderlies looking after him, and they have their work cut out to keep him down.

I have a very severe headache, being up all night, and being so upset. I feel heart-broken, and only wish to die. Would that I were never born, as I am so wicked.

He seemed to recognise my voice at the head of his bed, though he never saw me. But he patted the orderly's cheek and said, 'My dear little girl, you have come to see me. How are the kiddies?'

We all have a need to know that our criminals feel remorse, and here—not before time—is real contrition. It must be... The bedside tableau is Dickensian in its pathos, although there is an uneasy sense that Augusta has so far distanced herself as to milk it of its drama.

But then in one swift sentence she alienates us again:

Saturday, 29th July

Harry, lovie, my own precious sweetheart, I have a great disappointment in store for you, but evidently it is God's will to spare my hubby's life, and he is not going to die, Bucha darling.

Today he is quite conscious. The fever is only 99, but he is very weak. I am only allowed to stay two or three minutes at his bedside, and he does not say much; he seems quite dazed.

Even so, there is still some repentance left in her, although financial considerations do, rather grittily, tend to enter her thoughts:

Sunday, 30th July

My ever-dearest, very own precious Harry sweetheart, Bucha darling, many thanks for your loving, kind and

93

most welcome letter of sweet sympathy to hand safely this morning. I must confess that I do feel very sad and miserable to think I am the cause of so much suffering and expense to one who has never done me any harm in all his or my life, but only loved me tenderly.

Oh, Harry darling, I feel lonely, sad, down-hearted, dull and utterly unhappy and wretched. When my hubby leaves hospital, he is going up to Mussoorie I think, but he told me this morning he would not go without me and the children. Just imagine all the expense, and how can I leave the house and live-stock, and specially you, my own pet, lovie darling?

This last attempt has proved a dead failure, and means a lot of extra expense and trouble, no wonder my heart is sick within me, what with great disappointment and worry, lovie. They say 'Hope deferred maketh the heart sick,' my Bucha darling.

So you see, everything points plainly that we must part and forget each other, although Heaven knows it will be sore and sorry work, my own lovie, darling, my heart's own precious treasure.

You don't blame me at all, do you, darling? I have been very brave and have done my best, but fate wills it otherwise, and we must each do our duty where God has placed us, my Bucha darling. They have diagnosed my hubby's case as heat-stroke, lovie darling, and no one has the slightest suspicion of the truth, my own lovie. He is improving slowly but surely. He is very comfortable, and is lying there with the ice bag continually on his head.

Clark would not have placed any credence on Augusta's renunciation; he had heard it all before. For a fortnight, now, Edward's condition see-sawed, never showing the astronomic temperatures expected:

31st July

My hubby is getting on slowly, but surely. The tingling sensations in his feet and hands are just passing off, and he has a normal temperature, only feels weak. The ice bag is still kept constantly on his head, darling, and when I go and see him he talks quite naturally. Another case of heat-stroke was taken into hospital this afternoon, but the man is recovering.

9th August

Lovie darling, my own precious Harry sweetheart, my hubby was not doing so well when I called to see him last evening. He was not allowed out of bed, and his temperature had gone up to 100.6, the same as it was the night he was taken so bad. So instead of sitting outside, as you saw him, Bucha darling, he spent the evening in bed.

So, surprisingly, Clark, donor of compromising shoes, visited the invalid in his guise as friend of the family? Certainly, later events will show that Edward's hostility towards him lessened or became contained, but perhaps Clark merely accompanied Augusta to the hospital and watched from a doorway as she hovered over her sick husband.

Edward was a valued official, and the Comptroller of Military Accounts telegraphed every day to ask about his progress. The idea of a convalescence in Mussoorie was abandoned—Augusta was dead against it—and, on 14th August, Edward was discharged from hospital, on eight months' leave of absence from work, a weak and wobbly figure, to be sure, but still alive.

The next day was Clark's forty-third birthday, and, on the 14th, Augusta sent him a birthday letter of apparent resignation:

You are obliged to keep very quiet, and do things you would otherwise never do, and that is, control your feelings and temper, darling, and let things rest just to please me, and I know you will.

Everyone thinks they are doing a very foolish thing by sending him home so soon, as the heat is so great and there is fear of a relapse. It is so hard for me, Harry darling, and I only wish it was all over. You should pity and sympathise with me very much, my own darling. He is to continue the hospital mixture of quinine, pill and Mag.

sulph. three times a day; also two baths daily and keep
very cool.

*Surely*, she would not try again, having acknowledged the
evil of what she had done? With hindsight, however, phrases
even in this letter bear a double meaning. The ultimate truth is
that Augusta gave Edward a mere two days' grace to sit in the
garden and enjoy the company of his dear little girl and the
kiddies.

On Wednesday, 16th August, Clark was again a visitor to the
bungalow in Meerut. There is no actual evidence that he
brought with him any supplementary poison, but he had a
good reserve of atropine and cocaine. Additionally or alternatively, a quarter of the original 'heat-stroke' mixture still
lurked, sticky and yellow, in the corked scent-bottle hidden
away in a cupboard, and some, not all, of it may have been
drawn upon. The first half had been partly wasted in the mostly
rejected bowl of soup, but the quarter used up in the
diaphoretic had been very effective...

The relapse came to Edward Fullam on the afternoon of
Thursday, 17th August. It was very sudden, and Augusta
thought that no one would ever know what had been the
trigger.

Observant young Kathleen, eight years old at that time, saw
and heard what no child should have had seared into her
memory.

It was nice to have Father back home again. He seemed to be
cured. Then, that day, after tiffin, Mother poured some
medicine into his tea. He drank it, and said, 'Oh! Gus, you have
given me the wrong medicine.' Mother said she hadn't, but he
said his throat and tongue were burning, and he looked at his
tongue in a mirror. He said it was very hot. He ran off to bed
and called out for some ice and water. Kathleen thought he
said, 'Hospital...' He prayed in bed, and said, 'God have
mercy on me.'

On that same afternoon, Captain William Weston was
engaged in the harmless pursuits of an old duffer, when, at
around three o'clock, he received an urgent call from the
Fullams across the road. He found Edward frighteningly
unconscious, with rigid arms and legs, and his eyes red and

96

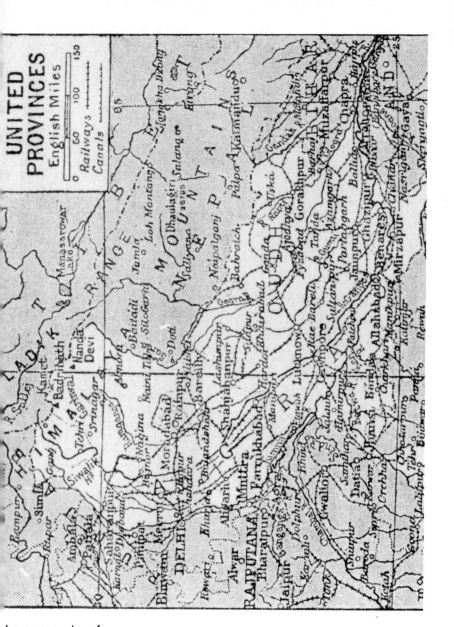

he geography of
he affair.

inflamed. Very alarmed, the Captain took him straight off to the section hospital.

Had she given him enough this time? Augusta prepared, again, for the vigil at the bedside, the public grief, and the private rejoicing.

## Chapter Seven

# Poor Little Me

For weeks, it was touch-and-go. The shattered wreck that had once been Edward Fullam, *burra sahib* of the Military Accounts Department, lay in a sweat-soaked bed and wept and suffered. Day after day, Augusta sat beside him and willed the staring eyes to close for ever.

Lieutenant Clark came too, several times, to gaze down thoughtfully at his prostrate victim, his bulky, healthy form looming over the frail shell of the quivering, twitching patient.

When, eventually, Edward was able to shape coherent thought and speech, he did not reproach his wife, did not question the sudden recurrence of his heat-stroke as a result of taking the wrong medicine. She was safe, again—safely reunited with a chronic invalid.

He was not even allowed to sit up until 19th September—one whole month after admission. Major Palmer, of the Royal Army Medical Corps, who was in charge of his case, was puzzled by his persistent muscular weakness, and discussed with his colleagues the possibility of the symptoms of the apparent heat-stroke being, in reality, an unusual form of onset of general paralysis of the insane—G.P.I.—the fatal third stage of syphilis. This idea was dismissed, however, because Edward did not exhibit other symptoms of G.P.I., particularly the 'imbecilic mind' which would have been expected. The diagnosis and treatment throughout were for heat-stroke only.

A complete breakdown of health was common enough in British India, and, with almost brutal promptitude, on 2nd September, the Medical Board sat to consider Edward's case:

2nd September

When I called to see my poor hubby this afternoon, I
found him not so well. He had passed a restless, wakeful
night, with little or no sleep, darling, and the excitement
of the P.M.O.'s* visit to the hospital this morning was too
much for his poor weak nerves. Besides, the Board sits on
the case today, and so all this put together is worrying
him. Oh! I tell you it is a most worrying time for him and
me, Harry darling.

The speedy decision of the Board was that Edward was no
longer fit for work, and ought to retire on pension. Augusta
despaired—ironically, really, when this was the end towards
which, once, supposedly, she had been moving. Trapped by the
netting of society, of obligations, of financial matters, dis-
entanglement from her union with a living husband proved, as
she must have known all along, to be unrealistic. She was no
nearer to the marriage with Clark which was her one, fixed aim.
Bitter as gall was the remnant of her life. She apportioned
blame. *Given the chance, though, she would still try again*:

3rd September

I should never have made such an attempt on his poor
life, which has resulted in cruel disappointment and
wrecking of his whole nervous system, brain and all.
Sweetheart mine, he can't even sign his pay bill, and so I
can get no money this month.

Bucha, lovie pet, you will be sorry to hear that the
Board sat yesterday on my hubby's case, and have
decided to grant him and his family, of wife and four
children, a free passage home to England, sailing either
from Bombay or Karachi by the second or third
Troopship, which will mean leaving India by the end of
October. Now I am sure this is the very worst news I could
possibly give you, Harry darling, my own Bucha sweetie,
but you know I am tied down to do whatever my hubby
and his doctors advise, so I can't act as I wish. You should
have made quite certain and sure of everything in that one

* Principal Medical Officer.

99

dose, my lovie darling, if you wanted me so much, and now I am afraid there will never be another chance to do the same thing over again, as he has a perfect dread and horror of this house, lovie darling, and begs and asks not to be brought here again. So I suppose he will go straight away from the hospital or something like that, my lovie. Of course I feel all this very much, and am worried. But if it is your fate and mine to be parted, darling, then nothing on earth can help it, Bucha pet.

I have been very busy and sat up last night making out a list of property for 'sale of E. M. Fullam, Esq., proceeding home'. I never bargained for all this trouble and worry, when I made that third and last attempt, as you led me to believe, sweetheart, for I fully thought and believed, that all would turn out satisfactorily, and that you, darling, would be a help and support to me in all things. But now, I am left all alone to use my own brains and to help myself, having neither my husband nor my own darling lover, to help or comfort me. I suppose it really serves me right, and it's making me very bitter towards the world in general, my own darling.

I sympathise deeply with you, darling, in losing me whom your loving heart has grown to love and worship so much, but I am helpless and powerless, you know that, lovie. I pray that God will always bless, guard and keep you.

With my heart's warmest, fondest and truest love and many millions of sweetest, loving kisses from your own true, constant, best beloved and dearest little sweetheart and Buchee darling.

Gussie.<br>(Till death).

My darling, be brave and ask God to hear us both in this dark hour of parting.

Encapsulated within this outburst is a reminder that life goes on normally:

Lovie, today is Katty's ninth birth anniversary, and she thanks you very much for your nice, kind little letter to her enclosed in mine. She is quite pleased with it, and desires her love and thanks. But certainly you must not send her anything as a present, my own Bucha darling, unless you wish to displease me very much indeed, then you can do as you like, but I tell you what, my darling, if you really wish to give her a present, let me give her a bottle of scent which you so kindly gave me, darling, and I can say that you sent it for her, while she was at school, and then afterwards you can replace it to me, if it so pleases you.

Augusta, for such a determinedly sensitive person, was always blind and deaf to incongruity, and failed to see the grotesqueness of commerce with yet another scent-bottle. You would think that the mere sight of one would fill her with nausea!

Impervious, ever-hopeful, Clark did not give up, but came tanking over to Meerut as often as he could, and from now on wrote fearlessly direct to the bungalow.

Augusta's letters at this time, as her home was stripped of its familiar furniture, and the phaeton sold, reached new heights of yearning, if plagiaristic, intensity, which show her to be as securely trapped by the romantic fallacy as by her matrimonial ties:

Your kind, loving and welcome letter to hand safely this morning, for which many thanks, darling. It is only one of the few more letters I shall receive from my sweetest treasure, and then never more will I see the dear, familiar handwriting with its firm, upward strokes, so determined and so characteristic of the beloved writer, darling!

What a shame that we two, who love each other so devotedly and passionately must part, perhaps never to meet again in this wide world, lovie. Oh, it cannot be, it is not possible, surely. The blue sky and flowers during day, and the moon and stars by night, would all be darkness and chaos without your dear presence, Harry darling, my one and only love, my King.

There is no more to say, Bucha. You are coming soon to

see me here, tonight you will be here, and I shall see your dear face, touch your hands and face, and see you smile. But all that will make it so much harder! Oh, God give me strength to bear this cruel, bitter blow of disappointment and parting, after all I have done. It is not my fault, Harry dearie, it is simply fate. I cannot write more. Much fond love from your loving little sweetheart and Buchee darling.

Gussie.<br>(Till death).

Clark's firm upward strokes were what she could not give up, and the more she pined the worse were Edward's chances of survival to pace the promenade of some imagined retirement haven in England.

A third omen now left its watching-post outside the fast-emptying bungalow and flew across town to warn Edward in his hospital bed. Self-referring, as ever, Augusta thought it came for her:

A bat fell on him from the roof last night, and gave him such a start, I wonder if that means anything, lovie darling, as you know I am very superstitious.

Clark himself was superstitious, and regularly consulted a fortune-teller by cards, named Miss Mugh. One of her forecasts was jubilantly confirmed by Augusta, on 6th September:

I was so surprised, lovie darling, to read the very first item in your enclosed future foretold. As it says you will soon have an important letter giving you news of my change of residence. Well, here it is, the important letter, and now wouldn't you like to know where your little Buchee darling is off to? What fun it would be, if you lost me even in Meerut, my darling? Shall I tell you, lovie? Well, I have taken two rooms at the Dak Bungalow, and am very busy shifting over there, Bucha. I shall live quietly for the month or so that my hubby is still detained in hospital, lovie darling, and after that we shall go away somewhere, to a nice quiet cheap place in India, not

England, as they have decided that my hubby must take pension if he goes to England, otherwise we do not get a free passage, darling. So he has no desire or wish to go to England, and neither have I. He is talking of settling down in Bangalore or some other nice place, but there is nothing at all definite, Bucha pet.

Of course the Fullams did not want to go 'home' to England. The Government's offer to ship them there was well-intentioned, but it was not appropriate to their circumstances. Neither had roots, only connections, in England; they were born in India, where many other family members were domiciled. India was home.

Bangalore,* in the far south of India, was a fine and healthy place, with its famous botanical gardens, 3,000 feet above sea-level, but Clark would rarely be able to make the long journey there from Agra. The brief spurt of hope died, and Augusta cast a cold eye on the hulk of her husband:

> 9th September
> I can't write any more now, and what is the use of my writing again? My husband is very ill, I am the only one allowed to see him, he never speaks to me hardly, but just lies with his eyes closed. He can't walk as you suppose, nor can he even sit up, but just twitches and jumps, and in the intervals stares like a lunatic.
>
> What a prospect! But I did it, and so I deserve a ruined life and a broken home, and no friends and no comforts.

Even though she had recently told Clark to go off and love someone else, obviously she did not mean it:

> Another thing that has turned my very soul, and made me bitter towards the whole world in general, darling, is the scandal which from time to time reaches my ears—I don't like to repeat all I hear to you, Bucha, for you naturally get very angry, and so I have to bear all my troubles alone and in silence, which, as you say 'eats into the very soul', and makes life so hard to bear.

* 'A kind of Indian Cheltenham'—Dom Moraes.

103

Clark, hardened frequenter of black hens in the bazaar, plays the card of suicide threat, and, in her turn, Augusta again dangles in front of him the manikin of convenient Mr H., now stricken with an embarrassment of the bowels. If it were not for the tragic figure in the hospital bed in the background, there would be a wry humour in this creditless exchange:

How you do beg and plead to be reinstated in my tender loving heart, Harry darling! What am I to say? You are a man to talk any one over, most of all poor little me, who although very forgiving and sweet and loving at times, can also change completely and be cold, bitter, hard, merciless. You know my true nature well, darling. You have not studied me for two long years in vain, and not to know that I am a very peculiar little person, very proud and distant at times (when jealousy grows) and most loving in ordinary surroundings.

*

No young lady could ever so eagerly expect her daily love-letters as I do, my darling pet, and I am more disappointed. But oh, Harry, sweetheart, this is all wrong, because you have your lawful wife, and I have my hubby, so it's that which worries me so, darling. I am so glad to hear my precious darling sweet is well, but you must not give way to sorrow or grief on my account, lovie pet. Please do not think of such an awful thing as a fatal dose for dearest self, should you love me for ever, darling. I know you are a brave, strong man, my own dearest soldier doctor, but it's only cowards who find a way out of life.

*

I wish you were not so madly in love with me, I really think you can smother all your passionate love, but you are such a headstrong determined man, my own darling. You are determined to win your little Buchee at any cost. I am sorry to say that Mr H. has also fallen in love with me, darling, but like a wise man he keeps away and does not come near temptation. He is a good chap, has been ill lately with dysentery. I shall tell you all and hide nothing when we meet, darling.

As if to remind them that this was no game that they had been engaged upon, baby Carrots happened upon its most grisly relic, and nearly died of it:

12th September

I did not write the day before yesterday, dear, owing to little Myrtle being ill. I went out on business, my darling, and fancy! she got hold of the bottle containing your famous liquid, which is so deadly certain, and luckily the cork was quite tight, but she sucked all round the cork and when I got home, I snatched it from the little pet, and scolded the *ayah* for unearthing things I had so carefully put away. Well, Myrtle soon became scarlet, and began to twitch a little, so I kept her in a cold bath and she gradually got much better. But you can fancy my state of mind, Harry darling, and I really thought I would lose her. She must have got very little, thank God!

Note the sarcasm. Augusta would not forgive Clark for the bitterness of the heat-stroke mixture. She had, incidentally, promised him that she would dispose of the scent-bottle only in his presence.

Meanwhile, Edward's escape to Bangalore turned out to be nothing but a mirage. Probably he was, anyway, too fragile for such a major undertaking. As he lay in hospital, his misery was compounded by the knowledge that his brother, William, was very seriously ill in Dehra Dun. In the state of uncertainty which gripped the whole family, a move to Dehra Dun, to support William, presented itself as a solid, constructive decision.

Augusta did not find the plan too objectionable, and Saturday, 7th October, was to be the day for Edward's discharge from hospital and journey by train to Dehra Dun. The *ayah* was to go on ahead with the children, on the Friday before. But William died sooner than expected, and, by his dying, altered the course of events in a manner way beyond any death-bed imaginings:

3rd October

Lovie, dearest, you seem to be quite perplexed by my
wire of yesterday afternoon, and I am sorry I worried you
so. But I did get excited hearing about Willie Fullam's
death, and then my hubby's sudden decision to go to
Agra, that I rushed off and sent you that wire. I hope and
trust you received my letter of explanation, my own
darling, and I wonder if you can secure that little place in
Metcalfe Road for us?

Sweetheart mine, I feel sure you will try and get a nice
suitable place in Agra, because you would like immensely
to have me near you, and this is such a good chance when
he is so eager to go to Agra for a change during the winter
months, darling. On hearing from you I shall write and
decide about the house in Dehra Dun. If we can't go to
Agra, we will go there.

* * *

Agra, where dwelt her King! Where, for love of Mumtaz
Mahal, his favourite wife, Shah Jahan decreed a funerary dome
of marble and jewels. Where, too, Mumtaz Mahal interceded
to obtain clemency for criminals condemned to death.

For Edward, though, Agra was the lion's den. His 'sudden
decision' to go there, allowing for the semi-guarded nature of
Augusta's communication, appears to be quite baffling, but it
is still possible to have a stab at reconstruction.

As the long-awaited rains crashed down, Augusta and Clark
crouched inside the half-way house of the *dak* bungalow,
engaged in agitated conferences. The balance had shifted:
Augusta had lost her drive, but Clark's reckless optimism had
increased. Augusta was willing for new means to be employed,
but saw no prospect of new opportunity. Indeed, on 4th
September, she had written precisely that: 'You must give me
up. I don't know how you have hopes of another opportunity.'

It was Clark, who, wildly and unrealistically as it seemed at
first, thought that, somehow, Edward could be spirited away to
Agra, but Augusta told him that the suggestion was an
impossibility, and asked him to abandon the idea.

As for new means, Clark had mangled his forensic books

again and was ready and waiting with a hoard of something special. Because he feared a post-mortem—especially in view of the recent, intensive medical attention focused upon Edward—Clark had turned from arsenic to alkaloid poisons, which would not be readily detectable. After the near-miss with the 'heat-stroke' liquid, he had alighted upon gelsemine, a very powerful alkaloid poison, extracted from the root of yellow jasmine. This he had been stock-piling from 11th September onwards—that early—and Augusta knew about it and had discussed it with him. Eventually, he had amassed at the very least 48 grains of the stuff. In fact, since the fatal dose is variously stated as one-fifth or one-sixth of a grain, one wonders if, as only a subordinate toxicologist, he had misread the textbooks!

So, by what power of persuasion or duress did they turn Edward towards Agra? We know for sure that he had been suspicious about Clark's relationship with Augusta. We know, although not with the same measure of certainty, that he had been suspicious about Augusta's tampering with his tea, but she had later back-pedalled about that incident and his reactions. He had never, with one possible exception soon to be revealed, complained to anyone that his wife and/or Clark had tried to poison him.

In his weakened condition, he was heavily dependent upon Augusta. He probably still loved her. He was a family man. She was attentive to him. She was a fine, improvising actress, and had not revealed to him the real expression in her eyes.

Clark was visiting him and showing every concern. Perhaps he was not such an awful feller (as some of his contemporaries are reputed to have called him) after all! Clark was a good doctor, to whom he was indebted for the lives of his wife and his dear little baby daughter. On his visits to the ward, Lieutenant Clark was impressive, respected, in his proper environment. Besides, Clark was a brother Mason. Masons might, at the very worst, flirt with one another's wives, but never, never, murder one another, except, by legend, for betrayal of Masonic secrets.*

* There is a theory that Mozart was thus punished for betraying secrets in *The Magic Flute*.

Shortly after her letter of 3rd October, Augusta wrote to Clark that they must be careful not to create jealousy, because Edward, *like a child, had trusting confidence in him.*

Augusta wanted to go to Agra. Edward must have known that. He was soft putty in her hands. He wanted to please her. Perhaps her displeasure frightened him, buffeted him.

In Agra, Clark would put him on his feet again. He, Edward, at home all day, could keep a close eye on things and nip any silliness in the bud. He knew that Augusta was a jolly fetching little thing, and perhaps it wasn't all Clark's fault; perhaps he himself had been a bit of a stick-in-the-mud.

If, in some far country of his mind, the truth lay buried like a mine, it was unacceptable, too frightful and incredible to contemplate. It has been suggested that he was imbued with the fatalism of the East. Another way of looking at it is that, a devout churchman, he trusted in God's Providence. If he went willingly, unprotected, into the lion's den, God would surely spare him—or not—as was His will. Equally, if he did what Augusta wanted, perhaps she, too, would spare him.

*Or,* the death of his brother could have been the final blow. Edward had been depressed for months—and going to Agra was a kind of suicidal act. Yet he entered with enthusiasm into the logistics of the move and sent messages to Clark, who was acting as Augusta's agent in the provision of accommodation, furniture, and travel arrangements, rather pathetically explaining the type of easy-chair that he liked.*

A kernel of the truth, or several truths, even contradictory truths, for the explanation of Edward's sudden decision, must reside somewhere inside these reflections. However, there was someone—Gunner H. W. Dixon, of the 64th Royal Field Artillery, who was acting as hospital orderly in Meerut when Edward was admitted—who claimed, afterwards, that he knew what had happened at Edward's bedside.

Dixon had looked after Edward, and they had become very friendly. Edward told him three important things: he thought that Clark had poisoned him; he did not want to go to Agra;

---

* The only surviving letter from Clark to Augusta, dated 5th October, 1911, was all about furniture. Every time the Anglo-Indians moved, they acquired new, often hired, items.

and he thought that if he went to Agra, he would be poisoned there—he did not say by whom.

Augusta, Dixon said, told the hospital staff that it would do Edward good if he went to Agra. Clark, too, suggested more than once that he should go to Agra. Dixon was once present when Augusta and Clark asked Edward to go to Agra, but he said he did not want to go until he was properly better.

Dixon's story seems to have been taken with a pinch of salt, because he did not, at the time, tell the authorities what he had heard. If he had dared to raise any doubt, Edward might have been kept back discreetly, and enquiries made.

Even so, Dixon had a reasonable explanation for his failure to intervene, quite apart from his lowly status in the hospital hierarchy: he simply did not believe Edward. Patients told orderlies all kinds of things, and they took no notice of them. Indeed, a paranoid delusion relating to a doctor is particularly common. Edward was never noted to exhibit delusions, but Gunner Dixon was not competent to diagnose whether or not a patient was deluded.

Major Palmer, who, it will be remembered, was the senior doctor in charge of the case, did not know that Edward was going to Agra when he left hospital. He thought that his patient was bound for the Hills, because he had been advised to avoid the heat of the Plains. The weather was still suffocatingly hot, steaming, humid—the vaporous air choked with noxious insects and the newly greening ground crawling with creatures it was better not to step upon.

Just about now, shrewd old Captain William Weston encountered Augusta, and was considerably surprised when she told him that Edward's disease had been diagnosed as general paralysis of the insane. That he would never have thought, from what he knew of the family, and it was not, anyway, a matter that a wife would have lightly let slip.

*   *   *

Saturday, 7th October, 1911. Complicated preparations had been made. At six o'clock in the evening, Edward left hospital. You could scarcely say that he was discharged. He was so weak

109

that Gunner Dixon carried him to the *dak* bungalow, where he was to rest for a couple of hours.

*Now are we in Harriet Staunton\* territory: by train and cab they carted her wasted frame to Penge, where no one knew her, to die the very next day.*

On arrival at the bungalow, Edward had to be revived with brandy. He begged to be left alone, and everyone tip-toed out of the room.

Dixon did not abandon his patient. Acting far beyond the call of duty, he stayed on and did not leave Edward until he had helped him to board the train to Agra.

The travelling party consisted of the Fullams, Clark, who had spent twenty-four hours at the *dak* bungalow, and at least one servant, notably Guru Buksh, an Indian Christian whom Augusta had engaged as a new bearer, six days previously.

The night-train to Agra via Ghaziabad and Tundla roared across the plains. Beyond the barred windows of the compartment, jackals howled in the Indian night. Edward slept.

---

\* Starved to death, in 1877, by her husband and others.

## Chapter Eight

## Eyeless in Agra

It was a hot evening in Agra, and the little girl, aged nine, lay awake in the sweltering bungalow at 9 Metcalfe Road. Outside, in the compound, undergrowth rustled and shapes slithered, while the fever-bird called in a rising crescendo, 'Are you ill? Are you ill? Brain fever! *Brain fever*!'

\* \* \*

The Fullams had arrived at their new home in the early morning of Sunday, 8th October. Edward had been allowed three last days, for the look of the thing, but now, by Tuesday evening, speed was of the essence. Clark was well known in Agra, but, as yet, the Fullams not at all, except in the gossip of the Subordinate Medical Service.

Edward chose to sit in the compound for dinner at 7.30. The sun had set, but the heat lingered. Still, all things considered, he didn't feel too bad. He was being well looked after. The burgeoning garden soothed his tired eyes and brain. Little Kathleen loyally sat beside him as he ate.

On this particular evening, Augusta herself, abandoning protocol, fetched with her own hands first his soup and then his meat from the cook-house. The cook and bearer were both put out by her behaviour—but then they knew that the memsahib was taking special care of her weak husband.

Edward finished his meal by the light of a lamp. Whining, flittering insects sang around his head. Funny, he felt dizzy and strange, and—surely—the food hadn't suited him. He had a pain, and he was very much afraid that he was going to be sick. It was unbearably hot, and he had to lie down. They helped him to stagger into his new bedroom, where he lay still and silent with his eyes closed.

111

Clark was there, and he and Augusta and Kathleen sat down in the dining-room for their dinner—for all the world as if they were the family and Edward a weird outsider. It cannot have been an enjoyable meal; the noise of Edward's violent vomiting soon percolated through the walls of the bungalow.

Edward cried out that he was ill, and Clark went in to him. Augusta did not join him, then or later. Guru Buksh was standing by. He saw Clark use a silver thing and some medicine, which he put into the sick man. 'Don't do that!' said Guru Buksh, who had so far only known Clark on his best behaviour and did not realise what risk he took. His instincts were right, too: many servants would not have questioned the actions of the powerful doctor-sahib. But Clark replied soothingly, 'This is good, his body is cold. It will make him warm.'

About half an hour after Edward was taken ill, Clark despatched Guru Buksh with a letter for the doctor who lived at a bungalow near the Agra Club. He did not name the doctor.

The bearer was new to Agra, and for quite some time wandered hopelessly along the Mall, apparently too shy to ask for the innominate doctor-sahib, or even for the Agra Club—anyone would have told him where that was.

Back at 9 Metcalfe Road, Kathleen was sent to bed. She shared her mother's bedroom, which was off the dining-room. The *purdah* (curtain) was up, and she could see her father's bed. She saw him vomiting.

In fact, although Clark and Augusta did not notice her as she slipped past, or ignored her, little Kathleen *twice* went in to her father. The first time, Edward was conscious.

'I am going,' he said. 'Be a good girl, and God will bless you.'

Then he said, 'Give my love to Lennie, and tell him not to fret.'

Then he asked his daughter, 'Where is Mother?'

'Shall I call her?'

'No, don't call her. I don't want her.'

The dying man, who had taken so many months to kill, closed his eyes, and Kathleen went back to bed. It was from there that she saw Clark as he poked the glass needle three times into her father's body—chest, arm, and shoulder. It was after that, when she heard the gargling noise, that she went a second time to stand beside him until the noise stopped.

'Gone!' Clark told Augusta monosyllabically, and cycled off into the night. On the Mall, he found the wretched figure of Guru Buksh, still searching for the Club. In Hindustani, Clark told him, '*Jao ghar. Sahib mar gia.*'—'Go home. The sahib is dead.' Back at Metcalfe Road, the bearer found Edward lying dead in his bed, and Augusta sitting on her own in the dining-room.

Clark went on to the Agra Club, where Captain J. S. Dunne of the Royal Army Medical Corps, a superior officer at Agra Hospital, was having dinner. He sent a waiter in with a message for the Captain, who left his meal and came out at once to the verandah. Clark asked him if he would mind visiting a friend of his, who was seriously ill. He did not say *dead*. The Captain immediately sent for his bicycle, and the two doctors, upright, sweating in the heat, pedalled off as fast as they could, to the quiet, dark bungalow.

Kathleen heard Clark pretending that he did not know that her father was dead. She heard him ask her mother how he was, but her mother did not seem to reply. Clark ushered Captain Dunne into Edward's bedroom, where the Captain found a dead man, still warm. 'I am sorry; I am too late,' he told Augusta. Clark offered no information about the dead man's illness, and, since there was nothing that he could do there, Dunne left within five minutes of his arrival, and presumably finished his interrupted dinner in the reassuring, panelled comfort of the Club.

Everyone at the bungalow was exhausted. The long day and the long deed were done. Kathleen went to sleep. During the night, she woke up and felt frightened. She called out for her mother, but there was no answer, so she went looking for her, and found her in the dressing-room, with Clark. Both were fully dressed.

'I'm frightened,' Kathleen told them.

Clark said, 'We are going into the other room, and there is something in there that will frighten you.'

The little girl knew that they meant her dead father, but it was not him she was afraid of, only the shadows and menace of being alone. She sought their company. 'Let me go with you. I won't be frightened.'

They let her follow them. There were two spare beds in Edward's room. Augusta lay down on one of them, with Kathleen, and Clark lay on the other. Between them, for the last time, on the bed in the middle, lay Edward's body, cold now.

Augusta was supposed to be a good mother, and perhaps she was—once, before Clark—but she had long ceased to put her children first. Kathleen was already affected for the rest of her life by what she had witnessed, and some other arrangement could have been made to spare her that last night and the waking at sudden dawn. The scene is quite as bizarre as Dr Pritchard's famous two-in-a-bed disposition—his dying mother-in-law, wearing a cap with a small artificial flower, and his wife, propped up beside her, dishevelled, similarly poisoned,* and soon to die.

Who slept, that night? Kathleen did. Augusta, probably, fitfully. Clark did, almost certainly. The next day was to be a busy one. There was delicate business to attend to.

At the hospital, Clark approached Captain Dunne and asked him if he would provide a death certificate for the man whose corpse he had seen the night before. Naturally, the Captain refused, since he had no knowledge of the fatal illness. Clark was not at all disconcerted; as an alternative, he put it to the Captain that he, as a subordinate, was empowered to give a certificate, but that it had to be countersigned by a medical officer.

Pleased to find a way out of an embarrassing situation, Captain Dunne said, 'Oh, I can do that.' After all, he had known Clark for a long time—apparently knowledge had not tempered his opinion of him—and had no reason to doubt his word. Clark whipped out a prepared certificate and watched inscrutably as the Captain countersigned his signature. The certificate read as follows:

Certified that Mr E. M. Fullam, who has been suffering from general paralysis for the past three months, had a relapse, and died from heart failure at 9.20 p.m. on the 10th October, 1911. Signed, H. L. W. Clark, Assistant

* He used antimony, and was publicly hanged in Glasgow in 1865.

Surgeon, I.S.M.D. Countersigned, J. S. Dunne, Captain, R.A.M.C.

'General paralysis'—the euphemism for G.P.I., and a total falsehood from start to finish. Clark probably appropriated the suggestion in Meerut Hospital, when he was snooping around Edward's ward. Augusta had rehearsed the lie to retired Captain Weston shortly before she left Meerut for Agra, as if she were preparing the way for it.

At 5 p.m. that day, 11th October, 1911, Edward Fullam was laid to rest in a cheap coffin in Agra Cantonment Cemetery. The haste was normal. The Reverend Ben Cotton, Minister and Chaplain of Agra, officiated. Augusta, Clark, and Kathleen attended the funeral—the little girl still not spared any sorrow. She observed that the only time her mother cried was when the coffin was closed.

\* \* \*

Back in Meerut, old friends and acquaintances from Quadrille days whispered the truth that could not be told. Louisa shuddered. So did Alick Joseph. Otherwise, in Agra, there was complete indifference. Kathleen knew too much—little Miss Nosey Parker—but she would soon forget. Augusta drew her to her side, and impressed upon her very strongly that she was not to speak about her father's death to anyone, or there might be trouble. It was also too sad to talk about. So Kathleen's bad memories were now officially secret, and that made them an even worse burden.

Lost without her father, the pitiful girl tried to creep closer to her mother, but, soon, Clark, who wanted Augusta all to himself, began to resent her children's claims on her affection, and took to beating them. That is in character, of course, and Augusta's own long-term prospects of surviving without bruises were slight.

For the moment, however, Agra was Paradise:

> 14th October
> I know you will love to receive these few lines from me this morning, because you count it a privilege, I am sure, to get my handwriting. Sweetheart mine, I felt so happy

115

and blissful last night, when we parted, and you called me your 'precious darling' and your 'Heart's own Queen'. Oh, darling, I retired to rest for the night so very happy and I thought to myself 'my Harry loves me and cares for me with a deep, true, pure love, more than anyone else on earth has ever loved me.' How good it is, my own darling, to be so dearly loved by a strong, tender man, it is 'more precious than rubies'. Harry darling, sweetheart mine, you know what a dreadful, anxious time I have gone through lately, in fact, we both have gone through. Is it any wonder then that I should look pale and washed out, my sweetie? You don't look pale or tired, but much happier and contented, and the very picture of strong, vigorous manhood, and just what a fine, muscular, sunburnt doctor should be, lovie Bucha. Now please don't you worry about giving me a tonic. I am all right and quite happy, darling, and you are my best and only tonic. I never dreamt that I could ever be so happy in this life, my Bucha darling, and I hope one day we shall both be happier even than we are now.

Sweetheart darling, let me take this opportunity of thanking you very heartily for all your kindness to me and mine since coming to Agra. How very good and thoughtful you have been, my heart's treasure. Every little detail for our comfort has been planned and ordered by you, darling, and I have watched and noticed it all and loved you all the more.

That was just three days after the funeral. A new pattern was establishing itself; after work, Clark now sped to Metcalfe Road for his dinner, and did not slink home until around ten o'clock. He made no pretence of living a normal married life.

16th October
Sweetheart, darling, I know that letter was written to me, during the stress and strain of your morning's work, and I cannot thank you enough, my own Bucha darling, for all the trouble you take over me and all the goodness you show towards me. There is nothing too good for me in your eyes, lovie, neither is there any sacrifice too great for

you to make. I only hope this devoted, passionate love of yours will last, my Bucha darling, even to the end of our lives on earth.

Sweetheart mine, what did Mrs C. have to say on your arrival home last night? Did she get very angry at your uniform being returned, darling? I am so sorry if you have got into any trouble and had her nagging tongue about your ears, my own lovie Bucha. Never mind, cheer up, my darling. With me it will all be so different; you will then know and realise what a home a true loving wife can make for a man.

Lovie, darling, today is just one year since we closed poor Mrs S.'s* eyes. What a lot we have gone through together. God bless my lovie.

Towards the end of October, upset by the news of her bereavement, Augusta's family—probably her mother and other kith and kin in Calcutta—urged her to return home. They obviously had no notion of her true situation, unless they were seeking to extricate both her and the innocent children:

Sweetheart mine, I have got an urgent call from my people to come home to them at once without delay. But how can I ever go far away and leave you, my ever dearest darling Harry, to mope and fret and live a solitary, unhappy, wandering, restless life? My place is most certainly here, by your dearest side, ever ready to help, comfort and cheer you with my love and presence, darling. I have made my decision and will not leave you, until you yourself turn me away, or turn from me. Then I shall leave Agra, never again to meet you, Bucha. May God grant that sad day may never come, dearie, although Miss Mugh fortells [*sic*] it so plainly. But rather may we two most loving and devoted sweethearts be drawn together by love, closer and nearer, in the sweet ties and bonds of matrimony, which is the sweetest slavery on God's earth.

Those who profess much practise little, and those who

* An old friend in Meerut.

practise always, profess not at all; thus strong love, like smooth water, runs deep with constancy and an abiding attachment making no show on the surface, by lying ever tranquilly at the bottom.

Rumblings from on high of a transfer to Delhi, or even faraway Aden at the southern tip of Arabia, may have indicated official disapproval of Clark for his liaison, or for just being Clark:

My ever dearest, very own precious Harry sweetheart, Bucha darling—

Many, many thanks for your most loving, devoted and always welcome letter handed to me by dearest self yesterday, and which I appreciate most thoroughly, my own darling. Bucha lovie, we were both made most sad and unhappy all day yesterday by the foolish light, frivolous talk of other people's tongues, darling. But what I only hope and pray will never come to pass at present, is your transfer to a distant station. Lovie darling, when I think how Miss Mugh prophesied a transfer for you soon, and to an unhealthy place, too, then I begin to wonder if the change to Aden will take place, darling. For Aden is a most unhealthy place, full of fevers. Oh, darling, our love will surely stand the test of waiting and separation even, if it so pleases the Almighty, who knows the depth of our love for each other. If you go away to Aden, then I only hope things will happen so that I may be able to accompany you, darling. I feel too much upset and sad to write more today, lovie Bucha.

> Gussie.
> Till death, my own precious
> darling, for nothing but death
> shall divide us, my sweet.

However, Miss Mugh's forecasts were premature:

13th November

  ' 'Tis well to be merry and wise,
  'Tis well to be honest and true,
  'Tis well to be off with an old love,
  Before you get on with the new.'

Love is a tender herb, which must be kept alive by great delicacy, it must be fenced from all inclement blasts, or it will droop its head and die.

A woman who truly loves asks but one question, whether he whom she loves gives her his heart in earnest, my own darling. Sweetheart mine, how things seem to be working together, in bringing us two lovers nearer and dearer together. You are not going to Delhi after all, and no signs of a transfer yet. I only hope we can go together, darling, when it really comes.

It is curious that the correspondence continued unabated, although there was now little let or hindrance on their daily intercourse. Only marriage would stem the flow of Augusta's quotations on her favourite subject. One would have expected Clark to be heartily sick of the written word:

As the atmosphere invisibly surrounds the earth, yet is felt by all, so love unseen, pervades every breast, though its temperature varies according to the heart that gives it birth.

When a man has made up his mind to seek a wife, neither the influence of others, nor surroundings, can deter him from the point, much less the possibility of non-acceptance. He will stake all or lose all, my very own precious darling.

My ever dearest, very own precious Harry sweetheart, Bucha darling—

Good morning, my lovie; how are you this bright, beautiful sunlit day? I am well and blooming, I am glad to say, and my heart is light, because my baby Myrtle is so much better. Oh, how clever and good and kind you are, Harry darling, to ease her so quick, break her fever, and put my most anxious mind at rest, darling. Sweetheart mine, Miss W. must have received your black-edged letter this morning. I wonder how she will answer it, my darling. I naturally feel very anxious over your old love and her correspondence, because I am sure she will never let you alone; her death-card was but a blind to renew your writing.

119

Well, let's see how things go? I am sure you would not care to be in my shoes, would you, darling? Sweetheart mine, I love you so passionately and devotedly, that I hate anyone else to step between us, darling, or draw your thoughts away from me at all.

Although Augusta's continuing jealousy appears to be unreasonable, it was, in fact, well founded, and Miss W. *was* a coiled serpent in her perfumed garden. Louisa Clark, who knew all, yet spoke not, considered that Miss W. was a force to be reckoned with. Still, Calcutta was a long way away, and Augusta went on wooing:

I am only too pleased to lift my pen and give you a few sweet loving lines today, if in so doing, you will find any pleasure, lovie. My own darling, why do you so love to get my letters? Do they remind you of those happy days when Mrs Clarkson was alive? Poor thing! She passed away very peacefully, and you have found a more lovable Buchee. Love, when mutual, gives and expects nothing less than the entire soul of man and woman, and enforces as an absolute duty that truth of which marriage is but the outward sign, seal, and ratification, viz., 'What God hath joined together, let no man put asunder ' Letters mean nothing, except that they are sometimes a natural relief to the heart, and the effort of pleasing a friend gives the writer good spirits in spite of himself. My own darling, I know you will say, 'You are a very mischievous little girlie,' but darling, you have a little gem in me, and the best girl in the whole world, so not another word, sir.

Harry, sweetheart, my very own precious lovie, darling pet, my troubles are not over yet, regarding the Depy. Comp., and the ten days' pay, and I will soon settle them, and knock the money out of the office. You must help me, Bucha darling, to go before the Civil Judge. There is nothing you would not help me in, I know, and you really spoil me by giving me always the very best of everything, lovie.

At some time during the two months after Edward's funeral,

Clark, of his own volition (more probably) or at her behest, transported to Augusta's bungalow a locking, tin dispatch-box containing the four-hundred-odd letters which she had written to him, and which he had so devotedly preserved, tied in bundles. As it happened, Louisa knew of the existence of the box, but she thought that it held letters from a number of women. No doubt it did, once.

It was pure craziness to keep the letters. Clark's original motives may well have been venal. Augusta valued them sentimentally. But now was the time to get rid of such speaking evidence of their crime. Did they both have a feeling of personal historicity, a sense that they wanted a record of a great and important adventure? Or did they each, even subconsciously, cling to the proof of shared guilt?

On 30th November, Augusta decided to do a little winnowing. Those letters which she burnt will have been *either* extra incriminating *or* sexually explicit. It was her idea, and she was slightly defiant about it:

> I am beginning your usual letter rather later than I do daily, because I have been very busy sorting out some of my letters from your box, darling, and have burnt about a dozen or so, I didn't count them. It's best to do this, Harry Bucha, my own lovie darling pet, sweetheart mine. I will walk over to see you again this evening, and hope I will be in no one's way, sweetie. Look not mournfully to the past; it cometh not back again—wisely improve the present, it is thine.
>
> Patience and perseverance overcome all difficulties, my very own darling. The great remedy which Heaven has put in our hands is patience by which, though we cannot lessen the torments of the body, we can in a great measure preserve the peace of the mind. So let us be patient and also brave, lovie Bucha. Harry darling, it is very interesting to read some of my letters of the past. How God has worked out all things so beautifully and brought us two most devoted and loving sweethearts close together, and given us freely to each other, here in Agra.
>
> The happy climax is still to come, darling, and let us hope and pray it will not be very far away, but will

terminate in our happy union and long married life, always together, my beloved.

I am quite sure we shall be very happy in our wedded life, my darling, for ours is a true love match, isn't it?

*Where* was she walking over to in the balmy Cold Weather evening? Surely she was not invading Louisa's matrimonial stronghold, weighing up the furniture, like any mistress in waiting? Could there have been small-talk and tea before Louisa moodily withdrew? Or did she never put in an appearance? Or was Augusta in the habit of turning up blatantly at the hospital?

Soon it was Christmas again. Christmas in Agra. No bearded Edward, beaming, handing out the presents from a loaded tree. Just tall, angry Clark, knocking the children about, excluding them from their mother's bedroom.

In the cemetery lay Edward now, remarkably well preserved. One down, one to go.

# Chapter Nine

## Badmashes

Louisa was waiting for them. And there was no decent interval.

Augusta—not Clark—had *already* renewed operations against her, before the New Year of 1912.

Budhu, Louisa's insurance policy, recipient of double wages, knew now what was afoot. One day, Augusta had called him to her bungalow, behind the Cecil Hotel, and tempted him with 50 rupees to put some powder in Mrs Clark's food.

His memory of the time of the incident was palpably defective. He placed it at about four months after he was seconded to the Clarks' home, to replace young Bibu—and that was in early May, 1911. Four months brings us only to August. The Fullams' move to Agra was in October—*six* months later. Therefore the likelihood is that Augusta's first strike was obscenely close to Edward's funeral.

It failed, anyway. 'I won't do it!' said Budhu, even though she pressed him hard, and wheedled, 'Don't be afraid, Dr Clark will see to everything.' Unconvinced, Budhu was stubborn: 'I did not take the powder which Mrs Fullam wanted to give me, and I left her place. Mrs Fullam did not show me the powder.'

Unlike Bibu, Budhu had his position at the hospital to cling on to: he had served there for eighteen years, and, no doubt, in some nearby hut a large family waited for him with open beaks. He simply could not fly away.

Several months passed without further devilry.

Powdered glass is not, of itself, a lethal poison—that was, and still is, a popular fallacy. Nor are ground diamonds. If coarse enough, powdered glass is merely a mechanical irritant to the mucous membrane of the alimentary canal, producing the symptoms of gastro-enteritis. Since, however, it has to be

123

ground finely to have any chance of escaping detection, it generally passes through the system harmlessly. It used to be prescribed as a vermifuge.

In India, the unskilled native poisoner turned naturally, after arsenic, to powdered glass. Often, the cheap glass bangles sold in every bazaar were pounded and mixed with curry, sherbet, or coffee. Even if ground fine, the taste remained gritty.

In about April, 1912, Clark *may* have succeeded in persuading wily Budhu to administer a small quantity of powdered glass to Louisa, following which she had an attack of 'dysentery'. However, Budhu's story is so ambiguous that it is better, here, to quote him word for word, in the original order of his sentences:

> One day Mr Clark came to the lamp-room in the hospital, where I was working, and took a chimney from my hand and asked me what could be the weight of it. He gave it to another man, Golam Rasul, and asked him to take it to his own bungalow. He made powdered glass out of this chimney and gave me three powders next day and told me to give this to Mrs Clark. Mrs Clark got dysentery. Mr Clark said he would give me fifty rupees when Mrs Clark would become very ill. I asked him the taste of the powder and he told me, 'It is nothing else than powdered glass made out of the chimney. Mrs Fullam has prepared it after consulting a book.' Mr Clark told me to take care not to put the powder in the food taken by the children, but put it in memsahib's food only. I opened the powders and felt they weighed about two rupees, and looked like sugar. I told Mr Clark that the powders were thick and could not be mixed with anything. He became very angry and abused me and told me, 'You are good for nothing.' He took the powders from me and kept them with him.

Clark may not have been the world's best doctor—or poisoner—but powdered glass was not worthy of him. He should have known better. Handicapped as he was, however, by Louisa's constitutional tendency immediately to vomit up violent poisons, he must have reasoned that she would be none the better for repeated attacks of gastro-enteritis. Augusta, crunching glass with cook's spice-grinder, or Clark's pestle and mortar—an electrifying image—clearly meant business, but, as far as Clark was concerned, it was an ill-conceived and half-hearted attempt.

Possibly, Alick Joseph, the letter-writer, heard about these activities. It is most unlikely that Budhu would have told no one. In May, 1912, Joseph found a new job as a clerk at the King Edward Hospital, Indore. Before he left, he decided that it was his duty to warn Louisa to be careful about her food and drink. First, he wrote her a cryptic letter:

> As I am leaving the station, I wish to have an interview with you. The couplet, 'Life is short,' recalls to my mind, and as such, no matter what comes in light, I am compelled. Perhaps it is Providential instinct, yet it is a spontaneous wish. Further I wish to tell you something confidential. Trusting you will be kind enough, with all my seeming fault, to give me a personal interview.

It is to be hoped that his surrogate love-letters to Augusta were not in such a clotted style! Poor, weak, human Alick Joseph: when, later, he faced Louisa, his courage failed him, especially since he had no proof of what he imputed to Clark. So he just made general converstion about his impending departure. Stony-faced, Louisa may well have guessed what Joseph's stammerings concealed, but it was her problem and hers alone to wrestle with.

Rupees had not tempted Budhu, so for his next attempt, Clark approached him from a different angle, threatening his most vulnerable part. He gave Budhu a bottle of 'medicine' and told him to give it secretly to the memsahib—or he would drive him out of the hospital. The threat worked—but only up to a point.

The incident of the *chota-hazri** tea occurred about ten days after Augusta had pounded up the glass lamp-chimney. One morning, Louisa awoke feeling slightly off-colour, and asked Budhu to make her some tea. Six rupees a month had little weight against expulsion from the hospital, and he poured some, possibly not all, of the contents of the bottle into

* Early-morning.

Louisa's cup. After one sip, she complained that it did not taste nice, and shortly afterwards she was very sick. She said to Maud, 'Your father is trying to poison me.'

Some time later, Clark again ordered Budhu to put some powders into Louisa's tea, but he refused. Dangerous and implacable, Clark then tried very hard to have him dismissed from the hospital as an incompetent servant, but he appealed to Louisa, whom he had poisoned, and who knew so, and she supported him.

There was in Agra a certain Mr Hearne, memorial and application writer, and for a fee of one rupee, provided by Louisa, he wrote two applications on Budhu's behalf: one to the Principal Medical Officer in Meerut and the other to Major Buchanan, in charge of Agra Hospital. They must have been eloquent, because he was allowed to stay on at the hospital. He was a survivor. For a time, too, he was released from service at the Clarks'.

In July, Augusta left the bungalow in Metcalfe Road and moved into a share of a bungalow in Garden Road, Cantonments, considerably nearer the Clarks. Louisa shuddered. In fact, Augusta found herself financially worse off as a widow, although she still had money of her own, and some retrenchment was prudent. She was not too proud, now, to accept from Clark presents more substantial than a pair of shoes.

In July, too, the incident of the poisoned pilau occurred. Budhu had been reinstated at the Clarks', and was serving at table. It was a hot night, and there was a guest to dinner— Assistant-Surgeon White, of the I.S.M. service, who was under Clark at the hospital.

The atmosphere was convivial, because Clark was not present, and because Louisa 'had hopes' of White for Maud. Silent and deft, Budhu brought each person a plate with food already placed on it. After just two spoonfuls of the rice, Louisa blenched, excused herself, and ran from the room. Everyone heard her vomiting. They followed her, and White gave her brandy for the severe pain in her stomach.

All through that night, Louisa vomited, ably tended by White and also by another Assistant-Surgeon, named Jacob. It never occurred to either of them that they were witnessing the symptoms of poisoning. Louisa did not tell them, nor did

Maud, nor did Harry, nor did Walter. Nor did Budhu, skulking in the shadows.

It was thought, afterwards, that Budhu had temporised, and put in the pilau only so much of the poison (whatever it was) as would make Louisa demonstrably ill, but not kill her. However, the substance was apparently tasteless, and Louisa could well have eaten the whole plateful, except for her body's sensitivity to poison. She thought that she had nearly died that night, and, by multiplication of the spoonfuls, she was very lucky not to do so.

After this spectacular failure, Budhu was shuttled back to the hospital, in disgrace on all fronts. Clark saw him there every day, though, and kept him, as it were, on ice. Wherever Budhu glided, guilty and soft-footed, he felt Clark's dark gaze upon him, complicit.

In August, when she had recovered, Louisa made one of her regular visits to young Harry, her son, left behind at his job in Meerut. It was a welcome respite from the strain of being an expendable wife in Agra. While she was there, she was evidently extremely depressed, and tried to make some sense of her predicament by writing a kind of numbered memorandum, which she may have sent, in the original, to one of her sisters in Calcutta.


### Louisa Clark's Memorandum

Meerut. 16th August, 1912, Friday

No. 1. Why is Mr Clark always angry with me and my three children?

No. 2. Mr Fullam died in Agra on the 10th of October, 1911, in No. 9 Metcalfe Street, Agra.

No. 3. Mrs Fullam has been living in Agra ever since her husband's death.

No. 4. All my friends in Agra tell me that Mrs Fullam is living with my husband as his wife for the last year when Mr Fullam was alive in Meerut.

No. 5. Mr Clark has got an increase of pay, from March, 1912, and he got a lot of back pay, but he only gave me a hundred, and I don't know what he has done with the rest of the money.

No. 6.  From the last four months Mr Clark gave me two hundred and fifty rupees, and keeps fifty rupees and sixty rupees sub-charge.

No. 7.  I have been told that Mr Clark has kept Mrs Fullam as his wife and allows her fifty rupees a month, and that she is going to get a baby very soon, and when I die he is going to marry her.

No. 8.  Ever since I have left Calcutta to come to Agra we have been transferred to many stations; first of all we came to Agra Fort, and when we were there we were all very ill, and I nearly died over there as my cook poisoned me; must be through Mr Clark's help.

No. 9.  We only stayed there a year, when we were transferred to Chakrata Hills, and we stayed there only a year, and during that time I was very ill and nearly died, as Gopi, the ward servant's wife, did witchcraft me very badly, that I broke out in sores all over my body.

No. 10.  We came to Meerut, and stayed there two years, or a few months more. There even I was very ill with a bad sore on my left cheek, that the Medical Officer had to come and see me twice a day. It was in this station that Mr Clark got to know Mr and Mrs Fullam.

No. 11.  We were sent to Delhi Fort, and we did not stay there long, as Mr Clark was only going on leave to Meerut to see Mrs Fullam, and the Medical Officer did not like him doing so; then he was sent to Agra, and we are there ever since; and would like to know very much how long we are going to stay in Agra, and to what other station we will have to go, as Mr Clark has become very wicked ever since we have gone to Agra, as he keeps very bad company.

No. 12.  When first we came to Agra from Delhi I brought a very good cook with me, but he ran away back to Delhi very soon after as he told me that Mr Clark gave him three white powders to give me in the tea, and if he did not do so that Mr Clark

Agra Club: interior with
ffed tiger.

Ihu: Clark's servant, wily
vivor, recruiter of
mashes.

Ram Lal: greengrocer with an alibi.

Mohan was a *bharboonja*.

would kill him, but he ran away and gave back the dry poison to my son, Harry.

No. 13. Last month* I was very ill, vomiting, as my cook gave me something in my tea. I dismissed him without giving him his pay.

No. 14. Last month I was very ill with vomiting all night the day of the *Sitla Mela*,† and if it was not for two assistant surgeons by the name of Jacob and White, I am sure I would have died that very night.

No. 15. On the 11th of August my son Harry came to Agra and brought my son Walter and my daughter Maud and myself away with him to Meerut, and he arrived in Meerut on the morning of the 13th, and we are feeling ever so much better over here.

No. 18. ‡I am perfectly sick and tired living with Mr Clark, and would like to live for good with my son Harry, as I fear he will be putting up the new servant to poison our food as soon as we go back to Agra.

No. 24. Mr Clark and his brother are selling their grand-father's house for six thousand rupees, and both the brothers will get three thousand each. What will Mr Clark do with all his money? Give it away

* It would be neat and tempting to conjecture that No. 13 refers to the *chota-hazri* tea incident, and that 'last month' is a mistake or misprint somewhere along the line for 'last May'. However, it is clearly 'last month' in two good sources, and Maud Clark was certain that 'some months' separated the *chota-hazri* tea and poisoned-pilau incidents. Also, Louisa *supported* Budhu immediately after the *chota-hazri* tea. The inference is that this July incident is a new, separate one, not recorded elsewhere, although, in that case, it is indeed curious that there is no mention of the *chota-hazri* tea anywhere in the memorandum. By the time of the poisoned pilau in July (the subject of No. 14, following) Budhu was definitely reinstated and bearing in the rice himself, and therefore the cook dismissed without pay may have been *another* cook suborned by Clark.
† Festival of Sitala, a form of the Mother-goddess, who presides over smallpox.
‡ Unfortunately, some sections of the memorandum were withheld.

to Miss W., Mrs Fullam, or leave it to his three children? His gold watch, and the seal are all at Mrs Fullam's house, with a box full of letters from different women. Will Mrs Fullam go along with him to the next station, or will she remain back in Agra? Such a wicked woman should be put to death.

No. 25. After Walter gets work to do,* and Maud gets married, won't it be better to separate from Mr Clark for good, and live with my son Harry, as I would be afraid to trust my life alone with him, as he is not a good man? I would be much happier away from him, and he could give me a good monthly allowance. I do not like him one bit now, since he has become so cruel to my dear children and myself. He does nothing towards making us happy, and never takes us out. The whole time he is in the company of wicked people, who are always seeking to do him harm. He may be going to the dogs if he is allowed to have his own way. Miss W. still writes to him, as she has a good hold of him.

Is there something in the stilted wording of the earlier sections which suggests a rehearsal of 'putting it in writing' to someone in authority? Anyway, even if it were so, she decided against it, and returned to Agra around September.

As for the 'getting' of a baby very soon, there is an uncanny prescience on someone's part, here, because Augusta *did* conceive Clark's baby soon after August. The exact, clockwork date of the conception would be 28th October, 1912. It is safe to assume that, if significantly premature, the baby would not have lived. Therefore, conception could not have taken place very far into November. If the baby were, in fact, late, conception would have been earlier in October.

There is an importance in these datings. Something terrible

---

* Evidently, Walter, the younger son, had left his position in the Military Accounts Department at Meerut in order to move to Agra with his mother.

was going to happen on 17th November, and it was later suggested that there had been an acceleration of the plotting against Louisa's life because Augusta knew that she was pregnant and wanted Clark to be free to marry her, so that their child could be born in wedlock.

According to Budhu, however, there had been a drastic change of plan long before the seeding of the baby. The poison-bottles had been corked, and a cruder method adopted. Riskily, other persons were to be involved—not hapless, trapped servants, but random others.

Poisoners, as they succeed, notoriously become grandiose and careless. Those who alter their *modus operandi* in midstream are even more vulnerable to discovery because, grown rash and careless, they are also unskilled in the new enterprise.

Budhu was incorrigibly approximate as to timing—but then he could hardly be expected to keep a diary—and it was at about the beginning of September that, he said, Clark first tried to draw him into the new project. He said, further, that he was working at the Clarks' bungalow at that time, which would put the occasion still earlier.

Clark's instructions were cruelly to the point. In Budhu's own words, Clark said to him, 'Get *badmashes** to kill the memsahib.'

A picked pack of *badmashes* was supposed to murder Louisa in her bed, and then disperse without trace, while Clark was elsewhere, establishing an alibi. The precise nature of the briefing is unclear. Augusta later claimed that Louisa was to be suffocated in her sleep, unmarked, so that she would be found dead of an apparent heart attack, the next morning. Illogically, however, in the same breath, she also stated that the attack was to look like a robbery.

---

* *Badmashes* (Urdu)—men of bad character; ruffians; the riffraff to be found loafing around the bazaars, available for skulduggery. Sometimes they doubled as household servants. Although they might join a gang, and there was some interchange, *badmashes* were not in the same league as the fearsome dacoits—professional, armed, murdering criminals who infested the countryside in large, roving gangs, robbing and terrorising the unarmed villagers.

131

A major snag, perhaps not put in advance to the quaking amateur assassins, was that Louisa did not sleep alone. Bedrooms in colonial bungalows were large and lofty, against the heat, and, as in the Fullams' bungalow, some 'doubling-up' was the norm. Maud slept in her own bed in Louisa's bedroom, and she was as alert and reactive as a spring-gun.

If things went wrong, and they were caught in the bungalow, *badmashes* made convincing burglars. A *badmash* was probably cheaper to recruit than a proved dacoit, although the going rate for a 'contract' was a disputatious subject. He was less dangerous to deal with. But he was not so good at vanishing into thin air afterwards. He was also, especially if over-stretched, more likely to make a bad hash of it!

There was no chance of hiring a single hit-man to do the job; prepared crimes were committed mob-handed or not at all. The aura which Budhu must have carried with him of familiarity with the darker side of the underworld of Agra proved to be misleading. The young heroes whom he unearthed were inexperienced, inept, and none too brave. Equally, tricky Budhu might have hoped for a blunder, for a falling-short of outright murder. But a wild flailing about can sometimes be just as lethal as a calculated assault...

The penalty for murder was hanging by the neck. *Badmashes* knew it. Clark knew it. Augusta never faced up to it; slow poisoning had been like a game to her. Perhaps, even as she allowed her bungalow to be used for the plotting of the killing, she did not fully understand the extent of her own culpability in what was there set on.

After some weeks of negotiation, Budhu had scratched together his gang of four. They were all very young men, and they all had a trade, and a veneer of respectability. Although two of them were 'known to the police', they were all familiar with honest toil and were not mere sweepings of the gutter. Their fixed abode tended to vary, but it was more than a rat-hole.

According to Budhu, the *badmashes* whom he recruited were named Sukkha, Buddha, Ram Lal, and Mohan.

Sukkha, aged 20, to whom he turned first, was a *darzi*—a tailor—who at that time had a 'shop' in the Lalkurti Bazaar, Agra. Budhu had known him for six or seven years—

since he was a boy. He was a cyclist, but lived to regret it...

Buddha (not to be confused with Budhu), aged 23, of the Sadar Bazaar, Agra, was variously described as a *banjar* (a pedlar) and a *kanjar* (a gypsy). He certainly purported to be a supplier of fresh foods to the military, and was intimate with at least one such supplier. Perhaps he slipped in and out of both roles. Budhu had not known him previously.

Ram Lal, aged 22, also of the Sadar Bazaar, was a *kachi*—a greengrocer. His father was a 'cultivator'—a farmer—and quite well-to-do. In due course, Ram Lal successfully denied that he was ever a part of the conspiracy. He had been questioned several times at a police station, and, two years before, he had been detained in custody on suspicion of the murder of a money-lender named Boota. Even so, these were not convictions. Budhu had known him for two or three years, and so knew of his reputation.

Mohan (also known as 'City Man'), aged 20, of Chakkipat, Agra, was a *bharboonja*—a corn-parcher (the trade by which grain is roasted over fire). He, too, was well known to the police, and had one previous conviction, for theft, for which he was whipped—'with a light rattan not less than half an inch in diameter', such punishment not to exceed thirty stripes.* He was therefore, technically, the most hardened criminal of the four, and he was, in fact, the most to be feared, although they all had their moments. He was a stranger to Budhu.

With our hindsight, it is amazing that Augusta and Clark were willing to entrust their very lives to the efficiency and trustworthiness of such a petty crew. If you were a *badmash*, you denied it, strenuously. Being a *badmash* did make you a bad person, but it did not make you a master criminal. There were too many people involved, and too many things that could go wrong. Budhu and his recruits were heedlessly forging a chain of evidence which snaked all over Agra like a poisonous weed, from bungalow to bazaar.

The blood-money was 100 rupees. Once Clark had set the sum, he refused to haggle, although the gang, from the start, resented the figure. Divided into four, it was not, perhaps, a great incentive. They were disgruntled accomplices. Budhu

* Section 392, Indian Criminal Procedure Code.

had no cut in the fee. His stake was to keep his job and stay alive. He was already guilty of the attempted murder of Louisa, and his situation was desperate. But he was a survivor, and Clark had underestimated him.

Clark's alibi had better be perfect. And what about Maud? What about young Kathleen? They had discounted her, at their peril, before. And Julie, the very important dog, who is now to be seen as such? Disregarded in the forward planning, she was to influence the timing of events, and to aid in the implication of her own master.

In November, Louisa paid another visit to young Harry, in Meerut, returning on the 14th. While she was away, Augusta wrote to Clark: 'Let us hope that when she returns, darling, our dearest hopes will be realised. Oh, how happy I should be!'

In anticipation, on Thursday, 14th November, the day of Louisa's homecoming, Clark went boldly and openly to the Bank of Bengal in Agra, and cashed a cheque on Augusta's account for the exact sum pre-empted—100 rupees in ten notes of ten rupees. The bank clerk, Kazanchi, remembered the transaction, and that it was Clark who endorsed the cheque. Any advantage in distancing Clark from the obtaining of the blood-money was thus effectively cancelled out. It was not a good beginning.

* * *

Sunday, 17th November, 1912. Kathleen Fullam was now ten years old. It was about eight or nine o'clock in the evening. She had been sent to bed, but she was wide-awake, listening. Clark was there, as usual. She heard someone knocking at the pantry-door. Clark let some men in, and they went into the dining-room, next to the bedroom which she shared with her mother and Myrtle.

She could not see them, but she could hear the voices of two natives. One was Budhu, who often came to the bungalow with medicines and letters from Clark. She did not recognise the other voice. The conversation was mysterious. The voices dipped and rose. The men said they had come for more money.

'You are always wanting money,' Clark replied. 'And you are taking so long to do what you have to do.'

'This is the last time we will ask for money,' they said. 'If you will give it to us tonight, it will all be finished by tomorrow.'

Her mother came into the bedroom and took some money out of her cash-box, which was kept in a trunk. She evidently did not notice in the gloom the sharp eyes which watched her. Kathleen had the impression that the money changed hands.

'When you come,' her mother was saying, 'the children will ask, "Who are those men?" What shall I tell them?'

The voice which she did not recognise answered, 'Say I am a *darzi*.'

As they were leaving, Clark asked, 'When I come in the morning, which door shall I knock at, and where will the servants be?'

Her mother told him, 'Knock at the front door. The servants will sleep where they always sleep.'

The little girl felt frightened, and alone. The air had thickened again into secrets and plotting, and this new bungalow was no safer than the first one in Agra, where Clark poked the glass needle into her father, and he died and was put in the cemetery. Just for company, she woke up baby Myrtle, who cried, of course. Her mother came in and got her off to sleep again. Then she went into the dressing-room—perhaps to undress.

Kathleen followed her there, a small shadow, and through the half-open door she saw two natives climbing down a tree and out over the wall of the outer platform of the bungalow— an unorthodox exit. She saw their faces, and, later, she identified one of them as Sukkha.

Night deepened. In the Clarks' bungalow, not far away, Louisa and Maud were asleep. A hurricane-lamp, turned low, radiated a dim, yellowish light in the long, high bedroom. Their beds were side by side, facing the door.

They had retired at around ten o'clock. Clark had left at some time between 5 and 6 p.m., and was still not back, but, as Maud would say, so what? He always had his dinner out, usually at that woman's table, and he was not missed. Before loping off to his surrogate family, he had told them to be careful about his pay, because there were thieves around. It was a one-off remark, and Maud remembered it.

For a husband and father worried by security, Clark left his home singularly pregnable. The main door into the hall from the verandah was not bolted, in readiness for his unwelcomed return. That was the way it had always been. The bungalow was positively riddled with entrances. There were two more doorways along the length of the verandah. One, with a broken pane of glass, led into a box-room. The second one led into Clark's bedroom, which, in turn, led, through a doorway, into the hall. Louisa's rectangular room lay at the back and was reached via two doors from the hall. Around the side, there was at least one other door—in particular, the one into the bathroom.

However, the wife and daughter were, in fact, wonderfully safe, as long as Julie patrolled her territory, her wedge-faced head pushing through *purdah* curtains and her claws rattling on the floors.

Wrong-doers feared a bull-terrier, and with good reason. There was a sensational case in Burma, some few years later, when an armed dacoit made the mistake of taking on one man and his 'bully'. Within moments, the dacoit lay dead, and soon afterwards the dog's owner was paid the substantial reward which had been on offer for the dacoit dead or alive.

Now it was time for Clark to stir from the Fullam bungalow and stage-manage the masquerade. Embracing a tremulous Augusta, in whose head, no doubt, there rode fantasies of knights setting forth to conquer, he cycled off first to the hospital for a final rendezvous with Budhu and his henchman, Sukkha.

Clark flourished some money—six sovereigns and ten rupees—but was too shrewd to let it change hands at that stage. 'When are those fellows going to be at the bungalow?' he asked, and Budhu answered him, 'When the moon goes down.'

## Chapter Ten

## The Red Gleam

Through the moonlit streets, with their huddled, sleeping figures, Clark pedalled off to the Agra Cantonment Railway Station, to set up his alibi. If you could call it that. Considering that he had had months in which to perfect it, upon investigation, as we shall see, it was so weak as to be positively incriminating.

Long before the climax, he should have abandoned his routine of arriving home at 10.30 or thereabouts, and established a new pattern of being a night-prowler. It was easy enough to prove that he was, literally, elsewhere, but not so easy to demonstrate a convincing reason for being away from home much later than usual. It is characteristic of the man that his planning and his research were shallow and faulty.

Ostensibly, he was bent upon a pre-arranged meeting with a friend who was passing through Agra on the midnight express—the Delhi mail train. In order to establish that purpose, he arrived at around 11.30, sat in the stationmaster's room, and made sure that Assistant Stationmaster D. F. Menzes knew exactly why he was there.

After the imaginary meeting—*for no such friend had been laid on*—as the train steamed out of the station, Clark cycled home at an appropriate speed, in the full expectation of finding there a dead wife, a hysterical daughter, a rifled bungalow, and an absence of *badmashes*.

But he had reckoned without the dog that *did* bark in the night. The compound was swarming with *badmashes*, and, inside, Louisa and Maud lay asleep and alive. The timing was going wrong. Clark stood aghast. The gang were afraid of the bull-terrier and refused to go in unless he removed her.

Julie had heard them arrive, soft-footed, heard them

scrabbling at doors and windows, whispering and arguing, and they would have to kill her first if they wanted to get in. Before they finished her, though, she would have notched her jaws into someone's throat. Two of the men had taken off their shoes, for stealth, and bare flesh cringed.

Strangely, perhaps, the dog's barking did not wake Louisa and Maud. Perhaps she always barked at night sounds, and they had learned to ignore her. Two upright, walking, not sleeping memsahibs might well have caused panic and flight—or a blood-bath.

It was afterwards supposed that Clark had stupidly forgotten the dog, but the issue is more complicated than that. Putting her outside before he left would have caused comment, especially since he had delivered a warning about thieves.

More likely, he had told Budhu that she would be closed in one room—probably his bedroom. There is no evidence that she was tied up. Budhu listened as she barked—they could not see her—but he could not make out which room she was in—Clark's bedroom or the hall, which was the ante-room to Louisa's bedroom. The dog seemed to be moving about, and he could not be sure that she was not loose. As he dithered, the other men had lost confidence.

Quickly, Clark slipped in through a side-door, dragged out the bitch by her collar, and shut her up in an outhouse. Not staying, then, he cycled off down the road to wait somewhere inconspicuous. No one saw him there. How adamant for death he must have been, to throw away a second chance for life in the space of time when Louisa still breathed. . . .

Newly brave, four determined assassins slithered into the slumbering bungalow. Not Budhu. He shivered outside. Perhaps his teeth chattered! *He* was not going to get involved in the actual killing, if he could help it.

Back they came for him, though. In the dimmed bedroom they could not distinguish memsahib from miss-sahib, and their instructions were to spare the girl (inimical as she was to her father). Budhu jibbed. He could glimpse the two beds through the glass door into the hall, which was lit by a lamp burning on the mantel, and he pointed out which was which.

They re-entered, but soon returned, not convinced. As yet, they had not been paid in full, and they wanted to get it right.

138

Budhu teetered and quivered; Maud might recognise him. Impatiently, Ram Lal* snatched a sheet† from Clark's bed and wound it round Budhu's slender, shaking body: 'Now you will not be recognised.'

Still the women slept on, undisturbed. Surely Clark had not drugged them? He had left home too early to administer an effective sedative, and he was, anyway, a poor secret druggist.

Budhu tip-toed in, a ghostly pillar, and identified Louisa. Then he put the sheet in the box-room, and watched either from the door of Clark's bedroom or from the door of Louisa's bedroom. Certainty deserted him, here.

The assassins split into two pairs, and assumed their positions. Ram Lal and Sukkha stood behind the *purdah* near Maud's bed. Ram Lal was holding a *lathi*.‡ Buddha and Mohan stood over the doomed woman. Buddha held up a lantern which had been filched from Clark's room. Light for precision.

A red gleam was supposed to flicker in the eyes of oriental killers. . . . High and inspired now that the moment had come, Mohan raised the thing which he had brought with him—a heavy, sword-like knife, as long as his arm. *He had kissed and worshipped it, and sharpened it on a stone.*

The sword dropped fast as a guillotine on Louisa's skull. It bit through tissue and bone in a terrible fissure, and as it fell it caught her little finger and snicked it clean away. She shrieked, and he cut into her again. She writhed, and rolled over. Three times the sword flashed and parted the living hemispheres of her brain. Blood welled over the pillow and engulfed the severed finger.

Maud woke. A native was standing beside her bed, with a stick raised above his head. From the corner of her eye she thought that she saw another man peeping round the *purdah* from the hall into the bedroom. Instinctively, she leaped out of

---

* Any reference to the participation of Ram Lal in the murder is only and entirely as stated by Budhu.

† The sheet was *not* used (by Clark) to stifle the dog, as Walsh hazarded.

‡ A bamboo stave, often shod with heavy metal such as brass or iron. Widely carried—not an illegal weapon.

bed, into the gap between the two beds, and faced the man with the stick.

Then she screamed, and he made a jump and ran away. Indeed, they all ran away, tumbling out of different exits, Mohan first, through the box-room, with his dripping sword.

Maud turned up the lamp, and went to her mother. Louisa was still alive, and sitting up, confused, with her unspeakable wounds. Weeping, the girl washed and bandaged her riven head. Afterwards, she bolted the front door and waited for her father. She was very suspicious. Louisa grew delirious, begged Maud not to leave her alone.

Minutes passed—about half an hour after the attack—and at last Clark was home, calling from the verandah for the door to be opened. Maud noticed that it was 12.55 a.m. by the clock in his bedroom. He never asked why the door was bolted. She told him. 'Come and see the state mother is in,' she said.

By now, Louisa was unconscious. Clark stood tall and strong at her bedside. "Louie, Louie, speak, what has happened?' he addressed the fragments of what had once been the young, hopeful nurse who had waited for him. There was no reply.

*He looked as if he was sorry.* Maud said so, and she, of all people, would have known true contrition in her father. If, for a moment, his eyes dazzled, he soon reverted to the charade: 'Come with me into the other rooms and see if anything has been taken.' Nothing had, in fact, been stolen—Maud's screaming had prevented the finishing touches. Only one thing was missing—the sheet, Budhu's shroud—and, later on, Maud found it rolled up in a ball in the box-room.

Clark made no enquiry about his precious money, did not seek to check it—an omission. He was more worried about the dog, or the absence of the dog. Making an excuse about going to see if any of the chickens had been taken, he went out to the fowl-house, near the servants' quarters, and returned with the bull-terrier, slipping in through the bathroom door. Subsequently, he asked Maud if the dog had barked in the night. When she replied that she had not heard any barking, he said that he would get rid of Julie.

Daringly, Maud remarked that on other nights her father had come home early, and it was funny that he should be late on that particular night. Uneasily, Clark trotted out his yarn about the travelling friend, without naming him.

During these various activities and exchanges, Louisa lay silent and still—untouched, untended by Clark. It was a full ten to fifteen minutes before he went away for medical help. First he sent in two subordinate doctors, one of whom was Assistant-Surgeon White, of the poisoned-pilau incident, and they rebandaged the bleeding crevices. There was not much that they could do.

Then, as was correct, he proceeded on to report to his commanding Medical Officer, and, on that officer's suggestion, to the police. On the way, however, he made a detour, an unjustifiable divagation, to Augusta's bungalow.

Kathleen heard his loud knock at the front door in the early hours when the moon had gone down. She woke Augusta. The bearer, who slept in the dining-room with the *ayah*, his wife, let Clark in. Kathleen stood beside her mother.

'Thieves broke into my house and nearly killed my wife,' he said dramatically. *Nearly* was the operative word. Augusta must have feared another half-death. 'What is the damage?' she asked.

'Her head is cut open and the brain exposed.'

Then he had a drink of water, and set off again on his duties. Augusta went back to bed.

By the time that Clark arrived at Laurie's Hotel, to roust out Major G. Buchanan of the R.A.M.C., it was very late—about 3 a.m. He announced to the startled Major that his wife had been murdered by a native in the course of a robbery, and asked him to go back with him to his bungalow.

*En route*, they called at the cantonment police station and collected the Head Constable, Safadar Hossain. They found Louisa still unconscious, with blood seeping through the bandages applied by the subordinate doctors.

The following morning, 18th November, after the sleepless night, Clark wrote up a 'report' for the police. Maud tried to contribute, but he told her—in the civil tones in which they always addressed each other—'Keep quiet. I will give my own wording.'

Soon afterwards, Horace Williamson, Superintendent of Police, Agra, sent along Inspector Smith of the Reserve Force, to investigate the extraordinary happening. Both were first-rate policemen and, at last, good brains began to concentrate on the Clark–Fullam connection.

Inspector Smith was sickened to find blood all over Louisa's bed (they must have been afraid to move her) and the little finger of her left hand, severed between the first and second joints, lying by the side of the pillow, as evidence.

The clearly dying woman regained consciousness for a couple of seconds, and spoke once, in Smith's hearing: 'Someone came to my bed last night...' but then her voice ended in a gurgle.

At about noon, she stopped breathing.

The Inspector took down a statement in writing from Clark. It was unsatisfactory. As a robbery, the atrocity was atypical and illogical, but it was Clark's alibi which thoroughly discredited him.

There was no witness to the imaginary meeting at the railway station. That was no matter in particular, although, no doubt, he would have been required to produce a person claiming to be the travelling friend. Such a ploy would have been well within his capacity.

It was, however, the evanescent identity of the friend that finished Clark with the police. When called to account, his considerable arrogant poise wavered, and after first naming the man as 'Joikim', he *changed the name* to 'Menzies'.

Piper Menzies of the Camerons was a champion draughts-player with whom Clark had corresponded on that favourite subject from 1907 to 1908, but, unfortunately for Clark, he had left Cawnpore for Home, with his regiment, in 1908! Was Scottish Menzies suggested to Clark's agitated mind by the name of the (almost certainly) Eurasian Assistant Station-master, D. F. Menzes?

It may have been his incorrect recall of the railway network that caused him to panic. At first, he stated that 'Joikim' was travelling through Agra from Delhi to Bombay, but apparently Agra was not on the route. 'Menzies', he then substituted, was a passenger from *Allahabad* to Bombay.

Inspector Smith called next on Augusta, and asked the name of the friend. Primed by Clark, with no carrier-pigeon available to bring to her the one, vital, new word, 'Menzies', she said 'Joikim'.

It was only a matter of time, now, before Clark was arrested, but first, the next morning, at 10.30, there was the post-mortem on Louisa Clark, which was performed by Dr J. P. Modi (L.R.C.P., Edinburgh), Lecturer in Medical Jurisprudence at Thomason Hospital, and Major E. J. O'Meara, I.M.S., Civil Surgeon, Agra.

The cause of death was fracture of the skull. There were three distinct cuts, caused by three separate blows. Three remaining wounds might have been caused by those three blows, but *could* have resulted from three other blows. The doctors did not test for poisons. Why should they?

On the same day, 19th November, 1912, Louisa was buried at the Agra Cantonment Cemetery, where also lay, not crumbled, the waiting body of Edward Fullam. Underground, hubby and Mabelle were neighbours again. By a strange quirk, the officiating chaplain at the funeral was H. *Menzies*.

While all this was going on, Augusta was sitting in the garden with Kathleen on the morning of the 19th, keeping up appearances. It was like the golden summer before a great war. She had a visitor, who, she told Kathleen, was a *darzi*. But Kathleen knew perfectly well that he was the Indian who had come on Sunday night. She spoke fluent Hindustani and, when her mother had left them alone together briefly, she challenged the man:

'You are not a *darzi*. I know who you are.'

He did not reply.

'Perhaps I shall talk,' she threatened him.

He put his head down, and said nothing.

Augusta came back with some rupees wrapped in notes, and gave them to him. 'Run, they are after you!' she said.

That afternoon, the police returned to the bungalow, with a search-warrant. If they had been watching the premises, they could have arrested Sukkha the *darzi* there and then, but they had not yet drawn in upon Augusta. They were concentrating on Clark.

Augusta would have received them imperiously. Knowing that Clark had been at the bungalow both before and after the crime, Inspector Smith was there to seek out anything which would strengthen his connection with the death of his wife, and also to ruffle Augusta's composure and to riffle through her possessions. From his enquiries, he knew by now what the relationships of the parties had been, but, at that early stage, suspicion of Augusta was rudimentary—although suspicion there certainly was.

Walsh has an attractive story, which has lingered, that the Inspector found nothing of any significance until just as he was leaving, when, by chance, his foot struck Clark's tin dispatch-box, repository of her letters, hidden underneath Augusta's bed.

The plain evidence, however, is that the police found the box routinely, in the course of their search, and, in fact, no competent policeman, equipped with a warrant, would fail to look under a woman's bed—even though that woman might have been intimidating in her small dignity.

Nevertheless, the diminution of the good story should not obscure the remarkableness of the discovery: Augusta had not disposed of the box of secrets. A turning-point had been reached in the still young investigation.

Inspector Smith wanted to look inside that box. Still defiant, Augusta argued that it belonged to Clark (as indeed it did) and asked for time to obtain his key. She would be seeing him, she said, the following morning. Keen now, ignoring her objections, the Inspector forced the lock, and found that the box contained a large number of letters, tied in bundles about seven inches thick.

Augusta turned bright red, and 'fell like a heap into a chair'.

Realising the potential importance of his find—as judged by the changed demeanour of Mrs Fullam—Inspector Smith knew that his superintendent had to be the first to examine it. He sent for a padlock, and Sub-Inspector Suraj Narayan, who had witnessed the search, bore the newly secured box away to the Government *malkhana*, or treasury, to be kept there overnight.

* * *

In his office, the next day, 20th November, Superintendent Williamson studied the tin dispatch-box. Other than the easy guess that the contents were an embarrassment of love-letters, he had no idea what they would reveal. Solemnly, he unlocked the padlock, untied the ribbons, and began to read. Hours passed as he read every single one of the letters—about three hundred and seventy of them, all in the same handwriting.

\* \* \*

The reading of the letters which should have been burned told the Superintendent that, in the words of William Roughead, great Scottish chronicler of crime, when he scented a case which would engage him to the hilt, he was 'in for it'.

Tucked away with the letters was Clark's pencilled draft of the false death-certificate for Edward Fullam. Speculatively, the Masonic betrayal would not have been lost on the Superintendent. He did not hesitate, but sent Inspector Smith forthwith to arrest Lieutenant Clark on suspicion of the abetment of the murder of his wife. A hypodermic syringe was removed from his bungalow.

On 26th November, accompanied by an Assistant Magistrate named Minson, in one of the extra procedural safeguards of the Indian law, Inspector Smith again searched Augusta's premises. This time, after the revelations in the letters, he was looking specifically for poisons, and he took away twenty-eight bottles and a box of Clark's which contained an empty bottle labelled 'one drachm gelsemium hydrochlor'.

Around this time, Augusta, too, was arrested.

And Sukkha, the *darzi*, came back for more rupees. It was the day after her mother's arrest. Kathleen was sitting in the garden, with only the *ayah*, now, for company.

'Look, that man has come again,' she said to the *ayah*. She felt angry. 'Go away! My mother is out.'

The police investigation gathered momentum. Enquiries were made at Meerut. Gossip which had been covert flowered into open ripeness.

On 6th December—nearly Christmas-time—they exhumed the body of Edward Fullam. Walter Sarkies, Edward's old friend and colleague from the Military Accounts Department, was asked to attend to identify the body. Appalled, he stood by as they raised the cheap coffin from Grave Number 130. The inscription on the headstone was 'Mr E. M. Fullam'.

When they opened the lid, the features of the body were in a state of decomposition, and unrecognisable. Sarkies saw some light-coloured hair in the grave, and Edward's hair had been light-coloured. The height appeared to be right. Guru Buksh— the bearer who could not find the Agra Club—was more successful as a witness; he identified some clothing as belonging to his late master.

Sergeant Charlwood, of the Government Railway Police, arranged transport of the body to the Agra Civil Hospital, where Major E. J. O'Meara, I.M.S., who had so recently catalogued Louisa Clark's mortal wounds, now performed the related post-mortem.

He, too, of course, alerted by the police, was looking specifically for poisons. As he prepared samples of hair, bone, and tissues to be sent to the Chemical Examiner, he noted that the preservation of the intestines, liver, diaphragm, and heart was remarkable, and consistent with the ingestion of some poisons, particularly arsenic. The muscles were very well preserved, and of a dark red colour.

The investigation became onerous. Superintendent William-son was relieved of his normal duties and placed on special assignment. Augusta and Clark indicated that they intended to fight all the way, and everyone concerned resigned them-selves to a long judicial process, embracing two separate trials.

By now, Augusta would have known positively that she was pregnant and that she could, therefore, expect to escape the death penalty, if convicted. Indian law followed the English exemption here, although not slavishly, as we shall see.

There is just one clue to her realistic doubt of avoiding conviction. In the year of 1912, the baby, Myrtle Phyllis, was adopted in India by a Mrs Cooper, and, oddly, her surname was changed from Fullam to Forster. The formalities of the adoption must have been completed with rare speed, after Augusta's arrest and, to be in 1912, before even the preliminary hearings in front of the Magistrate were completed. The inference must be that Augusta doubted that she herself would ever be in a position to care for Myrtle again. Her other children—Kathleen, Leonard, and Frank—were spirited away from public view and are also thought to have been adopted.* Only Kathleen, first, had to undergo the ordeal of playing a prominent part in the trials.

Aside from the saving pregnancy, Augusta had another trump to play: permission was sought in advance, and obtained, for her to be attended in court by a 'professional nurse', on the grounds that she was subject to 'occasional fits'.†

This is the first that we have heard of any 'fits'. Are we dealing, then, with a case of epilepsy? The subject has never been canvassed before. Could epilepsy to some extent explain and soften Augusta's vivid, excessive, and self-referring behaviour?

Where, then, is the reference to fits in her letters to her long-term lover— a doctor who attended her in the most intimate ways? While it is true that epilepsy was still regarded as a thing of shame, it seems unlikely that she would have been able to conceal such an affliction from Clark. On the other hand, not all of the correspondence was made public. Perhaps any mention of fits was censored, so that the rest of the family was not brushed with the same taint.

The only recorded occurrence that bears any resemblance to a fit is the 'faint' at the dance, after which she had to be revived with port wine and wrapped in a warm coat. She did complain of headaches. But what she was up to would have given anyone a headache.

Apparently, epileptics can be prolific letter-writers, with a 'hypergraphic style'.‡ Here, Augusta qualifies! Equally, though, memsahibs in their bungalows were known to enjoy copious, breathless correspondence—it was the norm.

* There were plenty of relatives about. Edward's deceased brother, William Arnold, had, on 2nd June, 1875, married Rose Baker Severs, and they had been blessed with eleven children. On the Goodwyn side, Lieutenant Alfred George Goodwyn and Maria Anne Rofs had had nine children. Augusta's sister, Dora Olive, already had one child, John Oscar Goodwyn Langlois, born on 17th November, 1909, and Paul Eric Goodwyn Langlois was to follow on 10th September, 1916.

† *Daily Telegraph*, 10th December, 1912.

‡ Observation of Dr Benjamin Zifkin, recorded by Herbert Lottman in his *Flaubert: a Biography* (Methuen, 1989).

Against epilepsy, one branch of her surviving relatives reports that all are in excellent health, and that, most certainly, no *congenital* form of the illness has shown itself.

There is a second possibility. None would deny that Augusta had an attention-seeking, hysterical personality. She herself positively relished what she was:

> I wonder if there lives a person in this world who understands my nature. I need all; love, attention and care. I simply cannot share with others. Just a loving, hysterical, weak little creature; but a regular handful. My Hubby says I am a wayward, wilful, headstrong girl.

Genuine hysterical fits, representing an unconscious attempt to dissociate herself from the proceedings, and from what she had perpetrated, might now have occurred, for the first time in her life.

The third alternative is faked fits. It would be quite in character for Augusta to feign fits, convincingly (for she showed unlovely guile and treacherous *voltes-face* during the trials), in a bid for sympathy. Clark might even have coached her—and she was ever his receptive pupil.

Her counsel did not, as it happens, put up any defence of mental impairment, but the mere presence of a solicitous nurse at her elbow, an unusual sight in the Indian courts, might have been calculated to exercise a silent influence.

George Wiggins, an English barrister-at-law, was briefed to appear for both Augusta and Clark in the lower court, as if they were united in one, interdependent defence stance. This arrangement was not to last.

Budhu was arrested. He quickly demonstrated a willingness to confess, and a disposition to incriminate all the others—including Augusta and Clark.

The four *badmashes* were still at large, but Superintendent Williamson was anxious to begin testing the evidence before the Magistrate, and an early date was set for the opening of the proceedings—Monday, 9th December, 1912. The missing men, as identified by Budhu, could be brought into court when they were picked up.

The news of the arrests and impending trials had spread right across the land, from Bombay to Calcutta. Over tea or tiffin, on the verandah, at the Club, all British India gossiped deliciously about the unprecedented scandal. Letting the side down was the deadly sin that dared to speak its name.

'The moral behaviour of all classes of Europeans should be extremely discreet, not only to preserve that inestimable blessing, health, but to command the respect of the native community.'*

The officers and agents of the Raj were cast to set an example and—quaint phrase—to hang together.

* George Bradshaw's *Handbooks to the Presidencies* (W. J. Adams, London, 1860–4).

## Chapter Eleven

# Indian Justice

Budhu was in handcuffs. Not so, Augusta and Clark. Four notional spaces were left in the dock for the fled *badmashes*. It was the morning of 9th December, 1912, and at 11.30 all available accused in the Clark case had been escorted by police into the hot, crowded, noisy court-room in Agra.

Such was the interest in the hearings that special tickets had been issued for admission. Everyone—British India, that is—wanted to see Augusta, and she had to endure stares and prurient imaginings. In Agra, a recent widow and known mistress of a married man, her social life had been restricted, but, had she been in court in Meerut, many of the goggling faces would have been uncomfortably familiar.

If the planned effects of the attendant nurse—protective and distancing in full, starched uniform—were to make Augusta appear fragile, not responsible for her actions, her own demeanour soon negated those benefits. She bore up very well—not swooning, but alert, combative.

Budhu was undefended. Not so, Augusta and Clark—George Wiggins was there for them. Charles Ross Alston (later knighted), an extremely competent English barrister-at-law appeared for the Prosecution. He was a small man physically and a good anecdote was told of him:

On one occasion when he was appearing in a case he was opposed by a great brawny barrister, also a European. As they were chatting together before they went into court the burly one said, 'Charles, I could pick you up and put you in my pocket.' 'If you did,' was the instant reply, 'you

150

would have more brains in your pocket than you ever had in your head.'*

The Joint Magistrate, J. B. Ormrod, presided. As an important preliminary formality, both Augusta and Clark claimed the right to be tried as European British subjects,† and the Prosecution raised no objection. The force of this obscure-sounding application was that, should they proceed to trial, as they surely would, they were entitled to be tried in the High Court before a jury, at least half of whom (out of nine) would be of 'European complexion'.

This privilege was a watered-down provision of the notorious Ilbert Bill of 1883, which had nearly caused a white mutiny in Bengal with its proposal that the few Indian judges qualified at that time should have jurisdiction over Europeans brought before the Court. The Act of 1884 was a compromise which aroused bitter Indian resentment, and the incident did much to vest Indian national feeling in a political form. It was a prelude to the formation of the Indian National Congress.

It has been said that what we might call the 'Ilbert' juries were so anxious to exhibit lack of racial prejudice that they tended to be over-severe towards the 'European British' defendants. In that case, Indians tried jointly with them could have expected extra leniency.

Already, before a word has been given in evidence, the special application illustrates the vast differences between Indian law and the English law on which it was founded. Codification‡ had seemed an opportunity to create a positively Utopian order and precision, but the criminal courts, dis-

* *No Ten Commandments: Life in the Indian Police*, S. T. Hollins (Hutchinson, 1954).
† Clark qualified. The definition was 'any subject of His Majesty of European descent in the male line born, naturalized or domiciled in the British Islands or any Colony, or any subject of His Majesty who is the child or grand-child of any such person by legitimate descent'. Section 4, the Criminal Procedure Code.
‡ The Indian Penal Code, composed by Lord Macaulay, with two others of lesser physical stamina, became law in 1860, followed by, and to be read with, the Indian Evidence Act, 1872, and the Criminal Procedure Code, 1898.

appointingly, presented a complicated and often chaotic spectacle of alien law introduced into a discordant cultural setting.

However, in this preliminary inquiry in Agra before the Magistrate, to determine that there are sufficient grounds for committing the accused to trial, we are, procedural variations notwithstanding, in known territory.

A committal inquiry in India was no mere formality but a full-blooded affair, with (often wild) cross-examination. There was no provision for a short-form committal (as was not, indeed, introduced in Britain until 1967), nor was there any restriction on newspaper coverage.

For reasons which will become clear, the evidence given before the Magistrate in the Clark and Fullam cases was fuller and often more telling than that given in the trials, with twists and revelations. It was reported most assiduously in Anglo-Indian newspapers. The trials, eventually, were abbreviated. Just as some cases, such as that of Philip Yale Drew* or the Bravo† affair, became trials by inquest, as it were, so the Clark and Fullam cases became a kind of trial by committal. Therefore, by deliberate choice, preference will be given here to the evidence in the lower court.

Without preamble, Ross Alston began to present his witnesses, put up by the police in, on the whole, a better logical sequence than in the customary nightmarish jumble that usually confronted hapless counsel. This was going to be a show-trial.

Traditionally enough, the first witness was a constable, Safadar Hossain, who described Clark's visit to the *thana*,‡ accompanied by another European gentleman, to report a robbery and an assault. Proceeding to 135 Cantonments, he found there a memsahib bandaged with a strip of cloth besmeared with blood.

George Wiggins did not rise. The Magistrate, bound to

---

* A swashbuckling actor suspected of battering to death a Reading tobacconist in 1929.

† Florence Bravo, suspected of administering antimony to her husband at The Priory, Balham, south London, in 1876.

‡ Sub police station.

protect the unrepresented Budhu, invited him to cross-examine. He declined.

The 'other European gentleman', Major G. Buchanan, R.A.M.C., a personage of some stature, neatly followed Safadar Hossain into the witness-box. He insisted that, when he came to him at Laurie's Hotel at 3 a.m., Clark used the word 'murdered'; Clark looked excited, spoke in a decided way, and gave a full description of the event.

Wiggins chose to cross-examine. The Major did not ask Clark at what time he had left his bungalow on the night of the attack. Neither did he ask Clark where he had been. Nor did he ask Clark by what route he had come to the hotel. Counsel appeared to be trying to bring in Clark's interim visit to Augusta, when he drank some water, to explain his late arrival at Laurie's Hotel. One would have thought, however, that the interim visit was not a matter to bring to prominence.

Again, Budhu declined to cross-examine, and the court adjourned for lunch. In the afternoon, Inspector Smith's evidence about the scene in the violated bungalow was brisk and to the point. He read out Clark's previous unsatisfactory statement, and said, also, that Clark had told him that his wife was a very bad-tempered woman, who constantly abused the servants.

Augusta, too, had made a statement to the Inspector, and he read aloud its hollow protestations: Mrs Clark was of a nagging disposition, but she knew that the Clarks were on amicable terms with each other.

Before recounting the discovery of the box of letters, Smith commented that if a man went from Clark's bungalow to Laurie's Hotel, he would go right out of his way to get to Mrs Fullam's bungalow.

The Court adjourned until the following day, 10th December, at 12 noon, when, not before time, the Crown had provided Budhu with an Indian lawyer, Babu Bijoy Shankar.

The Assistant Stationmaster, D. F. Menzes, said, in cross-examination, that, as Clark sat in his room waiting for his travelling friend, he spoke in an ordinary voice and showed no signs of excitement. There were no blood-stains on his clothing. Well, there wouldn't be, would there?

The next occupant of the box was Maud Clark, a principal

witness, bitter and bereaved. Her evidence was damaging in the extreme.

When at Meerut, she told the Court, she considered her father to be a great friend of Mrs Fullam's. He was very intimate with her. Her mother disliked the intimacy, and used to remonstrate with her father. There were quarrels over Mrs Fullam. Once, she saw her mother hand back to the postman a letter from Mrs Fullam to her father. The writing on the envelope was recognisable.

For many years *before* her family came to know the Fullams, her mother and father had many open quarrels. Her mother told her that her father entertained designs on her (Louisa's) life.

Sensationally, at this point, the Prosecution read aloud Louisa's 'memorandum', which had been found in a locked drawer in her room and was now identified by Maud. It was very damning in context, and it must have been excruciating for Maud to hear her mother's guileless, tormented musings.

After lunch, she was back to relive the night of terror. Then Alston brought her to the area of Clark's alibi. She never knew Menzies, nor did her father even mention that there was such a man as Menzies—a great draughts-player. Her family knew Joikim as an acquaintance in Meerut.

When pressed, she could not bring herself to articulate the last, plain, unnatural truth: she said that she could not give an opinion as to who was responsible for the attack on her mother. The Court rose.

The following day, at noon, again, Maud's ordeal continued. Cross-examination was inevitable. First, though, the Magistrate had some questions. For some reason, he wanted a better impression of the carnage, but Maud could only add that her mother was sitting up in bed and bleeding profusely. She appeared to have many wounds.

The Magistrate moved on to domestic matters. Her mother did *not* abuse the servants, but used to scold them when they did not work. Her mother had no dispute with the servants outside their ordinary work.

As for the lamentable marriage, Clark used to abuse Louisa violently, in front of Maud. Louisa had been annoyed, once, when Augusta came to breakfast at their home on Clark's birthday. On another occasion, when Louisa expressed annoyance at Clark's going to Fatehpur-Sikri* with Augusta, Clark threatened to kick her. When Clark used to call Louisa names, she retorted, 'You are that yourself,' but she never abused *him*.

Now Wiggins was on his feet. None could envy him. Previously, he might not even have guessed at the strength of the case against his two quite impressive and plausible clients. There was no disclosure of witness statements. His only expedient seemed to be to suggest that Maud had been 'got at'.

Accompanied by her uncle, she had left Allahabad (where she had presumably taken refuge) on 9th December, in order to give evidence in Agra. Police officers had met them on the way at Tundla, and then Inspector Wareham (C.I.D.), who was alone, had met them at Agra Fort. Wareham was present in court, and she pointed to him. He had gone with them from the station to the Carlton Hotel.

From the time of her arrival at the hotel, no police officer had spoken to her about the case. She was not aware that any officer had spoken to her uncle about the case. No relative had visited her at the hotel.

Wiggins changed tack. Certainly, she admitted, she sided with her mother when there were quarrels. Naturally so, because she and her brothers had all love and affection for their mother, and loved her more, since she treated them well.

During her stay in Agra, Mrs Fullam never came to their home (for breakfast). Maud did not know whether the relations between Mrs Fullam and her father were well known all over the station. She had no knowledge of her father's writing to Mrs Fullam, or to other ladies in Agra. No, her mother was not jealous of Mrs Fullam—a fine shaft, this—she had nothing to be jealous of!

It is difficult to perceive the reasoning behind this last series of questions, which did Wiggins' clients no credit, unless he were being remarkably subtle in seeking to demonstrate that

---

* A town 23 miles west of Agra, former capital of the Mogul empire, famous for its abandoned city, with ruined remains enclosed by a high wall, seven miles in circumference.

Maud was of a disposition to fudge the truth in certain areas, out of loyalty to her mother.

Lunch at 1.30 saved everybody, and Wiggins came back prepared for the safer ground of identification. Budhu was not, of course, his client, but his presence at the scene of the crime was against his own clients and, sure enough, Maud, in the dim lamplight did not recognise either the man with the big stick or the peeper from behind the *purdah*. Neither of these men was, in fact, Budhu, anyway.

Encouraged, Wiggins caused Maud to identify a letter which she had written to her uncle on 27th November, and which had, rather oddly, come into counsel's hands. The section which he thought helpful to his cause read as follows: 'Uncle dear, she did not die a natural death at all. Two native men came in the night between twelve and one on Sunday and murdered her.'

Finally after eliciting the extraneous detail that Clark had been to China when Maud was about seven years old, Wiggins sat down.

Now it was Babu Bijoy Shankar's turn to cross-examine, and perhaps to shine; he had only Budhu to defend and could pull out all the stops for him. He had been in court right through Maud's evidence, which included the *chota-hazri* tea incident and the poisoned pilau.

This is what Budhu's lawyer elicited. Budhu was first employed by Clark in his home. Clark also employed him for the second time. The memsahib used to pay Budhu six rupees from her own pocket. Budhu's duties were to cook food and serve as a table servant. There was a theft at the Clarks' bungalow in the previous year. That was all.

Alston opted to re-examine. He was worried by Maud's oblique answers to Wiggins' series of questions, but he was unable to improve matters, to shake her protective stance. Maud said that her mother did not care for (she meant 'about') the intimacy between Mrs Fullam and her father. Her mother was perfectly indifferent.

Turning to the letter to her uncle, Alston asked Maud what she meant when she wrote, 'Uncle, if you were here I would tell you everything.' Maud replied that she meant 'all about the murder'. Appreciating that the girl stopped short of naming her own father as the murderer—and, after all, she had testified to many matters which went against Clark—Alston did not persist.

Even so, the Magistrate then took it up. Had Maud any suspicion against anybody when she wrote in the letter to her uncle, 'It will all end very badly, I fear'? Maud said that she had no suspicion against anybody.

They let the girl go, and young Bibu, the honest cook, told the court about Clark's threat to strangle him unless he put some white powders in the memsahib's tea.

Harry Clark's ordeal, on the Thursday, was little less than his sister's. He deposed that his father was intimate with the Fullams in Meerut, and his mother objected to the intimacy. His father was in the habit of visiting Mrs Fullam in a *dak* bungalow in Meerut.

The stress of the occasion must have blunted Harry's memory, because it was his recollection that Augusta and Clark first came to know each other when he attended her in confinement. In reality, baby Frank had been long born when they met, and Myrtle was yet to be conceived.

He corroborated Bibu's evidence, and Maud's evidence about the poisoned pilau. Then Alston led him into the sensitive part of his testimony. His parents were far from happy together. His father did not care for his family at all. He had no love for his (witness's) mother. He doubted whether his father had any love for his children. This was because he thought that his father was running after another woman.

Clark used to abuse his mother—said Harry—in the most offensive language. She was far from quarrelsome, and of a very quiet disposition. She never neglected her household duties. Clark had struck her in Harry's presence. Clark had never complained of her misbehaving in any way.

The reason for Wiggins' introduction of China into the evidence was now to become clear. Out of gallantry, perhaps, he had reserved for the young man of 23, rather than the girl, some unpleasant material supplied to him by Clark.

Harry did not know if a particular quarrel at Dinapore was about his mother's (alleged) intimacy with Driver Shaw. Nor did he know if a child was born to her at Dinapore. He had a brother, John, who was born, and died, in Calcutta. He was not aware that John was the cause of any quarrel. John was born three months after Clark went to China.

Harry used the same terms as Maud had done—he did not, it was true, care very much for his father, because his father did not care for him. Once, his father wanted his mother to accompany him to Chakrata,* but she refused, as Mrs Fullam was also going there. Harry knew Mrs Fullam to be a woman of means. His mother said that she would get a separation. She was thoroughly disgusted.

After lunch, Wiggins continued. His mother had told Harry that she was going to be poisoned. Harry could not explain why no one had spoken to Budhu of their suspicions. When Assistant-Surgeon Linton had said that the powder passed over by Bibu was a slow poison, Harry had asked his mother to go away with him. She had refused, but gave no reasons.

Babu Bijoy Shankar took over, but made little headway. Harry said that his father, not his mother, engaged Budhu as a servant. Budhu used to make tea in separate cups and serve separately to each person at the table. Harry did not remember asking his father to dismiss Budhu after the tea incident. Assistant-Surgeon White did not tell Harry or his mother that there was slow poison in the tea or in the rice which made her sick. A bit of a point, at last—or half a point, since White was not present at the *chota-hazri* tea poisoning!

One wonders if Alston's next two witnesses had volunteered their information to the police, as good citizens. First of all, he produced a Mrs Wiele, who must have felt most uncomfortable in the witness-box. She knew Clark well for a short time, and met Louisa only once.

Mrs Wiele remembered that Clark had told her times out of number that he could get rid of his wife by some way or other. That was the main subject of his conversation. He abused Louisa, using very objectionable words. She had met Augusta once. Her acquaintance with Clark had ceased in June.

The cross-examination was kind to her, and, as so often in this case, merely sounded like an extension of the examination-in-chief. She said that she had repeated to Louisa a few of the things which Clark had said against her. Clark had told her

* A military hill-station, 28 miles from Dehra Dun.

158

that he wanted to get rid of Louisa because he was in love with two other ladies. When she told Louisa what her husband had said, Louisa had commented, 'My husband is a wicked man.'

Gleefully, the Prosecution re-examined, and Mrs Wiele said that Louisa had explained to her what she meant by wickedness.

The second witness of this stamp was J. Morton, another retired member of the Indian Subordinate Medical Department, who used to visit Clark frequently. Clark had several times complained of his wife. He had said, 'I wish I could get rid of her.'

On subsequent occasions, Clark had told Morton that Louisa had gone wrong while he had been away on the China expedition. He had also complained that she neglected him, and did not give him enough to eat. (So that is why he ate at another table!) However, Clark had never used abusive language about Louisa in Morton's hearing, and he had never said that he wanted to marry someone else. Wisely, this time, there was no cross-examination.

Friday, 13th December, after a whole week of evidence, brought forth the two post-mortem doctors. Major E. J. O'Meara testified first. He thought that the age of Mrs Clark was about fifty-five years. The condition of her body was distinctly stout. She must have been struck with a heavy weapon. The wounds on the skull were sufficient to cause death, and he judged that she would have become unconscious on receiving the blows, which were inflicted by a man who was very deliberate and accustomed to delivering such strokes.

Dr J. P. Modi deposed that, from the nature of the wounds, he could say that the striker intended to cause death, and that such injuries would certainly cause death. It was possible for a person with a fractured skull to have spoken, but it would have been unconsciously.

Walter Clark, now working in the Military Accounts Department in Meerut, was not kept long in the witness-box. He, too, recounted the familiar *chota-hazri* tea and pilau incidents, and the cross-examination obligingly elicited the extra data that Budhu had been their only cook at that time, that Clark had engaged him, and that he had gone away once and had been brought back by Clark.

159

Thus enlightened, the Court adjourned for lunch, and returned to examine the unhappy figure of Alick Joseph, the famous letter-writer, who had a new job as assistant accountant at Johns Mills, Agra. Volubly, he admitted his involvement, identified Augusta's handwriting on some of the letters shown to him, and rehearsed Clark's comment that Louisa was 'poison-proof'. Mrs Wiele and Mr Morton (who take on a gamier image than they had wished to convey in the witness-box) used to chaff him for keeping Augusta's letters. They also chaffed Clark about the letters, and he used to grin and laugh.

During Harry Clark's testimony, Alston had promised that he would, in due course, produce a letter from Augusta to Clark, giving extraordinary confirmation that the white powder in Bibu's unwilling hands, and said by Assistant-Surgeon Linton to be slow poison, was indeed slow poison.

Alston judged that he had now reached the effective point at which to introduce that letter. Indeed, it was as if the letters could no longer be held back but must be heard. They were going to assume almost a life and voice of their own, outside their originator.

This first reading of the letters, which gave the Court a foretaste of the rich, incriminatory hoard, was from the absolutely crucial and central letter of 27th April, 1911, which read, 'I don't think these powders are having any effect. What do you think? You say they must be given regularly and then you say you can't administer these to Mrs C. as regularly as you would like to.'

The chilling words froze in the stifling court-room, and Friday the 13th was over. That evening, a flustered Wiggins scurried between Augusta and Clark in agitated conference. There was a very strong feeling that a crisis had been reached, that it was a matter of *sauve qui peut*—preferably the lady.

The plan arrived at, and it bears all the marks of an extempore decision, although Augusta would already have been incubating certain notions for her defence, was that she would now make an exculpatory statement which, although it made dangerous admissions, did not amount to a confession. It would put blame upon Clark, but that could not be helped. Blame could also be heaped upon Budhu.

160

| When Died — Year | Month | Day | Christian name | Surname | Age | Quality, Trade, or Profession, &c. &c. | When Buried — Year | Month | Day | Cause of Death | Name and designation of person by whom Returned |
|---|---|---|---|---|---|---|---|---|---|---|---|
| 1911 | October | 10th | Edward McKeon | Fullam | 44 | Deputy Examiner, Military Accounts Department | 1911 | October | 11th | General Paralysis & Heart failure | Ben. Cotton, Chaplain |
| 1911 | October | 22nd | Seance Baylon | Body | 3 | Child of Henry Body Telegraphist | 1911 | October | 22nd | Diphtheria | Ben. Cotton, Chaplain |
| 1911 | November | 9th | Henry Neill | Johnson | 7 2/12 | Child of Mark Cornelius & Henrietta Johnson | 1911 | November | 10th | Meningitis | Ben. Cotton, Chaplain |
| 1911 | November | 29th | Eva Emolance | Young | 24 | Wife of Henry Young Telegraphist | 1911 | November | 30th | Blood Poisoning | Ben. Cotton, Chaplain |
| 1911 | December | 1st | James | Brotherton | 46 | Ordnance Department | 1911 | December | 2nd | Enteric fever | Ben. Cotton, Chaplain |
| 1911 | December | 30th | Isabel Catherine | Halkerston | 39 | Wife of John Halkerston | 1911 | December | 31st | Paralysis | Ben. Cotton, Chaplain |

I, the Reverend Ben. Cotton, Minister and Chaplain of Agra, do hereby certify that the foregoing (or annexed) return containing six Register of Burials belonging to and kept at the Church or Station of Agra within the Archdeaconry and Diocese of Calcutta, is a true and faithful copy of all the entries in the Register of Burials. In the year of Our Lord One Thousand Nine Hundred and Eleven, as therein entered and made between the first day of October and the 31st day of December.

Witness my hand,

Ben. Cotton, Minister and Chaplain of Agra

Edward Fullam's burial record, bearing false cause of death, as certified by Lieutenant Clark. (The surname is misspelt.)

Wiggins must have been in a state of disarray. Written proofs of what the accused would say in court were virtually unknown, and he found himself in the embarrassing situation of representing two clients where there was a conflict of interest. He would have to jettison one of them.

Saturday was still a court-day, and, early, at 10.30, *in camera*, the Magistrate began to record Augusta's statement. It was a much criticised principle of Indian law that the accused was not permitted to give sworn evidence on his own behalf. Britain had extended that right to the defendant in 1898, but had withheld it from the Indian courts. Instead the accused was permitted to make a statement from the dock to the tribunal, and to answer questions put to him by the Judge or Magistrate acting as a kind of French *juge d'instruction*.

At 2.45, Augusta had finished, and the public were allowed back into the court-room. Wiggins had a statement of his own to make. Since Augusta's statement went against Clark, he could no longer appear for her. He had chosen to stick with his male client. Or perhaps Augusta had rejected him.

Intrigued, no doubt, Ross Alston put up Assistant-Surgeon Linton to attest to the garlicky smell of Bibu's powders and his conclusion that they were one of the compounds of arsenic.

Strong now, disencumbered, able to go all out for Clark, Wiggins decided to have a stab at cross-examination, but Linton's opinion that, in fact, the powder would have had fatal results in about twenty minutes, did his client no good. It merely showed that Linton had been guilty of pussy-footing!

Paired with Linton, Assistant-Surgeon White proved the poisoned-pilau episode, or, rather, his failure to recognise it as such.

Then Harry Clark was recalled; he was wanted to identify his father's initials on the envelopes of the letters. While he was there, the Magistrate took the opportunity of examining him about his father's demeanour. On the day after his mother's death, Harry had met his father when he was going to hospital and Clark had said something on the lines of, 'I don't know why you children suspect me of murder. You all think your mother alone loved you.'

Alston rose to his feet: he proposed to put in Mrs Fullam's

statement made in court as evidence, and to be filed as an exhibit. No technical objection was raised. Augusta steeled herself to keep up a good front, as, in level tones, he began to read.

## Chapter Twelve

# Svengali Lives!

'I will begin at the beginning. I knew Mr Clark four years ago. He came over to our house frequently at 33 Warwick Row, Meerut, and fell in love with me there. He was very friendly with Mr Fullam, my husband, and treated all of us on several occasions professionally, always being very kind and attentive. I believe he must have had the power of hypnotism, for he made me and Mr Fullam do whatever he wished. He won my affections completely away from my husband. I became a tool in his hands. Gradually he came to dislike Mr Fullam on account of not getting his two sons, Harry and Walter, on in the office of the Military Accounts Department, where my husband was the *burra sahib*.

'Then he made a suggestion one day last year that he would make Mr Fullam ill. Mr Clark only wished my husband ill enough to make him go on long furlough out of the country, leaving me behind. That will show the purpose of the man. I do not know what I wrote in any of those letters, but I am now convinced that I must have been hypnotised. For I had no reason to harm my husband or go against him in any way. We were always a loving couple, and had a happy, comfortable home, I and Mr Fullam. I know my husband became ill, and I know he recovered. Mr Fullam got a fixed and determined idea to come to Agra, which also convinces me that he must have been under a state of hypnotic influence. Mr Fullam sent for Clark to come and bring him from Meerut to Agra. For he had great faith in him and trusted him implicitly.

'Four days after arriving here he became suddenly ill one night after having had his usual dinner out in the compound. I was not with him at the time. I wish to say that I was giving the children dinner in another room; Clark was with my husband, there was no one else with him, you see. Clark came into the room where I was, into the dining-room, and said to me: "He has got another attack. He is going fast." By this time my husband had walked to bed, Clark having helped him to bed. I and my servants went near my husband who was quite unconscious. I had a cook and an *ayah* and a bearer with me then in the bedroom. Clark was in the room too. I brought these three servants from Meerut, the cook went back there, and I still have Jhabia *ayah*, if the court likes to put down her name, and Guru Buksh bearer.

'It is so hard for me to say, as it is such a long story. Then Mr Clark biked off to get Captain Dunne immediately, and brought him back with him from the Club. Captain Dunne just came in time to see him expire. And Captain Dunne said to me, "Mrs Fullam, I am very sorry, there is nothing I can do." After examining the body and asking a few questions he went away. He certified that Mr Fullam died of general paralysis. That is about all my story.

'Mr and Mrs Clark did not live on happy terms, one blamed the other for their unhappiness. So I cannot say whose fault it was. I only know that Mr Clark was very fond of women, and had several love affairs both before and after I knew him. He won my whole love and trust. And I gave my whole life into his keeping. Now I find I have been duped, deceived and made a tool of. He spoke of doing away with his wife on several occasions. But I always dissuaded him from it. I had a great influence over him and he said he has been a better man since knowing me. I could not control his strong will, which was evidently to get rid of his wife. Lately she treated him very badly, and that made him very bitter against her. The children also were taught by her to hate him.

'He got Budhu into his confidence and bribed him and two other men to strangle her in her sleep. I am sure Budhu must have been in the house that night. For the dog knew him only, and I feel convinced that he must have called the dog outside while one of the others did the deed. I cannot say if all this is true. But Budhu ought to be able to speak. I am sure that he can speak. The two men went away to Delhi the next day. Budhu brought these men from some village and they were friends and associates of Budhu's, and I heard them say they were used to deeds like this. That is just what the Civil Surgeon said yesterday in the case, that the man was deliberate and used to striking blows like that. I was powerless to prevent it although I tried my best to do so. If I had warned Mrs Clark that night she would never have believed me, and she would have said I was abetting her husband in murdering her. She was very bitter towards me and my warning would have been of no avail.

'I know the intent of it; it was that these men would enter the house, Budhu to keep the dog quiet and to point out Mrs Clark to these other two men. They were to strangle her, leaving no finger impressions or blood behind. And to disturb the things so as to leave the impression that thieves had come in to rob. They evidently chose their own way of doing the deed. I know that they had planned to strangle her so I conclude that they took their own way of doing things. I never heard any talk about a weapon, or about cracking her skull.

'The bribe was a hundred rupees. The money was paid by Mr Clark. I do not know to whom. I do not think I have more to say except that I was a tool in Clark's hands. Now I find that his assertions of love for me were all false and perfectly untrue. I throw myself on the mercy of the Court and repeat again that I was utterly powerless to prevent him in any of his misdeeds which are very numerous. That is all I have to say. May God forgive him as I do.

'Once he told me about Calcutta where he had given her enough arsenic to kill ten men; she vomited freely on that occasion and got over it. I did not know him when in Calcutta. Two or three times he has given Budhu powders to give to Mrs Clark in Agra. This I know of my own knowledge. Whether Budhu gave them or not, I do not know. I have heard Clark speak about this matter of the two or three times he gave powders, but I did not see Clark give them to Budhu.

'Clark told the three men in my presence to kill her in her sleep somehow and leave no trace behind, then to rummage the boxes and things, to make it appear that thieves had been. If she was found dead in the morning, people would say she had a weak heart and went off in her sleep. These are the purport of Clark's words. There was nothing said about breaking her head open. It was to be a natural death in sleep, just as a person would go to bed and die in her sleep. That is all I know. I was powerless as if I had stopped them on that night, they would have taken another occasion, unknown to me.

'[When asked how Clark proposed to make Edward Fullam ill] Clark said he would send me a liquid medicine to give my husband. He did so, and I gave my husband only one dose; this medicine caused a rush of blood to the head. I sent for Captain Keene, Staff-Surgeon at Meerut; he came at midnight, stayed with Mr Fullam till morning and then had him conveyed to the No. 1 Section Hospital. Mr Fullam got better there under treatment, and after one month returned home. He was at home two days, and Mr Clark called to see us, and he became ill again with the same symptoms—heat-stroke.

'I wish to say that after two days at home mentioned above when my husband had again the same symptoms after Clark had been to see us, my husband just said "Hospital, hospital!" and fell back on the bed in a dying condition. A friend, Captain Weston, who lived opposite us, was sent for and he and I removed my husband to hospital in my own phaeton. He was very seriously ill for two months or more, paralysed and quite out of his mind. His brain appeared to have given way. I do not mean to say he was a lunatic, but he could not think much or long. Whilst there he got the fixed idea of coming to Agra himself and he desired that Clark should come from Agra and bring him. My husband was paralysed and helpless. He told me to wire to Clark to engage rooms at Agra and furnish them, which Clark did at No. 9 Metcalfe Road, Mrs Stone's house. My husband made me send a second wire to Clark asking him to take leave and come over to Meerut to bring him to Agra. Clark did this, coming to Meerut on the 6th October, 1911; we arrived in Agra on the morning of 8th October, 1911. Mr Fullam died on the night of the 10th October, 1911, at 10 p.m.

'I wish to say that Mr Clark gave my husband several injections in the presence of my servants and myself before going for Captain Dunne, in the night that Mr Fullam died. I cannot say what these injections were. But Mr Clark showed a bottle from which he had injected into Mr Fullam. I heard Captain Dunne say, "That is all right." Clark used a hypodermic syringe, filling it from the small bottle I speak of. The bottle was an inch long and the same in breadth, it was a fat bottle, and Clark told him that he had been injecting the liquid in the bottle.

'I would like to add that when Mr Fullam was dying he called out "Clark, Clark!" in a loud voice. Mr Clark held a table-lamp over him and leaned over my husband to hear what he was trying to say. Mr Clark caught these words from Mr Fullam's lips, "Look wife, children," but very inaudible and very thickly spoken, which shows that he trusted and believed in Clark to the last. I also wish to say now that when I wrote those letters I wrote them under Mr Clark's influence and not of my own free will.

'I would like if I may to state an instance of how he hypnotised Mr Fullam. On one occasion Clark came to Meerut to see us, believing Mr Fullam would be in office. It so happened that that day was a holiday; he found Mr Fullam and myself at breakfast and my husband told me he had no intention of going to office. Clark was surprised to find him at home and looked hard at Mr Fullam and said, "Fullam, you have a lot of work in the office; how is it that you are at home?" Mr Fullam quietly left the breakfast table and went into the dressing-room and dressed and cycled off to office. I tried to persuade Mr Fullam not to go, reminding him it was a holiday, and that he had all along promised to stay at home. He said, "Oh, there is too much work," and, "I'd better get through it." He stayed in office all that day till 5 p.m. from 10 a.m., which is another proof to me of Mr Clark's power to hypnotise. That is all.'

Svengali lives! Yet please let no one impugn the professional integrity of George Wiggins by the slightest suggestion that he had invented a defence of hypnotism for Augusta, and coached her in it—or even that he had flung it to her as a lifebelt.

Rather, this was her own artefact, the unaided product of her imagination—ingenious, perhaps, but ultimately absurd. This was her style, too, with its familiar, linked synonyms—'fixed and determined', 'duped, deceived and made a tool of'.

With perturbation, if not plain horror, poor Wiggins must have learned in conference what his interesting client was proposing to put to the Court. And once she had made that statement, she was stuck with it. Its abstractions were not like concrete facts which could be revised as evidence dictated. He may well have advised her to plead guilty, but she was set on having her jury. As he untied the grapplings and let Augusta's barque drift away alone, his relief was tempered only by the increasing peril of Clark's exposed position.

Hypnotism was a voguish topic, alive then in men's minds. In England, in 1907, the Medical Society for the Study of Suggestive Therapeutics had been founded. It might be said that there was a special awareness of the subject in India, where Dr James Esdaile (1808–59), M.D. (Edinburgh), who served with the East India Company in Calcutta and Hooghly, had achieved great fame in performing operations under hypnosis. His first such operation, and it was successful, was on a Hindu convict, in 1845. He was a good man, and it was a shame for him that chloroform and ether soon came to steal his glory. As a matter of fact, he admitted that he 'detested the climate, the country, and all its ways, from the moment I first set foot in it'!

Hypnosis as a defence to murder is still an open subject. Augusta must be one of its earliest exponents. Most authorities assert that a person cannot be induced by hypnosis to commit an act which, in full consciousness, he would consider to be morally wrong. However, there *are* experimental examples which refute this general rule.

Augusta would have appreciated the following passage, quoted by F. W. H. Myers in a paper to the Society for Psychical Research in the 1890s:

> The action may be *deferred* for hours or days after the suggestion is given. Professor Liégeois [a medical juris-prudist] gave to M. N. a paper of white powder, informing him that it was arsenic, and that on his return home he must dissolve it in a glass of water and give it to his aunt. In the evening a note from the aunt arrived as follows: 'Madame M. has the honour to inform M. Liégeois that the experiment has completely succeeded. Her nephew duly presented her with the poison.'

By way of variation, Augusta introduced the notion that the victim—Edward—was *also* under the influence of hypnosis and thus assisted his own death! But hypnosis was a desperate throw with which to explain away the mass of letters and the long period of the conspiracy.

A protracted course of conduct does not lend itself so easily to the hypnosis set-up as one, single, defined act. In the leading, modern case of Dr Carl Coppolino (1965), a prosecution witness, Marjorie Farber, claimed that she was in a 'waking trance' induced by the doctor for *one and a half years*. During this kind of dream of infatuation, she said, she injected a lethal drug into her husband and then stood by, as if spellbound, while Coppolino finished him off with a pillow. The New Jersey jury did not believe her.

Such niceties as the length of the period of the supposed hypnosis were not, of course, within Augusta's grasp. For her inspiration, she is more likely to have been relying on George Du Maurier's *Trilby* (1894–5) or other, derivative romances.

The dark character of Svengali in Du Maurier's coiling and seductive novel is calculated to appeal to her fantasising imagination, and Augusta's pliant memory could have stored away the saying that mesmerists 'get you into their power and just make you do any blessed thing they please—lie, murder, steal—anything!'

If, though, Augusta were asking the Court to believe that Clark was her Svengali, who 'had but to say "Dors!" and she became an unconscious Trilby of marble', she was vitiating the force of her claim by the other two, very concrete piers of her defence.

Thus, firstly, her discovered letters, however excused by a 'waking trance', linked her so strongly to Edward's poisoning that she was forced to fall back upon the 'intent only to disable' position, evidenced by a degree of conscious cunning. The second prong of her defence—total dissociation from Louisa's death—presented her in full possession of her reason and volition.

By now, it was five o'clock, and the Clark case was adjourned *sine die*. The Fullam case was ready to be taken up, and, after the brief respite of Sunday, on Monday, 16th December, the court-room was filled again with spectators. Budhu, naturally, was not involved this time, but languished in custody, brooding upon the words that Augusta had used against him. She herself had not found a substitute for George

Wiggins, and, in fact, remained unrepresented for the rest of the preliminary hearings, which appears to be most irregular. Financial considerations may have weighed with her, and her lack of counsel should not be taken as a sign that she had abandoned hope and resigned herself to the inevitable.

As before, Augusta and Clark claimed, and were granted, the privilege of being tried as European British subjects, and then Ross Alston launched into an opening address. Both accused were to be charged jointly with two attempts to murder Edward Fullam, and also, jointly, with his actual murder.

Although the Chemical Examiner's investigation had not yet been completed, the Prosecution suspected that the 'tonic powders' were arsenic, because Edward Fullam's symptoms strongly suggested that poison, and it was known, too, that Clark had brought arsenic powder in Agra, in the months of May and June 1911.

Counsel did not, at present, know what was in the jalapin preparation, nor, more crucially, what particular poison was administered to produce 'heat-stroke' in the July. As for the injections given immediately before death, Alston proposed that a powerful alkaloid poison which Clark procured from Calcutta early in September, 1911, was probably used. He would prove later on that Clark had bought 60 grains of this poison (gelsemine) from Calcutta. Forty-eight grains of it were found in his possession, suggesting that he had used some of it, as the purchase was made shortly before Edward Fullam's death.

Would that it were so simple! These were early days of over-optimism. As the evidence will go on to show, no such purchase at the vital time was ever proved in court, and the issue was abandoned.

Walter Sarkies, Edward's close colleague, was Alston's first witness. His evidence was guarded. To all outward appearances, the Fullams were a happy couple. He never heard of any quarrel between them. Mr Fullam had a quiet, retiring disposition, and Mrs Fullam was the same. He also knew the Clark family very well.

He attested to the exhumation, and, asked specifically about Edward's withered left arm, he described it as thinner and lighter than the right one. He had no personal knowledge as to whether Edward had paralysis, and Edward had never told

Sarkies that the thinness of the arm was due to paralysis.

Sarkies knew Clark's handwriting, because his establish-ment bills came to his accounts office. After Edward died, Augusta used to correspond with his office, signing her letters 'Gussie Fullam'. He saw those letters in his official capacity, and he thought that he would be able to identify her handwriting. Letters of a different kind were shown to him, and he did so.

The time had come for the reading of the letters. One after another, in graphic sequence, Counsel intoned the sizzling, tell-tale passages. Widely reported in India, and carried, less copiously, by British newspapers, the correspondence caused a sensation.

In due course, Augusta came to be regarded as 'the Edith Thompson* of Meerut', and the comparison is just enough. Their letters finished both of them, although there was less moral prejudice against Augusta *in the court*.

In each case, the letters appeared at their face-value to be powerfully evidential of an intent to murder. However, while Edward Fullam's post-mortem did, indeed, yield positive results, Percy Thompson's, performed by Sir Bernard Spilsbury, was negative, in spite of the sinister references to poison and broken glass.

The inherent ambiguity in the Thompson letters lies in the extent to which the mention of poison was all melodrama and erotic stimulus. At one stage in the Thompson case, too, there is the suggestion of the lover supplying 'something' to make the husband merely 'ill'. Ambiguity also lies in the uncertainty as to when Edith Thompson was referring to drugs designed to procure abortion.

Any inherent ambiguity in Augusta's letters lies, as we have seen, in the extent to which they *could*, academically, be interpreted as indicative of an intent to disable, not to kill.

Bywaters preserved the lady's letters. So did Clark. Bywaters kept them at his side, afloat, on the s.s. *Morea*. Augusta kept them under her own roof, similarly in a locked box.

---

* Both Edith Thompson and her lover, Frederick Bywaters, were hanged, in 1923, for the murder of her husband, Percy, stabbed by Bywaters in an Ilford, Essex, street.

The trial judge, Mr Justice Shearman, called Edith Thompson's letters of love and longing 'gush', and, no doubt, he would have found Augusta's effusions equally sickening. In neither case were they the expressions of a real lady, or a *'pukka memsahib'*. Curiously, although only a decade separates them, Augusta's style is positively Victorian against Edith Thompson's jaunty, flapperish evocation of Ilford and London in the 1920s.

Finally, Edith Thompson is acknowledged to have harmed her defence by insisting on giving evidence on her own behalf. Similarly, Augusta's statement (whether or not she insisted on making it) did her no good at all.

Late, at 5.30, sated with the reading and proving of letters in Ross Alston's objective, yet emphasised drone, the Court rose, but the next day, at noon, Alston was still producing them. At last, the weird, shaming recital was done, the shocked whispers stilled, and the Court returned to the blunt reality of witnesses.

Walter Sarkies was wheeled back in again, this time formally to identify Clark's handwriting, firstly in the form of the pencilled draft of the fake, 'G.P.I.' death certificate for Edward Fullam. Then he was needed to prove two important letters to a firm of chemists in Calcutta, Dr Bose's laboratory, 43 Amherst Street, most efficiently tracked down there by the police.

The first letter, headed 'Agra, 1st September' ran as follows: 'Dear Sir,—Will you very kindly send me by return post V.P.P.* two bottles of Nanala† as it is very urgently required. Yours truly, H. L. Clark, Assistant-Surgeon, I.S.M.D.'

There was a PS.—'Also will you very kindly send me twenty grains of the undermentioned drug at your earliest convenience as it is very urgently required:—Gelsemine hydrochloride. If you haven't this in stock any other alkaloid will do such as gelsemine nitidum, gelsemine alkaloid, gelsemine, but gelsemine hydrochloride is preferable to the remaining alkaloids.'

The other letter, dated 23rd September, was short and to the point: 'Dear Sir,—Will you very kindly send me by return post V.P.P., the under-mentioned, as it is very urgently required:—

* Value Payable Parcel. People paid for goods on arrival at the post office.
† A harmless patent medicine, containing phenacetin, etc.

Gelsemine hydrochlorate Mercks; one tube of 5 (five) grains.'

Sarkies was released, and Kathleen Fullam took his place, a small, brave figure, with her long, fair hair tied neatly in a ribbon—Alice in Wonderland in a court of law where the cards were a murdered father and a mother who had been taken away. She was wonderfully descriptive, with an excellent pictorial memory, as she relived the night of her father's death.

In the British fashion, as a minor witness, questioned kindly by the Magistrate, she had said that she knew the difference between telling a lie and telling the truth, and few present could have doubted the accuracy of her artless evidence about the glass needle and what Clark did with it.

When the little girl came to the moment where her father was about to speak to her his last, heart-rending words, she wept silently, watched by her mother.

Quite soon, she managed to continue, and her evidence was especially sensational when she explained that Clark pretended her father was still alive when he cycled off to fetch Captain Dunne. This was in direct contrast to her mother's statement.

Kathleen first related all the frightful things which she had seen to a Mrs Herbert, who had been looking after the children. She had not told anybody else, because her mother had told her not to, or she might get into trouble. The next person she told about her father was Mr Alston at the hotel. (So the police, after interviewing, or being approached by Mrs Herbert, had scrupulously held back from themselves interviewing the child.)

After lunch, Kathleen said that she did not tell her mother about her father's dying words. She did not like to tell her mother because she treated her father so badly. When he was ill in hospital in Meerut, her mother did not go to see him often. Kathleen felt sorry for him, then, and loved him more than her mother. In Agra, Clark used to beat her and her brother, although he used to treat them nicely in Meerut.

Wiggins had to do something for Clark, although it meant cross-examining a child: she did not hear Clark tell Captain Dunne that he had injected her father. She did not know then what injection was. She knew, now.

It was a good thing that Wiggins was no longer acting for Augusta, because his next question elicited the memorable comment that Kathleen did not see any tears in her mother's eyes that night, but she had cried the following day, when the coffin was closed.

This was the ideal, poetic moment for Augusta, bereft of counsel, to be asked if she wished to cross-examine her own daughter, and, so invited, she declined.

It only remained for Alston to establish that Captain Dunne could have spoken to Clark without Kathleen's hearing what he said, if he wished, and the long and emotional day was over.

The evidence on Wednesday, 18th December, was less highly charged, but, even so, very telling. First, though, the bearer, Guru Buksh, who had 'roamed' along the Mall Road, looking for the doctor's house near the Agra Club, had to be disposed of. He, too, was needed to attest that Clark knew that Edward was dead before Captain Dunne arrived, and although he could not be so precise as Kathleen, who had heard Clark say, 'Gone', he was well able to state that Clark told him to go home because the sahib was dead. Indeed, Kathleen's testimony had included the evidence that Guru Buksh had repeated to her, on the day after Edward's death, Clark's exact words to him: *'Jao ghar. Sahib mar gia.'*

The Postmaster at Agra, T. G. Chiodetti, was put up next, to say that, when he was stationed at Meerut, he knew all along that 'Mrs Clarkson' was Mrs Augusta Fullam. He identified a post-office book containing receipts for registered articles sent to her, care of the Postmaster, Meerut Cantonment.

Although Chiodetti was not transferred to Agra until 12th February, 1912, Alston also used him to prove a receipt signed by H. L. Clark for value payable on an article sent on 8th October, 1911, to Clark at Agra Station Hospital from Dr Bose's laboratory. This, said Alston, was the receipt for the package of gelsemine. More accurately, he should have said that it was for *a* package of gelsemine.

Inspector Smith described his successful searches of the two bungalows. Then Superintendent Williamson gave evidence as to some interesting discoveries. One was negative, but still interesting: he could not find Edward's case-sheets anywhere at the Meerut Hospital. There were hundreds of case-sheets for other patients. He did manage to find his diet-sheets for the

174

months of August, September, and October, but those for the last four days in July were missing.

The Superintendent had collected some medical books which were lying around Clark's bungalow in Agra and had sent them to Major O'Meara, not interfered with in any way. They included *Principles of Forensic Medicine, Tropical Disease(s), British Medical Journal*, Bedell's *Medical Jurisprudence*, and *The Encyclopaedia of Medicine and Surgery, 1904*. There was also a Park-Davies'* price-list.

Williamson identified a small bottle and some powder discovered in Clark's bedroom, and Counsel then read out the Chemical Examiner's report on these items. The bottle 'contained about a third of a teaspoonful of thick oily matter. A portion placed on the tongue produced an intense burning sensation. It contained no alkaloid.' Not very specific. But the powder was known—it was 'glass finely powdered'.

Rather well, Wiggins cross-examined, and got the Superintendent to admit that he did not enquire at Meerut Hospital about any case-books, as distinct from case-sheets. He had, though, asked for every available record from the hospital authorities regarding Mr Fullam's illness. Wiggins also elicited that, from his enquiry, the Superintendent found that Clark had had no official standing with the hospital since the spring of 1911, which negated the impression that Clark had been in a position easily to tamper with medical records. The Court rose at 2.30, after a short, but productive session.

December 19th was the day on which Augusta found her voice in court. Only a person equipped with unusual qualities of self-possession and sheer *chutzpah*—or perhaps the daringness of despair—will risk a spot of do-it-yourself advocacy in a crowded court-room. Augusta never was shy, but of a dramatic disposition, and she was not shamed or subdued by the public recitation of her most private letters. She had been watching the fairly mediocre display of adversarial skills and obviously thought that the role of Portia became her.

Her début came about when Gunner Dixon, who had befriended Edward when he nursed him in the hospital at Meerut, was called to the witness-box. He remembered that

* A well-known firm of pharmaceutical manufacturers.

Edward was unconscious, delirious, and vomiting on his first admission, and worse on the second occasion, with a swollen stomach. His evidence was extremely injurious to Clark, and Wiggins was bound to challenge his assertions that Edward had told him that Clark had given him poison, and that if he went to Agra he would be poisoned.

Wiggins did not press too hard, in his discretion, but certainly weakened the impact of Dixon's revelations by exploring the orderly's failure to report what Edward had told him. 'Easy!' said Augusta to herself, and her memsahib's voice trilled out in the hushed, fascinated court-room.

Yes, she elicited from Dixon, she did indeed visit her husband in hospital once or twice daily, and on one occasion she stayed the night there. She was attentive and kind. Edward was always pleased to see her, although he did not say much. He liked her to come and stay on. She used to cut up his dinner for him, but he did not ask her to do it.

Augusta's cross-examination was nearly over. She had had beginner's luck, and she should have left it there, but she then asked the classic one question too many. Did her husband say anything at all in the *dak* bungalow before his last train journey? Yes, Dixon rapped back smartly. He said that he did not want to go to Agra. It was when she was out of the room.

Like a true professional, Augusta recovered herself and pressed on as if nothing had happened. Edward was *not* afraid of her, nor did he complain about her. There she left it, but now she had a taste for advocacy, and her voice would be heard again.

Ross Alston was beginning to filter in what may be called his 'poison witnesses', in order, by proof of purchase, to prove Clark's possession of a series of poisons at times which fitted Edward's repeated illnesses and death.

The Prosecution was not yet entirely confident as to fine detail. It was no easy task to prove the nature of each wave of the poisonous attack. The case would have been tenuous indeed without the strong circumstantial evidence of the letters, which clearly signalled that *some deadly poisons*, never named, had been administered.

The arsenic stood up well, but the two 'heat-strokes' were tricky to account for, and the final poison or poisons used in

| Drug | | Supplier | Date in Clark's hands | Quantity | Evidenced by: |
|---|---|---|---|---|---|
| ARSENIC | | Baldeo Dass & Sons, Agra. | – May, 1911 | 120 grains | J. N. Bose, dispenser, in court: bought by Clark in person. |
| | | Baldeo Dass & Sons, Agra. | – June, 1911 | 120 grains | ditto |
| ATROPINE | | Banerjee, Agra | 23rd July, 1911 | 30 grains | Banerjee, in court: bought by Clark in person. Admitted by Clark, for use as 'embrocation'. |
| COCAINE | | Baldeo Dass & Sons, Agra. | – July, 1911 | 60 grains (One drachm) | Beni Madho Dutt, head compounder, in court: bought by Clark in person. Admitted by Clark. |
| | | Banerjee, Agra. | 27th July, 1911 | 115 grains | Banerjee, in court: bought by Clark in person. |
| GELSEMINE | | Dr Bose's laboratory. Calcutta. | 11th Sept., 1911 | 5 grains | Clark's letter dated 1st Sept., 1911, asking for 20 grains to be sent to him. Value Paid receipt for 5 grains, dated 11th September. Eventually, Clark admitted this purchase. Dr Bose, by interrogatory, admitted supplying. 5 grains only. |
| | | Dr Bose's laboratory, Calcutta. | ? 8th Oct., 1911 | ? 5 grains | Clark's letter dated 23rd Sept., 1911, asking for 5 grains to be sent to him. 'Chiodetti receipt' dated 8th Oct., 1911, proved by Postmaster Chiodetti, in court, *may* relate to this purchase, but not relied upon by Prosecution. |
| | | ? | ? | 60 grains | Empty bottle labelled 'one drachm gelsemium hydrochlor.' found in Clark's box in Augusta's bungalow, and 48 grains of gelsemine found in Clark's possession in a phial. |

TABLE OF POISONS PURCHASED BY CLARK

Agra were only a matter for informed conjecture. At this stage, Alston was still feeling his way, and quantities and dates did not always match up as well as he would have wished.

First the 'easiest' poison—the arsenic—bought by Clark in the May and June of 1911. It turned out that he had *not* had recourse to a grimy, illicit booth, distrusting, then, perhaps, the people of the bazaar. Instead, as a medical man, he had twice openly approached an orthodox chemist's shop, and had bought 120 grains of powdered arsenic on each occasion.

Babu J. N. Bose (not the Dr Bose of Amherst Street, Calcutta), dispenser in the firm of Pandaya Baldeo Dass, Agra, identified Clark's signature, entered in his presence, in his poison-book. Clark was well known to him, and he often purchased other medicines from the firm, but never, before or after, arsenic.

Then the 'heat-stroke' mixture. Babu Dabendra Nath Banerjee, druggist, Agra, identified a voucher, signed by Clark, for 30 grains of atropine in powder form, not in small crystals as also supplied, dated 23rd July, 1911. He knew Clark's signature well, because he often used to come to his shop and sign vouchers for various articles.

Atropine (belladonna) varies in its effect. Half a grain has proved fatal, but there was a rare case of recovery after fifteen grains taken by mouth. Thus Clark was making doubly sure! The symptoms are sometimes delayed. Eye-drops containing atropine have caused death. Clark, knowing that Edward was suffering from red, sore eyes caused by the arsenic, had, it will be remembered, proposed the application of poisoned eye-drops, but Augusta had rejected the idea, although not for reasons of altruism.

Interjecting with confidence, Alston drew the attention of the Court to the fact that a registered parcel had been sent to 'Mrs Clarkson' in Meerut on 26th July, 1911, from Agra, and the post-office receipt showed that the sender was Clark. This parcel nicely matches Augusta's enthusiastic letter of 27th July, which reads: 'Your kind and loving letter dated Wednesday, 26th, together with the small parcel containing the heat-stroke liquid, reached me quite safely at the P.O. this morning.'

Continuing, Banerjee identified three vouchers for 115

178

grains in all of cocaine hydrochlorate supplied to Clark, in person, on 27th July, 1911. It would be logically satisfying if this next purchase of poison, so close in time, also preceded the 'heat-stroke' concoction,* but it was supplied just too late, on the actual day on which the mixture was already in Augusta's hands and about to be dripped into the mulligatawny soup.

Even so, the Prosecution was, increasingly, holding to the belief that *some* cocaine was admixed with atropine in the 'heat-stroke' liquid. The ordinary fatal dose of cocaine is about fifteen grains. But death *has* followed two-fifths of a grain applied to the conjunctiva covering the eyeball!

* Walsh, or his contributing friend in the I.M.S., mistakenly dates this purchase 26th July.

## Chapter Thirteen

# Budhu Sings

Now it was the turn of the 'old duffer', neighbourly Captain William Weston, enjoying his moment in the spotlight. After all, doctors more highly qualified than he had failed to diagnose the cause of Edward's illnesses, and no criticism could be attached to him. He had done his best.

In 1911, he was called in to attend to Edward on three separate occasions. In June, Edward was vomiting, and Weston actually told him that he thought some discontented clerk in his office must have poisoned his tea. Edward said nothing in reply. He did say that he felt there was something wrong with his leg, as though he had paralysis, but Weston never treated him for paralysis, and never thought he had it.

In July, at three o'clock in the morning, Edward was pale and vomiting, and appeared to have heat-stroke. His pulse was intermittent, and his pupils were slightly dilated. Captain Keene, R.A.M.C., the Staff-Surgeon, sent for at Weston's request, sponged the patient's body with cold water, and sent him to the section hospital. He was delirious, with a temperature of 100 degrees. Weston visited him after a week, and found him sitting up and looking better; he advised him to stay in hospital.

In August, he thought that Edward was on the point of dying of heat-stroke. After rushing him off to hospital, he never saw him alive again. He knew Clark in Meerut, and he met him once in 1911, in the company of Augusta Fullam.

The old duffer bowed his way out of the witness-box, and Alston announced that, except for some formalities, he had finished his case, and asked the Court to adjourn the Fullam hearing until 6th January, when he would put forward medical evidence and the Chemical Examiner's report was expected to be ready.

The Magistrate agreed, and proceeded to examine the two accused by means of direct questioning.

First Augusta:

**Q.** You have heard the evidence in the case in regard to the alleged murder of Mr Fullam, your husband. What do you wish to say?

**A.** I have nothing to say. I wish to reserve my statement for the High Court.

**Q.** As regards the letters put on record said to be in your handwriting and read before you, do you admit they are in your handwriting?

**A.** Yes, they are in my handwriting. The envelopes were also in my handwriting and endorsed by Mr Clark. This is all I desire to say.

**Q.** These letters [exhibits shown] now shown to you: do you admit they are written by you?

**A.** Yes.

Then Clark:

**Q.** You have heard the evidence in the present case. What do you desire to say?

**A.** I have nothing to say at present.

**Q.** As regards the initial and the word 'answered' on these envelopes [shown to the accused] are they in your handwriting?

**A.** Yes, they are in my handwriting.

**Q.** I am now showing you these exhibits [these included the pencil draft of the false death-certificate, letters to chemists in Calcutta, and signatures on vouchers]—are they in your handwriting and the signatures yours?

**A.** They are all in my handwriting, and the signatures are mine, except the countersignature of J. S. Dunne.

**Q.** Do you wish to say anything as regards the points in the evidence against you?

**A.** I reserve my statement for the High Court.

**Q.** Regarding the nine powders referred to in the case, of which the Chemical Examiner said they were 'glass finely powdered', said to be found in your house, do you wish to say anything? [Powders shown to accused.]

**A.** At the time they were found I told Police Inspector Smith and Inspector Keegan that these and other powders that were lying on the table were used for my poultry. I say these are powdered glass prepared for the treatment of the poultry.*

Q. Do you desire to say anything about this bottle [shown] which according to the Chemical Examiner contained some thick oily matter and which when applied to the tongue produced an intense burning sensation?

A. Major Buchanan sent a small box containing a number of small and big bottles when he was going to Kashmir on leave. He asked me to keep them for him. This yellow bottle was lying among them in the box. I could not tell what it contained. Some of the bottles were labelled with his name and some were not.

Faintly, Clark's voice resonates for us: formal, punctilious, and giving notice of his intention to fight every point—to fight for his life.

It only remained for the Prosecution to put in those portions of Augusta's statement from the dock which had a bearing on the Fullam case, and the hearing was adjourned for two and a half weeks. Friday was a blank day, and then, on Saturday, 21st December, when the Clark case was continued, there were suddenly *five* prisoners in court: Augusta, Clark, Budhu, and two new, palpitating, abject accused—Sukkha and Ram Lal.

After 'vigorous search' in Agra—and it must have been, with *lathis* at the ready, combing the alleys and labyrinths of huts—the police had succeeded in arresting two of the *badmashes* named by Budhu. Now, handcuffed, they had to stand by as Budhu began to sing like the Indian equivalent of a canary!

He wanted, he said, to make a statement of his own accord, and all four of his co-accused listened with fear or rage, according to their temperaments, as he gave a detailed and believable account of the repeated poisonings, and murder, of Louisa Clark.

Augusta he did not spare in any way, and it may well be that he harboured considerable animus against her because of the

---

* Such a use was not inconceivable. Finely powdered glass could, speculatively, have been given as a purgative, and coarser fragments given as grit to aid digestion of food in the gizzard. For this information, the author is indebted to John Farrant, Editor of *Poultry World*.

way in which she had referred to his role and guilty knowledge in *her* statement. Her part in grinding up the glass chimney sounded particularly bad.

'One day,' said Budhu, in full flow, 'Mr Clark asked me in hospital to go to Mrs Fullam's bungalow in the evening. When I went there Mrs Fullam sent away all her servants and called me into the dining-room. I also met Mr Clark there. Both he and Mrs Fullam asked me, "Can't you arrange to kill Mrs Clark?" I said I would let them know later. This was about three months ago from today. I spoke of this to Sukkha [pointing, now, to Sukkha] and asked him whether he could do anything. The man Sukkha was then living in Lalkurti Bazaar. Sukkha said, "I will tell you tomorrow." But the same evening he came to me and told me, "I can't do this for a hundred rupees. I want more."

'I took him to Mrs Fullam's in the evening. We waited till Mr Clark and Mrs Fullam returned from an evening drive, and after they had finished their dinner they told me that they would speak to me after all the servants had left. When the servants left they called both of us into the dining-room. Mr Clark, Mrs Fullam and Sukkha had a long conversation there. Sukkha said, "First you will give me money, then I shall do the work." But the sahib said, "You will get the money when you do the work." To this Sukkha replied, "It can't be done like that."

'Mr Clark then told Sukkha, "I shall be waiting there. Directly you do the work you will get the money from me." Sukkha said, "You can give the money to Budhu." But Mrs Fullam said, "Budhu is not a very strong man. If you take the money from him he can't do anything." About four days afterwards, I told Sukkha that I was leaving for Delhi. He had better take the money himself from Mr Clark when the work was done. Sukkha then told me that unless he was paid in advance he would not do anything. Mr Clark stopped me from going to Delhi and told me, "You have not done my work."

'About three days after this he asked me to go to Mrs Fullam's bungalow in the evening with Sukkha, so I took him there and Sukkha talked with the sahib and memsahib. Mr Clark told Sukkha, "I shall give the money to Budhu in the hospital tonight at ten. Do the job tonight." Sukkha asked me to take the money from Mr Clark and rode off on a cycle towards the bazaar. I went to hospital to fetch a man. Mr Clark told me there, "I shall give you the money there [i.e. at the Clarks' bungalow]."

'At ten Sukkha and Mr Clark again came to the hospital on cycles. We all went out of the hospital. Mr Clark took six sovereigns from his pocket, and ten rupees, and showed the money to Sukkha, telling him he was going to give the money to me. Sukkha went away on a cycle, telling Mr Clark to give the money to me. I asked for the money. Mr Clark said, "No, they will snatch away the money from you. You will get it there."

'I met Sukkha near Buddha's house. Also Ram Lal was there. [He pointed to Ram Lal.] They asked me if I got the money. Four of us went to a spot where a new house was being built. The man that Sukkha had brought from the city was there. I don't know his name but I can recognise him. We all then went to a well. Buddha left us, went to a field and brought a large knife as big as my arm. Ram Lal took that knife from Buddha.'

At this precise juncture, Ram Lal, greengrocer, aged 22, toppled over in a faint and was carried out of the court-room, a soiled, white, limp bundle of misery. It might have been a strategic passing-out, but he had probably been kept standing in the dock, exhausted, and frightened out of his wits. It was four o'clock, anyway, and time for a brief, late lunch interval. Ram Lal was back in his place at 4.30, as Budhu continued inexorably.

'These four men asked money from me and threatened to kill me if I did not pay them. [After the killing] we then ran and came to the main road where there was no light burning. The four men demanded the money and I took them to the hospital. There I asked three men to wait and returned to Mr Clark's bungalow with Sukkha. There we heard the miss-sahib crying and heard the sahib shouting and calling somebody from a house just beside his bungalow. This sahib did not come.

'I told Sukkha not to worry about the money as the sahib would pay them all right next morning. I did not speak to Mr Clark at all and went home. Ram Lal saw me about eight times next morning in the hospital. When the sahib came to the hospital I spoke to him about the money. He asked me to tell the people to come to Mrs Fullam's bungalow at eleven o'clock, and they would be paid. I met Sukkha in the evening and he complained of not being paid till then. I do not know what happened afterwards as since then I have been in the lock-up.'

Budhu's part as supergrass was finished. Desperate to spill the beans—for he, too, was fighting for his life—he had let the killing words stream out of him like vomit. The Magistrate rose very late in the evening, and the Clark case was adjourned until 7th January, although, in fact, it did not get into court until the 10th.

Christmas in custody without cheer or company gave Augusta and Clark time to reflect, and time to scheme. Brought back to her hatefully familiar place in the dock for the resumption of the Fullam case on 7th January, 1913, Augusta had unfinished business to attend to. The festive season had wonderfully concentrated her mind.

The Magistrate called her up, and said, 'I understand that you do not now wish to be married to Mr Clark?'

'No,' she replied.

Apparently, she had made a previous application for permission to marry. However, it is more than likely that her request had been a matter of strategy, rather than a romantic desire for the union at last available to her. At first, as we have seen, she and Clark had presented a united front, but it had not been possible to sustain it. Her statement had been a long hymn of repudiation of Clark and all his doings, and, for consistency, she could scarcely be seen to wish to bond herself to such a monster of depravity.

On this day of public renunciation, her behaviour, even so, did not indicate that she had conceived a violent aversion towards the man who had previously held her in thrall. Shrewdly, a Reuter's Special Correspondent noted that the pair 'conversed constantly during the proceedings, and were apparently on the best of terms. Both the accused showed a markedly cheerful demeanour.'

Before opening the proceedings, the Magistrate read out a letter from Major O'Meara, the Civil Surgeon, asking Mr Ormrod to instruct the Chemical Examiner to test Edward Fullam's viscera for gelsemine hydrochlorate, strychnine, atropine, and cocaine.

Clark, advised by Wiggins, may or may not have been contemplating making a statement of his own at this stage, but the statement which he now volunteered appeared to be in direct refutation of the implications of Major O'Meara's letter.

He said that he was called to Meerut on 19th September, 1911, (a wrong date, to preface a tissue of wrong facts) to bring Fullam to Agra. The Medical Board had certified that Fullam was suffering from general paralysis of the insane. He was in a weak, exhausted condition, and had to be carried when brought to Agra, where his condition was continually getting worse.

For two days before he got a final attack, he told Clark that he felt as if he was going to have another attack. He continued with the medicine which he had brought from Meerut. His food consisted of slops. On the night of his death, Clark carried him to bed, and then dined in his own room. Fullam called out, 'Another attack is coming on.' Clark here explained that, when Fullam was first brought to Agra, Captain Dunne, R.A.M.C., was consulted, and advised that an injection of a mixture of ether, digitalis, and strychnine should be kept always handy to be used immediately when an attack was felt to be imminent.

Acting upon this, then, Clark at once gave ten minims of the prepared injection. Half an hour later, he gave a second injection of the same mixture of drugs. After the first injection, he had sent his bearer to the Club for Captain Dunne, and now he himself got on his bicycle to fetch the Captain. Eventually, he brought him to the bungalow, showed him a bottle, and told him that he had given two injections. He consulted the Captain as to whether he should give a third injection, and, as Fullam was by then in a very low condition, Captain Dunne advised Clark to do so. Shortly after that (i.e. in Dunne's presence) Fullam died.

At the suggestion of Ross Alston, the Magistrate asked Clark if he would like to state the parts of the body where the injections were given. They were, said Clark, in order, the upper left arm, below the heart, and the left forearm.

At the suggestion of George Wiggins, the Magistrate asked Clark if he would like to volunteer his reasons for injecting in those parts. Young Kathleen had testified that Clark had pushed the needle into her father three times in succession, which, at least in those days, was not orthodox medical procedure, and Wiggins was anxious to ameliorate this damaging point. His client was eager to assist: the injections were given in that way because Fullam was suffering from paralysis of the left side, and the idea was to stimulate his heart.

He himself, said Clark, made up the mixture as prescribed by Captain Dunne, and each injection consisted of three and a half minims each of the spirit of ether, tincture of digitalis, and liquor of strychnine. The bottle was labelled 'hypodermic injection' with the prescription in full inscribed on it. After Fullam's death, the bottle was kept in Mrs Fullam's bedroom, where it remained until the time of her arrest. Now he demanded that it should be produced to the Court, together with two other bottles.

It was a good bluff, but, as usual, it lacked forward-planning. Clark had the nerve to state that Captain Dunne, who was now in England, would be produced in the High Court, since he had seen Edward Fullam's condition!

Plausible, warming to his subject, he regretted that there was no chance of the Chemical Examiner's being able to detect digitalis. As for the dangerous area of the evidence of the previous 'poison-witnesses', Christmas homework had been done. The Magistrate prompted him, 'Do you wish to say anything about gelsemine at this stage?'

This was Clark's cue: he was going to admit receiving only five grains of gelsemine in 1911, and to account for it by legitimate use. In the September, he said, he was asked by a man named Hewson, who was in charge of the regimental coffee-shop,* to treat one of his staff who was suffering from rheumatism and neuralgia. Ordinary treatment proving in-effective, Clark sent to Dr Bose of Calcutta for five grains of gelsemine and also for Bose's speciality, Nanala.

These duly arrived, and Clark mixed the gelsemine with a one-ounce bottle of the Nanala. He then took ten grains of this compound, mixed it with five grains of caffeine, and made it into powders for Hewson's servant.

Clark said that in 1912, when, of course, Edward Fullam was dead, he had bought 54 grains of gelsemine from Bose, together with Nanala, and had used them in that year. He gave the names of various patients whom he had dosed with his concoction.

---

* A peculiarly Indian institution, really a kind of club, with the emphasis more on the conversation than on the light breakfast served at an earlier hour than the regular breakfast of the day.

'You have accounted for about six grains of gelsemine,' the Magistrate remarked helpfully and blandly. 'The balance of 48 grains is in the hands of the Chemical Examiner.'

'That is so,' said Clark, encouraged. Now the cocaine. He was a doctor, wasn't he? From a different firm, which he did not name, he bought, in all, 118 grains of cocaine, in 1911, for use in medical practice. He was probably referring to the previous evidence of Banerjee of Agra that, on 27th July, 1911, he had bought 115 grains of cocaine. As a favour, he gave 54 grains of the 118 to a native veterinary practitioner, who was otherwise unable to obtain cocaine. He refused to take any payment for it. He did not know the name of this native vet, nor could he remember the date of the gift.

Finally the atropine. Clark admitted the purchase of 30 grains of atropine from Banerjee's, of Agra. He used it, he said, in a liniment for Hewson's useful servant, that being then a perfectly respectable if slightly risky procedure. Three drachms of belladonna liniment applied to the lumbar region once made a healthy, 30-year-old man extremely ill, 'quite off his head', with widely dilated pupils and a pulse of 120.*

'Clark has now given explanation of all the gelsemine, atropine, and cocaine proved to have been purchased by him,' the Magistrate commented sagely.

'It would be interesting to know what has become of all the patients who took the gelsemine,' Ross Alston contributed mildly.

Clark's reply had an element of bathos: 'Hewson's servant was a very bad case. He died about October or November, 1911, a month or a fortnight after my treatment. I am not sure of the date.' If the servant so little responded to Clark's special therapy as to die, then it was surprising that he would have continued to prescribe it! But then, the servant was a very bad case.

The Magistrate wanted to know why Clark bought atropine in such a large quantity. Because, he explained, it came much cheaper in quantities of half a drachm. As a dubious rider, he added that he gave the cocaine to the lucky native vet in Augusta's presence, at her bungalow, where he kept his cocaine (together

---

* Taylor's *Principles and Practice of Medical Jurisprudence* (J. & A. Churchill Ltd, 1957).

with other dangerous *materia* such as her love-letters).

Augusta then wanted to add a small ornamentation of her own to Clark's statement. She could account for the missing bottle of Captain Dunne's injection mixture. The police had not found it at her home because Clark had removed it from her bedroom shelf in order to treat a lady who was living next door. Her name was Mrs Godfrey, and she suffered from fits, she believed. Clark used the same injection on this lady and saved her life on two or three occasions. The bottle never came back from the Godfreys' rooms. The two quart bottles mentioned by Clark should still be in her bungalow.

How strange that Clark had omitted to mention Mrs Godfrey! Did Augusta notice the stir in a corner of the courtroom as a police officer was dispatched to interview the convenient lady? As a matter of fact, neither side produced her—perhaps, like Hewson's useful servant, she was no longer alive.

After lunch, Beni Madho Dutt, head compounder of Baldeo Dass and Sons, Agra, from which firm of druggists Clark had bought 240 grains of arsenic, produced the cocaine register of his city branch, which recorded the purchase by Clark of one drachm (60 grains) of cocaine in July 1911. This is in addition to the 115 grains of cocaine supplied to Clark on 27th July by Dabendra Nath Banerjee. If only the exact day in July were knowable, this other lot of cocaine might pre-date the preparation of the 'heat-stroke' mixture.

Superintendent Horace Williamson was called to sharpen his previous formal evidence regarding the finding of medical books at Clark's home. One of these, *Principles of Forensic Medicine*, was marked almost as plainly as if Clark had kept a diary of his activities. There were pencil lines beside paragraphs on chronic arsenical poisoning, and the corners of pages referring to cocaine and atropine were turned down.

In another tome, *Lyon's Medical Juriprudence*, the page on which gelsemine was dealt with was pencil-marked *and* turned down. Frequent underlining appearing throughout the books, Alston said, was confined chiefly to poisons and drugs which caused abortion.

Handwritten comments of the *'Very Good'* and *'Note This'* type were absent—nothing for long-suffering Walter Sarkies to identify—and, naturally, Williamson had to field Wiggins' suggestion that some other hand—even the Superintendent's —might have tampered with the books. Thereupon, Williamson proved the finding of the empty bottle labelled 'one drachm gelsemium hydrochlor' in a box found in Augusta Fullam's possession and said to belong to Clark.

The network of evidence was beginning to form an impressive pattern, and, flustered, perhaps, Clark rose to improve on his statement of that morning. On thinking over the matter, he now wished to say that he gave Fullam only *two*, not three, injections. He now remembered that when Captain Dunne had arrived, he found Fullam either dead or almost dead, and no third injection was given. A poor performance, which perhaps he sought to counterbalance by the admission that he had, indeed, purchased the drachm of cocaine proved by Beni Madho Dutt.

The following day, at the outset, Alston asked the Magistrate to note that Clark had been shown the 28 bottles found by the police at Augusta Fullam's home. Neither the injection bottle nor the two mysterious quart bottles were among them. No one mentioned Mrs Godfrey: it is very strange.

Importantly, the Prosecution then put in interrogatories* taken by the Calcutta Presidency Magistrate, who had been issued with a commission to examine Dr Bose, the druggist to whom Clark had twice written for gelsemine. Bose admitted that he had supplied five grains, but only five grains. He 'did not refer to' the other 54 grains said by Clark to have been supplied by him in 1912. Was he asked, then?

Alston's first witness of the day was Major O'Meara. His expertise was to be more stretched, this time, than it had been when he was detailing Louisa Clark's brutally simple injuries.

---

* 'Whenever, in the course of an inquiry... it appears to a District Magistrate that the examination of a witness is necessary for the ends of justice, and that the attendance of such witness cannot be procured without an amount of delay, expense or inconvenience which, under the circumstances of the case, would be unreasonable, such Magistrate... may dispense with such attendance and may issue a commission to any District Magistrate or Magistrate of the first class, within the local limits of whose jurisdiction such witness resides, to take the evidence of such witness.' Section 503, the Criminal Procedure Code.

After dealing with Edward Fullam's exhumation and post-mortem, he was led into the opinion that, 'having carefully considered certain letters on the files of the court, the symptoms are compatible with chronic arsenical poisoning.

As for the two 'heat-strokes', considered in the light of the parallel letters, could any poison have caused such symptoms? 'Yes, any poison coming into the belladonna, hyoscyamus,* or stramonium dhatura† group would cause those symptoms.' A dose of atropine could cause the temperature indicated in the letters, as also the delirium and loss of consciousness, great weakness, feeble pulse and flushing. It could, perhaps, cause the temporary paralysis.

Asked what symptoms Edward Fullam exhibited which were not consistent with genuine heat-stroke, Major O'Meara replied that the temperature was inconsistently low. It should have ranged anywhere between 107 and 111 degrees, possibly even higher. Under efficient treatment, such a temperature, in a case of heat-stroke, might come down very quickly. It might easily be down to 100 in two or three hours, or even less than one hour.

Atropine usually gave a temperature ranging up to 101 or more, but generally somewhere between 99 and 100. With atropine, the skin would be dry, whereas in heat-stroke it would be moist, clammy, and pale.

Alston was still conjuring with cocaine, but Major O'Meara's experience could not extend to aid Counsel's speculation that mixing cocaine with atropine would tend to raise the temperature higher than atropine alone. He could not say.

But what he *could* say—and this was crucial—was that there was nothing in the evidence on the file to suggest that Edward Fullam was suffering from general paralysis of the insane.

At long last, the Chemical Examiner's report had arrived, and the Magistrate read out his findings. There was, as expected, no trace of alkaloids—no atropine, cocaine, gelsemine, or strychnine. In half a thigh-bone, however, the Examiner had found 0.15‡ of a grain of arsenic. This was not, in fact, one of those cases where the body was saturated with arsenic, and none was detectable in the hair or in the earth inside the coffin, but still, arsenic there was.

---

* Henbane.          † Thorn-apple.          ‡ *Not* 0.015, as in Walsh.

## Chapter Fourteen

## Doctor Gore Testifies

Pressing home his advantage, Ross Alston read aloud interrogatories taken from Major Palmer, R.A.M.C., now stationed at Jutogh.* There was no mention of general paralysis of the insane. Edward Fullam had been sent before the Medical Board because he was a perfect wreck and would never do a day's work again. His life was hanging on a thread.

He had exhibited slight symptoms of paralysis, but, so far as Major Palmer's information went at the time, he thought the illness to be heat-stroke. He had, with other doctors, considered the possibility of heat bringing on paralysis, and later he had treated the patient for cerebral paralysis—the result of minute haemorrhage caused by heat.

There *was* dilation of the pupil of the eye, but the full effect of atropine, if it had been administered, might have been masked by eserine [an alkaloid extracted from the calabar bean, employed by West African natives in trials by ordeal for witchcraft, which causes contraction of the pupil].

Still fighting, Clark elicited from Major O'Meara, the next witness, the opinion that a severe attack of heat-stroke *frequently* brought on paralysis. Re-examined by Alston, Major O'Meara said that nothing in Major Palmer's interrogatories indicated G.P.I. The statement that Fullam was a wreck was more consistent with his being poisoned. (Arguable!)

Augusta rose to her feet, primed, surely, by Clark, for her letters do not show the necessary sophistication to ask, as she now did, if a person might have delusions following heat-stroke. The Major agreed.

* A small town with cantonment, three miles west of Simla.

192

Augusta Fullam's burial record, showing the ironic cause of death. (Her age is given incorrectly.)

The Pilot's grandson: Henry William Hope, son of Augusta Fullam and Henry Clark.

Cool and logical, Alston extracted his last point from his witness. If Fullam's paralysis had been caused by poison, he would not have had a relapse after leaving hospital, unless more poison had been administered.

The fruitful session was over. Augusta and Clark were in some disarray. The following day, Ross Alston put in a photograph of Edward Fullam, and closed the case for the Prosecution. Neither of the accused wished to call witnesses in the lower court.

The Magistrate gave Clark a last chance to add to his statement in the light of the further evidence adduced against him, and he was very ready to do so. A letter from Hewson, of the regimental coffee-shop, had been shown to him. Dated 20th September, 1911, it reported his rheumatic servant's death on the previous day, 19th September, and therefore, Clark realised, his request for gelsemine in his letter to Dr Bose, dated 23rd September, was obviously too late to be for the treatment of the (dead) servant.

That is why Clark now said, weakly, 'About the letter of Hewson, I wish to say the date is wrong. It should be dated *October* 20th. As far as my recollection goes, I started treating Hewson's man on September 27th.'

Clark was helped, here, in his calculations, by Dr Bose's evidence on interrogatory that (in spite of Clark's two separate letters) he had provided only five grains of gelsemine—received, said Clark, on the day when he started the treatment, i.e. 27th September.

Augusta was invited to comment on the evidence, and she contributed a kind of mini-defence, an epitome or abstract which woefully ill-matched the concrete details of the case against her. 'I wish to speak about the tonic powders which I gave my husband. I did not know what they were composed of.' Clark had said they would make Mr Fullam slightly ill, only enough to destroy all sexual power in him. (This is a new line, with a whisper of the Bravo case* in it!) Otherwise she

---

* It has been suggested that Florence Bravo gave antimony to her husband, Charles, with the intent only to inhibit his sexual appetite. A similar suggestion was made to account for Dr Crippen's administration of hyoscin to his demanding wife, Belle Elmore.

would not have given them to him. They never harmed him but did him a lot of good.

She also wished to say that Edward went to Mussoorie on account of the heat. He stayed there for only ten days because he could not get more leave. The day when he got heat-stroke, he had done a lot of gardening in the afternoon, without his hat, and had then complained of his head. She had warned him to come in and be careful of the sun.

There is an oddly *ad hoc* quality to these proceedings, in that Alston was now permitted, in refutation, to ask the Magistrate to read out the epistolary passage regarding heat-stroke—'Do you think, lovie darling, that the same symptoms could be produced on someone we know?'

Silenced, Augusta reserved her defence, and the Magistrate then framed a charge, under Section 307 of the Penal Code, that Lieutenant H. L. W. Clark and Mrs A. F. Fullam jointly attempted to murder Mr Fullam at Meerut during or about April, May, June, 1911, by administering a poisonous drug. Both the accused pleaded not guilty.

Secondly, under Section 302 of the Penal Code, they were charged jointly that between 27th July and 11th October, 1911, they committed murder by administering a poisonous drug to Mr Fullam at Meerut and Agra. Not sure of the exact drugs, the Prosecution viewed the 'heat-strokes' and the *coup de grâce* as one continuous process. Again, both the accused pleaded not guilty, and announced their intention to call witnesses in the High Court. They were, thereupon, formally committed to the High Court at Allahabad for trial.

Since there was still plenty of court time left, the Clark case was reopened, and the Indian prisoners, who had been held in readiness, were marched into the dock. Budhu, Sukkha, and Ram Lal had been joined by Buddha, arrested before Mohan. Buddha is not reported to have had any form of legal representation before the Magistrate. Nor had Sukkha.

Maud Clark, brought back because she had given her evidence before the three *badmashes*, as described by Budhu, had been caught, looked 'lengthily' at the accused, and pointed out Sukkha as the native with the big stick who ran away from her bedroom. Amazingly, Sukkha the tailor piped up to cross-examine, and got Maud to say that she had seen only one man.

Kathleen Fullam, who had been waiting, too, told the Court all that she had seen and heard. She identified Budhu, whose voice she had recognised, and, walking boldly across the court-room to point him out, also Sukkha, who had told her mother, 'Say I am a *darzi*.' Both Sukkha and Budhu tried to shake her in cross-examination, but with no success.

She told Wiggins, who was now representing Ram Lal, as well as Clark, that she definitely did see the faces of the two natives as they climbed over the bungalow wall. Kathleen had, in fact, previously picked Sukkha out on an identification parade, and she was still certain about him. At an earlier parade, she had picked out a man who, she thought, was Budhu; they had not told her if she was right.

At this stage, the Magistrate had a statement to make: he had received a letter from the Chemical Examiner to say that he had found no poison in Louisa Clark. There is no evidence that her body had been exhumed, and one must assume that her viscera had been preserved from the post-mortem—perhaps routinely.

The Prosecution next produced a coffee-shop attendant who testified that Ram Lal was in Agra at the time of the murder, in order to refute the alibi which, it was already known, he intended to plead.

Before the Court rose, Alston, still pursuing the gelsemine and Hewson's servant, said that he had caused enquiries to be made and had ascertained that the date of the man's death was 22nd September, precisely the day before Clark, on 23rd September, had sent to Calcutta for the drug. Therefore, Clark was slightly right—the letter from Hewson dated 20th September with the date of death given as 19th September *was* wrong, but only by three days. Not wrong enough.

Back in court the following day, Clark was fast on his feet with a change of statement to make. Again, the Court was lenient, and solemnly recorded his new version; it appears that these statements from the dock, tempered as to the continuing evidence, could be altered *ad infinitum*.

He had made a mistake on Wednesday, said Clark. In fact, he had received the five grains of gelsemine in reply to his *first* letter, of 1st September, in which he had asked for twenty grains. As it happened, he had never received any of the drug in reply to his second letter, of 23rd September. By way of proof, he here put in a postal receipt to show that he had indeed received a parcel in reply to his letter of 1st September.

Ross Alston studied the receipt. It did not, he pointed out, specify what was in the parcel. To make things even more uncomfortable for Clark, the Magistrate had a pertinent question for him: in that case, who was the person for whom he had ordered five grains of gelsemine on 23rd September? It was, said Clark, for another patient, not named in court.

At this juncture, and it may well indicate the beginnings of a loss of confidence, Augusta and Clark withdrew the names of two witnesses apiece whom they had, on the previous day, cited to appear in the High Court.

The hearing reverted to the Clark case. No one cross-examined Kazanchi of the Bank of Bengal, who proved Clark's encashment of Augusta's cheque for 100 rupees. Nor did Wiggins tangle with the aptly named Dr Gore, Assistant Chemical Examiner and bacteriologist, whose surprising and sinister new evidence, not previously adumbrated by Alston, showed Clark in an almost ridiculously villainous light.

Last October, 1912, said Gore, Clark came to his laboratory and asked him for some cholera culture, saying that he wanted it for some experiments on animals, as he had a cholera specific which he wanted to test. Animals do not get cholera. Gore put him off with some harmless water microbes, because Clark evidently knew nothing of bacteriology and real cholera culture would have been a very risky thing to place in his hands. Clark was not joking.

On the Saturday before Louisa's death, Clark appeared at the laboratory again, and asked for more culture. He had obviously found that his wife was 'cholera-proof'! He said that he had tried the former 'culture' on fowls, dogs, and cats, and they had all contracted cholera, but had been cured by his specific. For verisimilitude, Clark added that, even so, calomel had proved more effective than his own specific.

To make the point quite clear, Alston elicited the opinion that cholera would certainly follow if a human being were given cholera culture. Genuine culture would produce cholera if added to most foods, unless too hot or too acid.

Sukkha was proving a lively accused. He was denying to the police his ability to ride a bicycle, as a way of refuting Budhu's evidence against him, and therefore the Prosecution dredged up a cycle agent, Munna Khan, to prove that Sukkha used to hire a bicycle from his shop, to go to the *dargah*\* Shall Ullah. Switching his tactics, Sukkha got him to agree that he usually hired a bicycle on Thursdays—not on a Sunday.

Aware that the underlinings, not annotations, in Clark's forensic books were not totally satisfactory evidence, Alston called Assistant-Surgeon Jacob to say that *Principles of Forensic Medicine* was his book, and that he had lent it to Clark before July, 1911, in an unmarked condition.

Superintendent Williamson came back to depose to finding an envelope containing powder, reported by the Chemical Examiner to be arsenic, in a box belonging to Louisa Clark. This pathetic piece of evidence, kept by Louisa, must have been part of Bibu's consignment.

On 11th January, Williamson announced that he had established the identity of the seventh accused, Budhu's man from the city, who had wielded the sword. His name, Mohan, had been added to the charge-sheet, and, from information supplied by Sukkha—who was now, for his next trick, seeking to usurp Budhu's position as informer—Williamson applied for a warrant for Mohan's arrest.

The Prosecution put in some last letters. One of them, written at the end of September, 1912, read, 'Get hold of Budhu and bring him to me if you can as there is no time to be lost.'

Augusta was asked if she had anything to say, and she was ready with a sequence of refutatory points—all carefully noted by Alston to work on before the trial, although she probably did not realise that.

Referring to the cheque for 100 rupees, she said that she first gave it to her bearer to cash, but, owing to a discrepancy in her signature, the bank twice refused to cash it. Then Clark got on a bicycle and cashed it to save her further trouble. Out of the 100 rupees, she paid 47-8 to Hall and Anderson, Calcutta, for a value payable parcel which arrived on the day before Mrs Clark died. Another 20 rupees went to pay the Bishop Cotton school bill (for Leonard), dated 17th or 18th November. She

\* Shrine.

used the balance for household expenses. There was still some of the money left in her box when she was arrested.

She would like it proved that her dressing-room door was always kept shut at night. Kathleen had said it was open. Kathleen was a very timid girl, and could never have gone to the door to see anyone, as she would not have got out of bed. Also, the box said by Kathleen to have been opened by Augusta, to take out money for men, made a loud noise when opened, and could not have been opened without waking Myrtle. Kathleen had very weak eyesight. She did not know Budhu well enough to recognise his voice. In any case, she could not have heard anything—she was asleep.

As for Kathleen's story about the *darzi* coming to the bungalow for money, as a matter of fact, two tailors called that morning, and she paid one of them 2-10 rupees, and the other 7-12, for work they had done. The tree which Kathleen said the men climbed down on the Sunday night grew on the platform of the house and not from the road. No man could climb down. It was a sheer wall, with nothing to climb upon. 'Then,' she added, 'the watch-dog I have, which is a very good one, would never allow men to climb over the wall.'

On the Tuesday morning of the tailors, she had had another caller, a European, the undertaker, who had discussed the monument which she was placing on her husband's grave. A nice touch. She admitted writing all the twenty or so letters filed in the Clark case. But she had an explanation for the reference to getting hold of Budhu as quickly as possible: her son, Frank, had an ulcerated throat—they feared diphtheria—and Clark sent some medicine by a stranger who could not find her bungalow. She herself had an appointment that afternoon and was in a hurry. Therefore, she concluded triumphantly, she asked for Budhu to bring over the medicine.

Augusta reserved her defence for the High Court—although she had already said more than enough. She was, for example, already regretting having in her first statement admitted that Clark told three men in her presence to kill Louisa.

Clark, who was now asked if he wished to make any statement, had bent his mind to the embarrassing problem of Piper Menzies of the Camerons—his 'alibi'—who had so inconveniently left for Home in 1908. About a month before

Mrs Clark's murder, he said with a straight face, he had received a letter from 'R. Menzies', Cawnpore. The hand-writing was very similar to that in the letters from Piper R. Menzies filed in court. The signature was very similar. 'I have lost this letter. The police searched for it but it could not be found. This letter informed me that the writer was going to Bombay from Cawnpore via Delhi and would be passing through Agra cantonment and would like to see me at Agra station.'

After making a search of the train and *not finding Menzies* (for what else could he say?) he returned home. Maud described the thief with the stick as dressed in a long, white coat, dark waistcoat, and big, white turban. Clark was upset by the events and went to inform Mrs Fullam what had happened. He got there at about a quarter to two and only stayed five minutes. (He was into his stride, now, and attacking old points which rankled.) 'I got to Laurie's Hotel about 2 a.m. Major Buchanan sent for a gharry* and there was half an hour's delay.

'My daughter told a falsehood when she stated in court I prevented her speaking. I found my dog, Julie, in the hall room with my daughter when I got home that night. On the morning of the *16th* I gave my wife out of my pay 250 rupees, which was her monthly allowance, keeping for myself 110 rupees. I warned her to be careful of the money as I had heard of thieves about Agra. The only thing missing from the house was the money I gave my wife on the 16th, which was not in the box in my wife's room on the morning of the 19th.' (This is the first we have heard of missing money. Maud did not mention it.)

He reached a peroration which moved no one: 'All my children are against me and have been so for years. I never instigated anyone to murder my wife. Thieves murdered her and ran away, being alarmed by the cries of my wife and daughter. The whole case is false against me and I am innocent of the charge.'

Unmoved, indeed, the Magistrate peppered him with questions, and his denials came thick and false. Budhu was

* A box-like carriage with small wheels. Vehicles of this type plied for hire.

lying, because he was very strict with him at the hospital. Bibu was lying. Joseph was lying; he had never drafted any letters for him. He got to Major Buchanan long before three o'clock. He knew nothing about the arsenic found in his wife's box. Kathleen was asleep when he was at Mrs Fullam's. He always went round to her house every evening and locked all the doors, because she was afraid of thieves. He was sure the dressing-room door was shut that night.

Now the terrible, incriminatory passages in Augusta's first, hasty statement, which screamed out the half-truth. Clark had thought up a defence: she had made the statement when she was annoyed with him, and none of it was true. Risible this may seem, but the fact is that juries, daily, accept such explanations.

Clark sat down, played out, a desperately worried man, with no allies to support him, and still cursing himself about the Menzies mistake.

Budhu, upon enquiry, stood by the statement which he had already made, and had nothing further to add. Sukkha denied all knowledge of the murder. Ram Lal stated his alibi—he was at Karauli with his brother. Buddha said that he went to Delhi on 6th November, and did not return until after the manoeuvres in December. He was arrested at Muttra on his way back to Agra, and knew nothing about the murder.

Duty done, the Magistrate proceeded to frame charges. Budhu, Ram Lal, Sukkha, and Buddha were jointly charged under Section 302 of the Indian Penal Code with having committed the murder of Mrs Clark with a sharp instrument. Augusta and Clark were jointly charged under Sections 109 and 302 of the Penal Code with abetment of the murder. Clark named only one witness—Menzes, the Assistant Station-master.

One week later, on the afternoon of Saturday, 18th January, all six accused were brought into court for the Magistrate to deliver his formal committal order, which covered 41 pages of typewritten matter.

Before Mr Ormrod began to read, Clark wished to make public his reason for not calling Captain Dunne, as had been his original intention: since he was now in England, the cost would be too heavy. Of course, as he now realised, the idea of calling him had been sheer, reckless braggadocio, and he could only hope that the Prosecution would not bother to incur the expense.

The Magistrate summarised the good prima facie evidence against all six for the actual murder of Louisa Clark, and went on to say that he had not charged Clark, Mrs Fullam, and Budhu in regard to her *poisoning*, because he was not satisfied that the point could be tried jointly with the circumstance leading to the attack, especially since Ram Lal, Sukkha, and Buddha had nothing to do with any attempts to kill her by poisoning.

'There is good prima facie evidence, however,' he stated, 'of the administration of poison to Mrs Clark. That can be considered by the Honourable High Court and a separate charge instituted or an additional charge can be framed. I accordingly commit all the accused for trial* under Section 213(j) Criminal Procedure Code, to the Honourable High Court at Allahabad.'

As he pronounced the finite and solemn words, and Augusta and Clark felt the nearer approach of the end of the affair, it was observed that their good humour had deserted them and they both 'showed some emotion.'

Meanwhile, on that same day of committal, missing Mohan the *bharboonja* had been arrested. The reward of 500 rupees for his capture—five times the murder-fee—is an indication of the importance of the case to the Raj. Murdering a woman in her bed in a cantonment bungalow was only too reminiscent of the Mutiny.

Mohan had missed out on the court proceedings, and therefore, on 23rd January, a separate, miniature committal had to be set up on his behalf—a hearing within a hearing. Ross Alston was temporarily absent on other matters, and, in his place, Superintendent Williamson had instructed Sahib Rahim Husain.

Wiggins had been appointed to represent the seventh

---

* Under Indian law, Augusta and Clark had to be sent up for two consecutive trials. The general rule, by Section 233 of the Criminal Procedure Code, was that 'For every distinct offence of which any person is accused there shall be a separate charge, and every such charge shall be tried separately.'

accused. His jumbled hand consisted of Clark, with his already discredited alibi, Ram Lal with *his* alibi, and now Mohan, who was also to plead that favourite Indian defence. It was just about all right, in the lower court, for the look of the thing, but in the High Court, where conflicts might become apparent, there would have to be separate apportionment of counsel.

Inspector Smith and Dr Modi, disgruntled, no doubt, were obliged to re-evidence the crime, and Narain Singh, constable of the Agra police, dramatically described his arrest of Mohan. Acting on information received (and the informer may indeed have found himself considerably richer afterwards), he went to Achnera, and saw Mohan sitting in a train about to start for Bharatpur. 'I pounced on him,' the constable said, 'and got him out of the train. The constable on the platform came to my assistance.'

Wiggins cross-examined, and, in reply, the constable carried on: 'I have been in Rakabganj *thana* about five years. I know accused well. He has been convicted once before, and his house has been searched in several cases. Accused gave a petition shortly after conviction that the police were troubling him.'

Superintendent Williamson deposed that he had ordered Mohan's arrest—following *Sukkha's* statement to the police—on 20th December, 1912, the day before Budhu made his statement in court. (Budhu, it will be remembered, claimed that he did not know the name of the City Man, or perhaps he was just too afraid of him.) Mohan was brought to him by Narain Singh, under arrest, at the Agra Club, on 18th January.

Williamson sent the prisoner to the court compound, where he was placed with 21 Indians on an identification-parade. The Magistrate, Mr Ormrod, presided, and it is interesting to observe the primitive early precautions taken to prevent abuse of the procedure. Hobbling in leg-irons, Budhu, brought out of custody to identify him, was 'previously taken away a long distance from the spot where Mohan was placed among several men'.

The Superintendent testified that Budhu successfully identified Mohan, and he was corroborated by Mozaffir Hussain, *peshkar** of the Joint Magistrate's Court, who said that, as

---

* A minor court-official.

Budhu picked Mohan out, he had stated, 'This is the man who struck Mrs Clark with a big knife.'

The City Man was not reticent in his own defence, but made a glib and fluent statement: 'I was not in Agra. After I was convicted for theft, and whipped, I made an application to the District Magistrate and I did not want to stay here after this. I went to a village called Nanbari. Next day, I returned to Agra to take away my property. Then I met a man who offered to get me employed. He took me to Gwalior and we stayed at Mullaji *kerai** for two days. My companion then went further up and I returned to Agra and went away by *ekka*† to Hathras. There I worked at my trade as a *bharboonja*.

'From Hathras I returned to Agra. Next day I walked to Bichpuri and there took a railway ticket for Bharatpur. At Achnera, Narain Singh arrested me and brought me to the court compound where a man whom I do not know came and caught my hand in token of identification. This man had not previously seen me that day.'

At Mohan's bolt-hole in Agra, to which, by his own story, he had repeatedly returned during his restless odyssey, still smarting from his whipping, the police had found, and produced in court, a lump of the yellow ochre with which *sadhus* (mendicant Hindu holy men) mark their foreheads. The import was that Mohan had been, or intended to be, in disguise. He failed to adduce an alternative reason for possessing yellow ochre. It was no part of the equipment of a corn-parcher.‡ The big sword was never found, but existed for a long time in the imagination of all those who heard the evidence.

The police ferreted out Mohan's tracks and burrows, and, on 28th January, he was brought back to court to be charged under Section 457 of the Indian Penal Code with having committed burglary in the ordnance bungalow on the night of 28th November, 1912—ten days after the murder. This was

---

* Inn.
†.A small, two-wheeled pony trap.
‡ A certain criminal tribe in the United Provinces used, at this time, to go about in bands, all disguised as *sadhus*, committing many thefts. Their disguise was so effective that they deceived even the priestly class.

just, as it were, for starters; on 3rd February, Mr Ormrod delivered his committal order against Mohan, saying that 'Budhu's evidence shows the part taken by Mohan in the murder. Mohan pleads an alibi and asks for the production in the High Court of the register of arrivals and departures kept up at Serai* Mukaji in Gwalior together with the clerk who keeps the register and made entries therein on November 16th and 17th, 1912. Mr Wiggins, who appeared for Mohan, informed me that it was doubtful if the Gwalior State would allow the register to leave the state limits.'

By English standards, the 'hard-cheese' attitude to Mohan's alibi is unfortunate. Here was a disadvantaged Indian, committed on trial for his life, his alleged to be the hand that struck the killing blows, in a most important criminal case. Even if not George Wiggins, harassed, out of his depth, *someone* should have been seen (to continue *vulgatim*) to bust a gut to check out the alibi. To be sure, Gwalior was one of the Native States, and ruled by a maharajah, but all the States recognised the suzerainty of the British Crown, and, however intricate the red-tape, its petty officials could and should, have been overruled. No such tussle was ever made public. It is too far-fetched to suggest that Mohan knew there would be administrative difficulties about his alibi, and relied upon its mere assertion to interpose a reasonable doubt into the minds of the coming jury.

On the last day of January, unaccountably postponed, perhaps trapped in the maw of the Chemical Examiner, the Prosecution had exhibited a phial of gelsemine, together with a broken syringe. Here, at last, was the 48 grains of gelsemine found in Clark's possession, and, now, he admitted ownership, repeating his previous contention that he got it from a Calcutta chemist, between March and June, *1912*.

Clearly, the phial was not dated, and Alston never did achieve his stated ambition of proving Clark's acquisition of 60 grains of gelsemine shortly before Edward Fullam's death, let alone prove that some of the contents of bottle or phial had been injected into Edward by Clark. The empty bottle, labelled one drachm of gelsemine (60 grains), must have been the origin of Alston's hopes. The very fact that it was found in Clark's

* Village.

box, in Augusta's bungalow, connects it powerfully with the crime, although it does not appear to have been dated, nor marked with its supplier. Dr Bose did not admit to supplying any more than five grains.

On that same day, 31st January, the Clark case had arrived at a milestone: the Magistrate had sat to tender a pardon to Budhu, under Section 338 of the Criminal Procedure Code, in compliance with an order received from the Allahabad High Court.

Budhu was now officially adopted as 'approver', and, freed by the pardon from the muzzled status of prisoner in the dock, was in a position to give evidence on oath for the Crown.

The use of an approver was a cherished bastion of Indian law, carefully sanctified by the Criminal Procedure Code and more clearly defined than the hazier 'turning King's Evidence' of English and Scottish common law. Without approvers—so the theory went—there would have been such a scarcity of convictions that 'the wheels of justice would have ground to a halt.'

Truth was a slippery commodity, because few crimes were committed single-handed, and multiple suspects or co-accused would take part in a kind of confession-race to get chosen as approver. If not so adopted, the miscreant would retract his confession! Confessions to the police, however, were not admissible in evidence: there was a wide gap between such a confession and a formal confession before a magistrate.

The device appeared to work well enough, in that there was a heavy burden on the approver to present a fair simulacrum of the truth. If he failed to make a 'full and true disclosure' before both the lower and the upper court, he was deemed to have forfeited his pardon, and also to be liable to prosecution for giving false evidence.

As soon as he had practised his new role, by giving evidence against Mohan, Budhu was stowed away 'in similar custody as the other accused persons'. By law, he could not be detained in police custody.

Augusta was moved across country by train to Allahabad, to await trial. In prison there, she consulted with new counsel, and it was they, it must be presumed, who advised her to write the last-ditch letter which is reproduced here in facsimile. With firm upward strokes scratched in thick, black ink, its inflated phrases read as follows:

205

Allahabad.

12<sup>th</sup> February 1913.

To The Joint Magistrate

Dear Sir —

I have been considering our many cases & feel perfectly distracted & worried in mind so much so that I feel it is my duty in the sight of God & for the sake of all justice & truth, to turn "King's Evidence" on both cases.

May I beg you therefore kindly to forward this my appeal to the Honble High Court;

Allahabad, for due
consideration –

    I remain
      dear Sir,
     Yours faithfully
     A. Lullam

Allahabad.

12th February, 1913

To
  The Joint Magistrate.
Dear Sir,—
  I have been considering over my case, and feel perfectly distracted and worried in mind, so much so that I feel it is my duty in the sight of God, and for the sake of all justice and truth, to turn 'King's Evidence' on both cases.

  May I beg you, therefore, kindly to forward this my appeal to the Honble. High Court, Allahabad, for due consideration.

          I remain,
            Dear Sir,
          Yours faithfully,
            A. Fullam.

She used the vernacular 'turn King's Evidence' as more appropriate to her case and status.

Her request was denied. There was already an official, pardoned approver in the Clark case, who was standing up well to the stress of his exposed position. There was, the Prosecution thought, sufficient corroboration of his assertions against his accomplices. In the Fullam case, there were still shaky areas, but there was adequate corroboration, particularly in the form of the letters.

Budhu was not a principal in the Clark murder, and he had acted under the duress of Clark's threats. The spectacle of Augusta, a scarlet principal, walking free under a pardon would have affronted public opinion. The justiciary must, by now, have been aware of her pregnancy, and they knew, therefore, that they would be spared the embarrassment of hanging—or considering the hanging—of a memsahib in her shame.

# Chapter Fifteen

# Till Death

The great, grim palace of the High Court in Allahabad, the capital of the United Provinces, was a clattering, chattering, incongruous sort of place in which to stand trial for your life. In the Hot Weather, crows used to fight and scream over the bowls of water kept for moistening the *tatties*,\* to cool the parching hot winds which blew through them.

The big Sessions Court was packed with spectators, marshalled by the police, on Wednesday, 26th February, 1913, when the Fullam trial opened. Clark, seen as a 'tall, well-built Eurasian' was dressed in black, a widower. Augusta wore a coat and skirt, and a solar topee—that badge and signal to the jury of her Europeanness.

Sir Henry Richards,† the Chief Justice, presided. Counsel for the Crown were three: A. E. Ryves, Government Advocate (afterwards Mr Justice Ryves), M. Malcolmson, Assistant Government Advocate, and Ross Alston. Counsel for Clark were E. A. Howard, and O. M. Chiene. Wiggins had gone, and one can but ask, who sacked whom? Counsel for Augusta were Richard Kaikhusroo Sorabji and A. H. Hamilton.

The two charges reflected the Prosecution's continuing uncertainties over the poisons: they were that 'in or about the months of April, May and June, 1911, at Meerut they attempted to murder Mr E. M. Fullam by administering to him a poison; (2) that they murdered Mr E. M. Fullam between the 27th July, 1911, and 11th October, 1911, by administering a poison in Meerut and Agra'.

---

\* Screens, often made of grasses, over doors or windows.
† Sir Henry George Richards, K.C., 1860–1928. Called to Irish Bar, 1883. Puisne Judge, India, 1905–11. Chief Justice, 1911. Retired, 1919. Recreations: hunting, shooting, polo. No publications.

Both the accused pleaded not guilty, 'speaking distinctly and with no apparent nervousness'. It was thought worth mentioning that they were accommodated with seats. Augusta was attended, now, by a European wardress. Theoretically and presumably, the 'Ilbert' jury were unaware of Augusta's failed King's Evidence manoeuvre, but so strong was the grape-vine in British India, and so small the community, that a slight doubt remains.

Ross Alston's opening speech took up the whole day, and even then he had not finished. He was, as he well knew, addressing a jury who already had more than an inkling of the facts of the case, due to the detailed coverage of the committal proceedings by the widely read Anglo-Indian newspapers such as *The Pioneer*,* printed in Allahabad.

He came quickly to the letters, explaining that the Prosecution had filed eighty of them in evidence, and that the rest had been brought to court and were available to the Defence.† They showed the gradual working of the woman's mind, how from little she went to more, and from more she went to the extreme step of writing boldly and without mincing matters of the intention of taking the life of her husband.

As for her defence in the lower court that she intended only to make her husband ill, and also her claim that Clark had hypnotised her, the jury should listen to the letters and then put to themselves the question, 'Is there a trace in these letters of a woman writing involuntarily and contrary to her natural inclinations, or do the letters show that Mrs Fullam went into this matter literally *con amore*, that she was up to her neck in the conspiracy to murder her husband?'

Counsel found the feminine mind unfathomable to the male understanding. This woman did not mind killing her husband but, when the attempt miscarried, she was troubled at seeing him suffer. He did not attempt to deal with the psychology of the letters. They were beyond him. It was for the jury to decide with what object she administered the poison.

* On which Rudyard Kipling had worked as reporter and assistant editor.
† Some letters, like Madeleine Smith's, were thought at the time to be 'obscene'.

There was not a suggestion in Mrs Fullam's description of her husband's health to justify anyone's seriously considering for a moment the question of general paralysis of the insane. That disease ordinarily ran a course of four to six years.

Ross Alston could not prove positively to the jury, he admitted, how Edward Fullam was killed, but he would put before them the circumstances of his death, on which he thought that they would be forced to the conclusion that Clark and Mrs Fullam *did* kill him. If the jury were not satisfied that the evidence proved that something new was done in Agra, they would have to consider whether death was not the result of what had been done in Meerut.

Counsel told the jury that the Prosecution case was that there was a double conspiracy to kill both Fullam and Mrs Clark, but whether or not the second part of the plot was carried out was not a matter to concern them.

After reading many of the chosen letters, which were somewhat drained of the impact which they had made in the lower court, Ross Alston commented that he could not understand anyone's saying that Mrs Fullam was acting entirely under the influence of Clark. The letters showed that she met him on equal terms, if she had not actually got the whip hand of him.

The following day, Alston produced a model of 9 Metcalfe Road, in order to demonstrate young Kathleen's lines of vision from her bedroom. There was no doubt about it, he said: when Fullam did not want Kathleen to call her mother to his side, he must have known what was being done to him.

Before he used the hypodermic syringe, Clark went into Fullam with a glass, which, the girl thought, contained brandy, because she had heard Clark ask for brandy.* She said that Clark tried to force a spoon from the glass into her father's mouth, but could not get it in. Whether he would not open his mouth, or his teeth were clenched, could not be said. Nor did they know what was mixed with the brandy.

Kathleen's evidence met with extraordinary corroboration; she said, in effect, that Clark gave Fullam three injections, and Clark, in his statement before the Magistrate, admitted that he

---

* This was to be new evidence.

211

had given three injections. Being a medical man, he knew perfectly well that no doctor would give three injections at once. That was why he said that the injections were given at half-hourly intervals.

Counsel came next, with private triumph, to a topic to which Clark was particularly sensitive—the intervention of Captain Dunne. There had been time to summon him back from England, and he was now a Prosecution witness who would refute Clark's blatant lies; he would say that he had never heard of Fullam before being called to the death-scene.

Fullam was buried (Alston continued), and there the matter ended. All that was known in Agra was that a gentleman who had gone there a few days before, very ill, had died. No one knew the Fullams in Agra. It might have been a very different thing if the death had taken place in these circumstances in Meerut. No doubt a great many tongues would have wagged, and something would have come to the ears of the authorities, which would probably have led to an immediate post-mortem. Not so in Agra.

Smoothly, Alston moved into the most difficult part of his case. He did not know what was in the injections. A portion was not kept for analysis. Clark admittedly got five grains of that most violent poison, gelsemine, on 11th September, 1911, after writing off for twenty grains of it on 1st September. There was a Value Paid receipt, dated 11th September, to evidence that purchase of five grains. The Prosecution had not, though, been able to prove that Clark got the five grains which he had ordered on 23rd September.

This is all very curious. No such Value Paid receipt dated 11th September had been reported in the body of the evidence to date, nor was it to be. There *was* the Value Paid 'Chiodetti receipt' by which the Postmaster proved a package of gelsemine sent from Dr Bose's laboratory to Clark on 8th October—the day on which Clark arrived back in Agra with Edward, after travelling all night. Early on, Alston had set great store by that receipt, but now it was never mentioned.

Dr Bose's establishment evidently took rather more than a week to process an order for a dangerous drug, and, at that rate, the 'Chiodetti receipt' *could* represent receipt of the gelsemine ordered on 23rd September—but Alston does not rely on it. Was it defective in some way? Alternatively, was its date wrongly reported? Could its true date have been 11th September, so that the original 'Chiodetti receipt' and Alston's newly introduced receipt are, in fact, one and the same item?

Alston was on firmer ground with the purchase of arsenic, neither challenged nor admitted by Clark, and with the atropine purchased on 23rd July, 1911, too early convincingly to be for an embrocation for Hewson's servant; but he was still a little vague about the cocaine. When Clark sent the 'heat-stroke' liquid to Mrs Fullam at Meerut, Alston said, he had in his possession cocaine which could have produced all the symptoms which Fullam showed when he had his two attacks. But, as we have seen, there was no proof of such *prior* possession. The purchase on 27th July was too late.

Counsel closed his speech with a few choice passages from the letters, and began to call his witnesses. Augusta's barrister, Sorabji, unwisely drawing on Walter Sarkies' intimacy with the Fullam family, elicited the unwelcome information that Kathleen was a very clever child for her age. She was fond of books, and she used to recite little stories, remarkably well.

Postmaster Chiodetti proved by his register that a registered parcel was sent to 'Mrs Clarkson' at Meerut on 20th July, 1911. What can this have been? The letters provide no clue. The 'heat-stroke' liquid was not dispatched until 26th July.

With the permission of the Chief Justice, Clark elected to cross-examine Captain William Weston himself, and did not do too badly. Even though Weston thought that Fullam might have been poisoned on the first occasion when he was called in, he did not treat him for arsenical poisoning.

The Captain had no knowledge of atropine or cocaine poisoning (was it foolish of Clark to imply his own knowledge?) nor could he suggest from his experience any poison or poisons that would produce symptoms which he noted in Fullam on the second and third occasions. Sorabji got him to admit that he was not aware that Fullam suffered from chronic indigestion, and on that note, with Clark and Augusta still full of fight, the court day was over.

On Friday, the third day of the trial was crammed with strong and important evidence. The star witness (apart from Kathleen, who was always a star) was Captain Dunne, but, before him, came Major Palmer, R.A.M.C., in person, instead of by his interrogatories from Jutogh. Alston questioned him closely, and he had to refresh his memory from notes. When he first saw him in hospital, Edward Fullam was unconscious, with a purplish face, and his arms and legs were working in convulsions. His pupils were slightly dilated, and his temperature was above normal. It definitely looked like heat-stroke.

The next day, he was conscious, but his mind was a child's, emotional, easily moved to laughter or tears. For five or six days, there was slight general muscular weakness, not definite enough to be called paralysis in the popular sense of being unable to move a limb. He would say it was slight paresis. Fullam was still in a very weak condition when he left hospital.

When he was readmitted, with the same symptoms, the muscular weakness was much more pronounced. This was puzzling, but it was *not* a case of G.P.I. Assuming that his death in October had been from that cause, his illnesses in July, August, and September would have shown the mind almost of an imbecile.

In retrospect, cocaine and atropine could have produced the strange symptoms. Such a mixture would not greatly raise the temperature. But, with atropine poisoning, there should have been considerable dilation of the pupil, and Fullam showed only slight dilation. It varied in cocaine poisoning: there might not be any dilation. Eserine (which inhibits dilation) was kept in all hospitals.

The persistence of muscular weakness was quite consistent with chronic arsenical poisoning, which might also explain the mental condition. The amount of arsenic found in the thigh-bone indicated that there had been a considerable deposit of arsenic in the body originally.

Hamilton cross-examined for Augusta, trying to show that Major Palmer's grasp of Edward Fullam's case was limited, but it turned out that there were, on average, only 25 in-patients at the hospital. The G.P.I. myth would not lie down: Hamilton sought to make capital out of Edward's withered arm, but Palmer would not allow more than that it was a long-standing affliction.

Howard cross-examined for Clark, very effectively. Fullam had had two or three set-backs in hospital, which were more consistent with heat-stroke than with poisoning. Further, Palmer admitted that there was a form of heat-stroke in which the temperature did not rise significantly, although this was not the type—the only type he had met in India—for which he had treated Fullam.

Then Alston put Captain J. S. Dunne, R.A.M.C., in the witness-box. His unequivocal evidence, a turning-point in the trial, not challenged, was going to be an unpleasant experience for Clark, but for Dunne himself the giving of it was going to be, almost certainly, the worst moment of his professional life.

The Captain's testimony was, quite simply, devastating, as he told the jury that he was fetched from the Agra Club to tend a man who was already dead, whom he did not know, whose case Clark had never mentioned to him, and for whom he had never prescribed any stimulant to be given by hypodermic needle.

To Dunne's extreme discomfiture, the Chief Justice now took over, and read out the false death-certificate, signed by Clark and countersigned by the Captain. Dunne explained how Clark had, most cunningly, persuaded him to countersign, but the Chief Justice would have none of it. There was no acceptable excuse, and Sir Henry Richards was determined to administer a public rocket. Captain Dunne had signed the certificate without having seen the man before, and, said the Chief Justice, he hoped this case would be a lesson to him for the rest of his life. A doctor should never put his hand to anything of that kind without being personally acquainted with the matter.

The rocket was reported in newspapers at Home and in India, and it was hard on a captain of a distinguished service. It was almost unfair: both Dunne and Clark were brother officers of the Raj, and Dunne was entitled to trust Clark's representation that it was correct for him to countersign Clark's subordinate signature. It was the Captain's rotten luck to get caught in Clark's wheels.

Clark must have been violently discomposed by Captain Dunne's revelations, because, after Gunner Dixon's evidence about Edward's fear of moving to Agra, and Guru Buksh's tale of Clark's use of a 'silver thing', he suddenly stood up and said that he would like to say something. But this was not the

215

Magistrate's Court, and the Chief Justice made him sit down.

Now it was Augusta's turn to suffer, as Kathleen was brought into the big court-room and placed—not seated—near the jury. She gave her evidence as bravely as before, not flinching, until, again, she could not speak for tears when she came to her father's dying words, his injunction to be a good girl and to tell Lennie not to fret. The Court rose before Alston had completed his examination-in-chief.

Saturday, 1st March, 1913, was the fourth, and unexpectedly the last, day of the Fullam trial, which had looked set to continue for days. Augusta had chosen to wear a veil. At first, the evidence proceeded normally. Kathleen finished her Grimms' tale, agreed with Hamilton that her mother was kind to her, and was taken up to the bench to stand by the Judge, like Alice in Wonderland again, looking up at the King of Hearts.

It is somehow right that, in a looking-glass way, it was only now, when she had already given her evidence, that the Judge should ask if she knew what it was to tell a lie. In an English court, she would not have given a single word in evidence before the Judge was satisfied as to her competence. Sir Henry wanted to know how she first came to tell Mrs Herbert about the night when her father died. They were talking about her father's death, she said, and she told Mrs Herbert that it was all stories for Clark to say that her father told him to look after her and the other children. There was no cross-examination for Clark.

The evidence proceeded smoothly. No one was in a hurry. Not before time, Hewson, of the regimental coffee-shop at Agra, was called to examine Clark's weak, amended claim that he had procured gelsemine on 11th September, 1911, to treat the sick servant. In fact, Hewson could not help the Prosecution much. He was as vague as his incorrectly dated letter had suggested. He testified that he had asked Clark to attend to the man at the end of August, or the beginning of September, and the man died twelve or fourteen days later, after taking medicine which Clark said he had got from Calcutta.

Assistant-Surgeon Jacob, Inspector Smith, Superintendent Williamson, and Major O'Meara followed one another into the witness-box, the Chemical Examiner's report was read, and

216

Alston read the statements which Clark and Augusta had made before the Magistrate. Then, suddenly, the whole atmosphere in the court changed. Augusta was unmoved, steady behind her veil, but Clark was seen to be 'agitated'.

After Alston had announced that the evidence for the Prosecution was closed, Clark leaped to his feet and told the Judge that he wanted to make a statement. His two counsel, one must suspect, were considerably startled by this development. They had been expecting to present a full case for the defence, but Clark had set off on a course of his own, and they could only sit by, helpless, as his statement blossomed into a kind of qualified confession. Augusta's two counsel must also have felt extremely apprehensive.

The Chief Justice helped Clark. 'I shall ask you a few questions,' he said. 'Do you admit that you received and answered the letters from Mrs Fullam?' 'Yes,' Clark replied.

The Chief Justice continued: 'These letters tend to show that Mrs Fullam was systematically administering poison to her husband under your directions from the 20th April, 1911, up to the time he went to hospital the second time. Do you wish to give any explanation of that?'

The court-room must have gone very quiet, a vacuum within all the clamorous outside noises, as Clark controlled himself, and made this admission: *'I wish to say I am wholly and solely to blame. I being the stronger will had her under my control and whatever I asked her to do, she did. She did not do it of her own free will.'*

It would be pleasant to be able to report that Augusta wept at these gallant words, but she was still a steely, stocky figure in the dock beside him, her mind still racing to preserve her poor little self.

'You did send her poisons?' the Judge prompted.

'Whatever drugs were given I sent. She acted under my influence. She is not to blame for what she did. I am to blame for the whole thing.' Clark further admitted that it was he who suggested the bringing of Edward Fullam to Agra.

'Your own admissions, the little child's evidence and Guru Buksh's evidence all show that you gave injections to Fullam after he became sick subsequent to his taking his last dinner at Agra. The letters which have been given in evidence show that

217

both you and Mrs Fullam were very anxious that Fullam should die. Therefore it may be said that you were very unlikely to give him those injections with a view to saving his life. Have you any explanation to give with regard to that?'

Clark braced himself, and then poured out a most remarkable version of the killing of Edward Fullam, which *was* a confession, but still backed off from the Crown's construct of what had happened as evidenced by the letters and the purchase of poisons.

'May I begin from the very beginning, your Lordship? At first I had the intention only of making him sick and by giving him small doses of poison at Meerut to get him sent away on long leave from the country. The last dose he got in July made him very ill, and he was in a very bad condition when he came to Agra.

'I felt sorry for him, because he was simply a wreck. I simply administered four drachms of antipyrine before dinner to kill him and that is what really killed him. The injections I gave him were what I said, digitalis, strychnine and ether. The doses were too small to counteract the effects of the antipyrine. I gave him four drachms of antipyrine, and that is what played on his heart. The two injections I gave him were not enough to counteract the antipyrine, and that is how he died.'

Surprised, sceptical, the Chief Justice strove for truth and got a dusty answer. 'You mean you became sorry for giving him the antipyrine, and gave the injections to save him?' he asked.

'No,' said Clark. 'The injections were to show I was doing something for him. I knew it was impossible to do him any good when he was in that condition, but the injections did not kill him.'

The Chief Justice: 'I understand you to say you intended to kill him, and did kill him that night?'

Clark wriggled: 'After having him in Agra for three days, I knew he would not improve—he was too far gone. He was a wreck, and I wanted to put him out of trouble and misery. I had pity on the man, then. I blame myself for what I did in Meerut.'

'Is that all?'

'That is all I have to say.'

And that is the last we hear of Clark's voice—a more subtle

218

one than might have been expected from his poor academic record. In a few words, with the introduction of another drug—antipyrine—he has introduced a new dimension into a case which is already stocked with a positive pharmacopoeia of poisons. Although Clark was shielding Augusta, this could have been the poison which she, not he, applied to Edward's last dinner.

Antipyrine (phenazone), a coal-tar derivative, is a synthetic analgesic and antipyretic. Toxic symptoms can follow ten to fifteen grains in a sensitive subject. Four drachms, or 240 grains would be a massive dose. Symptoms vary in individual cases, and may include cyanosis, vertigo, collapse, sub-normal temperature, coldness, sweating, delirium, and convulsions preceding death. But vomiting is not given as a usual feature, and Edward's reaction to his dinner in the compound was violent and repeated vomiting, and he complained of the *heat*. He was weak but fully conscious when he spoke to Kathleen.

Euthanasia, however, performed to release a sufferer from an illness *caused* by the mercy-killer never has been, and never will be, a viable plea. Clark was clutching at the hope of some clemency, and, in fact, the death penalty was generally applied quite sparingly.\* Even if, though, he could convince the Court that there was a reasonable doubt and that he lacked the guilty mind of the intent to murder, there was still the spectre of Louisa's brutal murder looming over him.

At this stage, in an English court, Augusta's counsel would have asked for, and been granted, an adjournment in which to discuss the new position in which his client found herself, but this was a tough, brisk Indian court, and the Chief Justice turned immediately to Augusta and began to examine her.

Clark had tried hard not to implicate her, but she was now very much alone and isolated. Clark might have given in, but she herself was in no mood to surrender. *Her* counsel, too, had to sit by, helpless, as she improvised and parried the Judge's shrewd questions. She spoke very clearly.

'Mr Clark', she said, 'suggested that I should give the powders. I only gave my husband a half or quarter dose, and not the full dose. I was willing to give the heat-stroke mixture

\* *The Company of Cain*, Al. Carthill (Blackwood, 1929).

after I had heard of Sergeant Dunne recovering from heat-stroke in hospital.'

The Chief Justice pointed out that one of the letters showed that she it was who first suggested the giving of something to produce the symptoms of heat-stroke. Augusta was well up to that: 'It was after Clark had visited me and talked it over with me.'

He pressed on: 'In a large portion of your letters you complain that the tonic powders were not rapid enough, and you ask for something to bring on a crisis.'

'The tonic powders were doing him good.'

'You complained of that in your letters.' The Judge was sharp. 'Do you wish to give any explanation of your complaint that they improved his health?'

She was stubborn: 'Because I was anxious to make him ill only.'

'In your letters you suggest that Mrs Clark must be removed, too. Do you wish to give any explanation of that?'

She had nothing to say.

Chief Justice, winning: 'In one letter you warn Clark he must not free himself from Mrs Clark in so soon as a month because it would look bad in the eyes of the world. Do you wish to give any explanation of that?'

Augusta harked back to her statement in the lower court: 'Yes, I warned Mr Clark not to hurt his wife, not only on that, but on several occasions.'

Chief Justice: 'According to the evidence of your little girl, it was immediately after you had given dinner to your husband in Agra that he became very ill again and vomited.'

'There was nothing in his dinner. Mr Clark gave my husband a dose of medicine before dinner.'

Chief Justice: 'You yourself have admitted that you saw Clark giving the injections to your husband at Agra. Do you wish to give any explanation?'

'I saw him giving the injections and he showed me the bottle.'

And that was all! A mere travesty, however searching the questions, of the full exploration of the defence of an accused under oath in the English legal system. Defence counsel, deeply despondent, upon enquiry, did not intend to call any evidence. What witnesses could they have called? Captain Dunne and

Hewson were dead ducks, called by the Prosecution.

Ross Alston, in his closing speech for the Crown, now found himself faced with a curious situation. Augusta's was still and definitely a plea of not guilty, but Clark had just admitted that he was, in Alston's words, 'criminally responsible' for the death of Edward Fullam.

Clark had said that death was produced in a way which the Prosecution did not suggest with certainty—counsel continued —and it was a question whether death *was* produced in that particular way, or whether that had been said by way of helping Mrs Fullam. Clark probably thought that it was his duty to help her, because he knew that if he had not kept those letters, in all human probability, Mrs Fullam would not be before them.

He would remind the jury that many passages in her letters showed the desire to kill and not a desire to make ill. He asked them to act upon the plain English of her letters. If they could see anything in them which suggested that she was never at any time a party to the idea of killing her husband, they would, no doubt, bring in a verdict to that effect, but he thought that they would find great difficulty in putting such an interpretation on the letters, taking them as a whole.

If the jury were of the opinion that the whole of the circumstances, including Mrs Fullam's conduct on the night her husband died, her indifference to his illness and his sufferings, the absenting of herself from his room, satisfied them that she was in fact a consenting party to the killing of her husband, they would have to convict her as well as Clark.

It was not a brilliant speech, expressly short, but perfectly fair. Alston gives the impression of having been taken slightly off-balance by the unexpected collapse of the Defence. Augusta's barrister had it all to do for her, and his well-prepared speech was the best forensic performance of the trials.

Sorabji asked the jury to consider the woman's character. They had got from various witnesses that she was not a bad woman. The first letter showed that she was fighting against a tremendous temptation. There came into her happy life a person like Clark, and she became like wax in his hands. That certainly represented their relations at that time. It was quite evident at this early stage that she had no intention whatever of doing any harm to her husband.

Then began the second stage, with her pleading with the 'old coaxer' to break off relations. Counsel contended that he was entitled to say that the first suggestion of harm did not come from her, but from Clark. On 19th April, she wanted to break off relations with Clark after the first hint that something ought to be done.

Sorabji's explanation of the tonic powders was that, up to that time, Clark had not suggested anything actually harmful but he wanted to get her into the way of giving medicine to her husband, and, so far as Mrs Fullam was concerned, she believed that she was giving him nothing more than a tonic which made her husband better. (This was naughty of Sorabji. It was taking Alston's injunction not to go behind the plain English of the letters too far. It would have come better from Augusta herself.)

If this woman had made up her mind to kill her husband, on the 24th, they would not expect her to be writing on the 25th* about being jealous of the attentions which he had paid to other women at parties.

Judging by the letter of 26th April, Counsel said he thought Clark then suggested that Fullam should be made ill. It was, Sorabji said, not easy for him to say so much for his client at this stage, but there *were* things to be said. This woman had everything to lose and nothing to gain by her husband's death. He was a man drawing a comparatively handsome salary for people in that position in life.

Various circumstances showed—Sorabji contended—that she only gave Fullam the 'heat-stroke' liquid when she believed that it would not kill him but simply keep him in hospital. There was another point in her favour. She was sent the whole dose of some medicine, the contents of which she could not know. The man who was giving the medicine was a doctor. She could not be supposed to have any knowledge of drugs at all. And she reduced the doses to half and a quarter of what Clark sent on different occasions. Was that the conduct of a woman who really wanted to kill her husband?

* This letter of 25th April is not available.

Moreover, in one of her letters, she showed tremendous remorse. She had had her wish, and Fullam went to hospital, but she had not realised what his sufferings would be. Then they found she was putting ice to his head and calling a doctor. Her anxiety was evidently that he should get better.

The only evidence that she gave him poison between his two admissions to hospital was that of the little child—'Oh! Gus, you have given me the wrong medicine'—and he did not think on that evidence they were justified in coming to the conclusion that poison was given then.

Coming to the last stage of the case, Counsel argued that Mrs Fullam's conduct on the night of the tragedy was, in fact, quite consistent with his theory that she did not want to kill her husband. She had written that she was like wax in Clark's hands and, when in Agra, she was absolutely under his control. Clark had suggested that she should come to Agra with her husband because he felt that she was not carrying out his instructions, and he wanted to see to matters himself.

If she had had a guilty mind on that night, and had been helping to kill, she would have been going in and out of her husband's room frequently, in order to make evidence to show that she felt it tremendously. Her staying away was *not* evidence against her. It was in her favour that she did not go into hysterics. There was a stage beyond tears where no tears would come at all.

Counsel did not put it that, necessarily, this woman was very sorry that her husband had died, but he did put it to the jury that she was stunned and surprised. A man who believed that he was probably about to die would be likely to tell them the truth, and he asked the jury, therefore, to rely on Clark's statement that Mrs Fullam was a tool in his hands and entirely under his control.

In conclusion, Sorabji asked the jury to say that Mrs Fullam was certainly not guilty of the charge of murder, and that she just fell short of being guilty of attempted murder, because she gave only small doses of the mixture sent by Clark, and that, at the most, she was guilty of having done a most terrible and awfully rash act in giving these things of which she did not know the full danger.

Sir Henry Richards, the Chief Justice, summed up against

Augusta.* This was one of the cruellest murders that had ever
been investigated. His charge would, he was glad to say, be an
extremely short one, because, having regard to the statement
made by Clark, a very large part of the case was now ended. He
did not want to say very much about that, but possibly one
might think that Clark had done perhaps the only thing he
could have done in the peculiar circumstances in the case. But it
did not at all follow that all he had said even in this last
statement was true.

Of course it did not necessarily follow that, because Clark
murdered Fullam on the night of 10th October, Mrs Fullam
also murdered him. The Judge wanted to get rid of a few little
matters which might confuse the jury. In the first place, they
must take it from him, as a matter of law, that there was no
evidence in the case which would go to show that Mrs Fullam
was not responsible in law for the murder of her husband [he
was referring to the Svengali defence!] if she in fact joined with
Clark in murdering him.

There was no evidence in the case that would justify the jury
in holding that she was so under the influence of Clark that she
could not resist murdering her husband, and that she was
unable to help giving these poisons.

It was also no part of the duty of the jury to apportion the
blame between these two people. This might be a question
which could be argued at considerable length. Some people
might say that a kind, good father and a kind, good husband
was entitled to be protected by his wife who had yielded herself
up to his Masonic friend and brother; that he was entitled to
look to his wife for protection, instead of her, on her own
admission, administering to him, not once, but many times,
poisons that were causing him most terrible suffering.

The jury had not got to apportion the blame. They must
settle that between their own consciences and God Almighty. If
the letters showed that Mrs Fullam had made up her
mind—although she might have had occasional twinges of
conscience—that she would murder her husband, and if they

* Because Clark's statement was treated as a plea of guilty, there was
no final speech to the jury by his counsel. Nor, later, did the Court
hear counsel in mitigation before sentence.

found that she brought him up to Agra into the presence of the very man who finally did murder him, and who for months had been supplying her with the means of administering poisons to him at Meerut, they would be entitled, but not bound, to infer from that that she was a party to the murder.

They had seen the little girl, and had heard her give her evidence. It was entirely for the jury to form an opinion as to the value of that evidence. Fullam, who had been brought up to the house furnished and hired by the man who was carrying on an adulterous intrigue with his wife, was given his last meal by his wife, who, on her own admission, had been giving him poisons in Meerut, and, shortly afterwards, he became violently sick.

Then, on her own admission, Mrs Fullam saw Clark administering those injections. Whether they were harmless or not, he could not say, but, in his statement made that day, Clark did not even pretend they were for the purpose of relieving the dying man's pain, but simply for the purpose of showing that something was being done.

If the jury believed what Mrs Fullam said in her letters and her own statement made that day, she undoubtedly did attempt to murder her husband, but they must distinguish that matter from the actual murder. If, however, she was there on the 10th October, and she knew that Clark was murdering her husband, and she was willing that Clark should so murder him, she was, in the eyes of the law, guilty of murder, and it was not for them to say who was the more to blame.

They had the evidence of the little girl, they had Mrs Fullam's conduct before the murder, and the attempts which she made upon Fullam's life earlier—if they believed them to be attempts of murder—and they had her conduct on the night of the murder: these were all matters which would justify the jury in coming to the conclusion that she was present, knowing her husband was being murdered, and so willing. On the other hand, if they had the slightest reasonable doubt—not any ridiculous doubt which would not for a moment affect them in the ordinary affairs of life—they should give her the benefit of it.

With the Chief Justice's tones of moral indignation ringing in their ears, the nine members of the jury retired for ten

225

minutes before they returned with a unanimous verdict of guilty against both the accused, on the two charges of attempted murder and murder.

Augusta's counsel handed a document to the Judge, and asked him to consider it before passing sentence. This referred, as the Chief Justice surely knew, to Augusta's pregnancy, but it was, anyway, 4.30, and he said that he would pass sentence on another day. The two prisoners were immediately removed through a back door, as a large crowd had gathered in front of the court-house. Clark's life was now trickling away, like poison from a green glass bottle.

## Chapter Sixteen

## Under the Neem Tree

Being sentenced to be hanged by the neck till you are dead must induce the most profound feelings of unreality. The furnishings of the court-room, and people's faces, must spin and swim. The incredulity, the sensation that it cannot be happening, the visual image of the dangling figure—*me*—must be overwhelming.

Augusta's public tears were rare, last seen when Edward's coffin was closed, but she sobbed aloud as the Chief Justice pronounced the death-sentence.

On that same day, over one hundred miles away, in Lucknow, Edward's fourteen-year-old nephew, Richard Everett Fullam, was found drowned in the tank* at La Martinière College, where he had been a scholar. He was buried two days later by William Lachlan Bell, Minister and Chaplain of Lucknow Cantonments. The cause of death was 'Accidental drowning'.

It was Monday, 10th March, 1913, the day set for the opening of the Clark trial, but also the day for sentencing Clark and Augusta. Asked for their plea, the four Indians claimed to be tried† for the murder of Louisa Clark. A plea of guilty in such circumstances was almost unknown, and Indian counsel would hardly ever advise that course, or his client would think him to be in dereliction of his duty.

During their eight days' disgrace as convicted prisoners, Clark and Augusta, however, had lost their will to fight, and no doubt they had been discouraged by their legal advisers from

---

* A lake or pool, often artificial.
† The plea of 'not guilty' was not recognised by the Criminal Procedure Code.

continuing their defence. Still, they were both unpredictable, and their counsel might have felt a degree of wariness until they had pleaded guilty to the charge of abetment* of the murder of Louisa Clark.

The Chief Justice was now in a position to dispense a double judgement. Clark stood up straight and tall as the Judge addressed him:

'On a previous occasion you were convicted by the jury for the murder of Mr Edward Fullam. No other possible verdict could have been given on the evidence. The sentence of the Court is that you hang by the neck till you are dead. In this present case, the murder of your wife, you have pleaded guilty. I convict you on that plea of guilty and the sentence of the Court is that you hang by the neck till you are dead.'

Clark received the sentence quietly, and sat down. Augusta then stood up, and the Judge intoned the same bipartite sentence, without the comment about the evidence.

Although the Judge had no intention of hanging her, for one moment of panic Augusta herself must have wondered if things could still go wrong. Indeed, and it may have been kept from her, technically, under Section 382 of the Criminal Procedure Code, the Court had a very frightening power—'If a woman sentenced to death is found to be pregnant, the High Court shall order the execution to be postponed'—but the Judge also had the power, if he thought fit, to commute the sentence to transportation for life.

Reassuringly, she heard her barrister, Hamilton, calling Dr Cearns, who had examined her (there was no impromptu 'panel of matrons'), and he was testifying that she was pregnant.

Chief Justice: 'Mrs Fullam, it has been proved to my satisfaction that you are quick with child. Not because there are any mitigating circumstances connected with the two murders with which you have been found to be guilty, but in consideration of the condition which you are in, and on that

---

* Abetment was a useful section (107) of the Indian Penal Code, widely used. It corresponded to the English offence of being an 'accessory before the fact', and differs from present English law, where an abettor is one *who is present* assisting or encouraging the principal at the time of the commission of the offence.

consideration only, I commute the sentence in the case of the murder of your husband to penal servitude\* for the remaining term of your life. In the other case also, the murder of Mrs Clark, for the same reason, I commute the sentence into penal servitude for the remaining term of your life.'

Augusta and Clark were then removed from court, and parted for the last time. The four Indians, Sukkha, Ram Lal, Buddha, and Mohan, were waiting for their trial, and a jury was briskly empanelled from the 'majority of Europeans' who had been summoned in readiness to compose an 'Ilbert' jury if Augusta and Clark should elect to be tried.

It was thought greatly to the advantage of the *badmashes* that, shielded by their association with Augusta and Clark, they had a High Court judge (indeed, the Chief Justice, himself) and jury all to themselves. Otherwise, they would have been tried in the ordinary way at Sessions (a lower court) by a Sessions judge, without a jury.†

Ahmed Karim, an Indian barrister, or *vakil*, had been provided by the Court to defend Sukkha, Buddha, and Mohan. Another *vakil*, Mahomed Ishaq Khan, appeared for Ram Lal, separately and privately briefed.

Counsels' task—and it was one in which they were well versed—was to persuade the jury that Budhu, the approver, was lying in naming their clients as members of the conspiracy. The corroborative evidence to be adduced by the Prosecution was strongest against Sukkha the *darzi*—naturally so, since he, with Budhu, had been an instigator, and there was also identification evidence against him. The other three were more elusive. It was not, apparently, unusual, for a defence of alibi

---

\* The substitution of penal servitude for transportation to some hellish penal settlement caused comment, but, in fact, in a very unusual case, the Judge was drawing upon Act XXIV of 1855. The substitution was applicable only to Europeans and Americans, 'by reason of the difficulty of providing a place to which such convicted persons could be sent with safety to their health.' Thus, Walsh was wrong when he called penal servitude 'a sentence unknown to Indian law'.

† Although sitting with three or four Indian Assessors, whose opinions, if helpful, yet had no legal effect.

*and* self-defence to be set up simultaneously, but these were to be orderly proceedings in a grave and important case.

Ross Alston, in his opening speech for the Prosecution, made no secret of the fact that Augusta and Clark had been removed from the trial. Indeed, the truth could scarcely have been concealed, since, quite apart from the previous publicity, the pair were frequently to be mentioned as abettors of the murder, and the jury would be bound to infer what it might from their absence from the dock. The knowledge that two participants in the crime had already been disposed of was, of course, most damaging to the remaining four, but it could not be helped. Ross Alston indicated that it would be unnecessary to call a considerable amount of evidence which he would, otherwise, have had to be put before the jury.

If, he went on, the jury believed that Budhu had told the truth about Sukkha, it would be for them to ask themselves why he should not have told it regarding the other men, unless these men could give some sort of explanation as to why he should have mentioned their names if they had nothing whatever to do with the crimes. Up to the present, Counsel knew of no such explanation .

Ahmed Karim, as he had to, challenged the identification of Sukkha by both Maud Clark and Kathleen Fullam, but did not shake either of them. Then Budhu, the approver, was put up, and he produced a good, consistent performance, avoiding the red gleams of hatred from the handcuffed prisoners in the dock. There were some small, but interesting variations from his first statement in the Magistrate's Court. One passage contradicts Augusta's previous statement in which she claimed knowledge of only two *badmashes*: 'Mrs Fullam asked how many men there were and Sukkha said four. Mrs Fullam said: "If you four take the money from Budhu, what will he do?"'

A new point, which Sukkha's counsel could have made use of, was Budhu's assertion that, at the time of preparation for the murder, when Clark was flourishing six sovereigns and ten rupees, Clark and Sukkha came to the hospital gate to meet him, *both riding on the same bicycle*. If Sukkha was the passenger, that went towards his denial of being a cyclist!

Budhu also expanded his account of the gathering and arming of the gang: he had gone some distance beyond the

230

*kotwali,** and met Ram Lal and Sukkha. Budhu had known Ram Lal for two or three years. They took Budhu to Buddha's house, close by, entered, and saw a man sleeping there. After about a quarter of an hour, all three went away, taking Buddha with them. Budhu had not known Buddha before that night.

Beside a house that was being built near the Lalkothi Bazaar, they found another man, sitting in the shade of a stone. This was Mohan. Budhu pointed to him in the dock. They all four then set off for the *maidan†* and sat down, and then Buddha went into a field and brought out a big sword, which he showed them, and said, 'Come along.' There was a big neem tree‡ on the artillery parade-ground, and they all went and sat down there for a long time, and then they went to the Clarks' bungalow.

The following day in the High Court, they had still not finished with Budhu, the approver. As he wound up his tale, he repeatedly named Ram Lal as an active participant. There was a major discrepancy, not missed by Sukkha's counsel: Budhu said that Ram Lal stood over Maud Clark's bed with a *lathi* in his hand, whereas Maud thought it was Sukkha who brandished the big stick.

As a curlicue to the tale, Budhu now remembered that Sukkha had told him that he had pledged his property in order to give Mohan ten rupees. They must have been very frightened of Mohan. In reply to a question from the Chief Justice, Budhu stated that Clark knew none of the four men, except Sukkha, the visitor to the bungalow.

Mahomed Ishaq Khan sought to discredit Budhu by a roundabout route; why, out of all the fifty or so servants employed at the hospital, did Clark select him to pick the *badmashes*?

'I talked to him more than the others and also worked at his house.'

'Did the sahib know you were a *badmash*?'

'No.'

* The chief police station of the city.
† Open space of common land, sometimes a parade-ground.
‡ *Azadirachta indica*, a sacred shade tree, under which village elders sit, meetings are held, and plots are hatched.

'Did he know you were an associate of *badmashes*?'
'No.'

Ahmed Karim, burdened with his three clients, took over, but he, too, made little progress, and Budhu emerged unscathed. Hazari Mal, a poultry dealer, was now called to corroborate Budhu's evidence as to the gathering of the *badmashes* for the deed, and, on the whole, his testimony was quite strong. He was immovable about the date—17th November—because it was only two days before he went to Delhi with the Royal Artillery on manoeuvres.

Buddha, of the same trade, had been living with him for a month. (That would go with Budhu's tale of meeting at 'Buddha's house'.) At 7 p.m. Ram Lal and Sukkha called at his house. Buddha, who had been out, returned at 7 or 8 p.m., and Ram Lal and Sukkha took him away with them. No mention of Budhu, who, by his own account, had been in attendance.

Ahmed Karim did rather well. The two men did not enter Hazari Mal's house at all, whereas Budhu had said that they went inside and saw a man asleep there. Also, it was too dark for Hazari Mal to see the men clearly. Mahomed Ishaq Khan was less successful: it was Ram Lal who shouted for Buddha.

The Chief Justice joined in, and he and Ram Lal's counsel together interrogated Hazari Mal. He had known Ram Lal for a long time. That is, he had seen him at work in the bazaar, but had not spoken to him. He knew everybody in the bazaar. He knew Ram Lal by his voice. But it was a dark night and he could not see him.

The Sessions Judge at Agra once wryly observed that the alibis relied upon in his court fell into three main categories: the marriage feast, the purchase of a bullock at some distant fair, and the visit to the medical dispensary. By variation, Buddha had claimed to have followed the regiment on manoeuvres, but now Ross Alston produced Sajjad Husain, of the coffee-shop of the Seaforth Highlanders at Agra, who said that he went into camp with the regiment on 6th November, 1912. He knew all the contractors who used to supply eggs and fowls to the coffee-shop, but these did not include Buddha. He did not even know Buddha, whose alibi was now a thing of tatters.

Ram Lal's alibi next. The only witness found, or willing, to disprove it, was not so satisfactory as the coffee-shop manager.

It was all too vague. This man was Nanak Chand, a *zemindar*, or landowner, of Lalkurti, Kachipura, Agra, who had known Ram Lal for ten to twelve years. He had needed some vegetables for his daughter's marriage feast at Kachipura on 20th November, and, three or four days before the ceremony, he saw Ram Lal and ordered vegetables from him. He also saw Ram Lal at Kachipura on 20th, 22nd and 23rd November. In the Magistrate's Court only, he had said that Ram Lal was actually present at the feast, and his uncle, Kanhia Lal, a contractor, had been brought to corroborate that detail. At this point, the court day ended.

The following morning, Alston still had one witness with new evidence. This was Narain Singh, the constable who had pounced on Mohan in the train for Bharatpur. In the lower court he had not been reported to state, as he now did, that there were bloodstains on Mohan's *dhoti*.* Mohan's story was that he had had a 'quarrel' with someone at about the time of the murder, during which his lip was cut, and he had wiped it with the *dhoti*.

The case for the Prosecution ended, and then the Chief Justice turned to examine the desperate, defiant prisoners. Sukkha had always had a tongue in his head, and he stubbornly denied everything that was put to him, before coming out with an obviously prepared attack on the police.

Superintendent Williamson, he said, had told him that Budhu had been made a witness for the Crown, and that he, too, could be one. Sukkha told him he knew nothing. The Superintendent then went away, and he was stripped, and cold water was poured over him by the *Daroga*,† who also made him drink milk with *bhang*‡ in it. The *Daroga* said that he must say what he was told to say.

Then they made him sit in a buggy, and they took him to a place he did not know. Then they were taking him to the park. There were a number of gentlemen there and he was made to stand among about twenty men. He was only pointed out by those brought to identify him at the instigation of the police.

---

* Loincloth.
† Sub-inspector in the Indian Police.
‡ Indian hemp, i.e. *cannabis*.

He knew that Budhu only mentioned his name at the prompting of the police.

The Chief Justice was not at all disconcerted by these allegations: torture by the police was regularly complained of. The favourite techniques alleged were beating with stinging nettles, tying a pot of wasps to the naked body, the Chinese water torture, and the forced inhalation of cayenne pepper. By 1913, such accusations rarely stood up to investigation, but a spot of 'slapping', as it was called, was a commonplace.

Sukkha said, now, that he had complained to the Magistrate about his treatment by the police, but the Judge would have none of it. He told the jury that they could take it from him that this part of Sukkha's statement was a pack of lies. If Sukkha had made the slightest complaint to Mr Ormrod, it would have been taken down in writing and proceeded upon at once.

In refutation, a third-class magistrate of Agra, named Minson, who had interviewed Sukkha before taking him to the Joint Magistrate for his formal statement to be recorded, was called by the Chief Justice. Minson had found Sukkha to be in his right mind, not drugged or ill-treated, and both Superintendent Williamson and Suraj Narain Singh, the *Daroga* in question, denied Sukkha's allegations. And that was the end of Sukkha's chance—wasted, really, in attacking the police; for, although it may have been the only defence he knew, it was the wrong occasion, and the wrong tribunal, for such antics. His denials, at least, had been fiery and spirited.

Ram Lal, examined next, claimed simply, with, it must be assumed, a convincing dignity, that on the night of the 17th he was with his brother at Kirauli, fifteen miles away from Agra. He did not elaborate, but relied upon his counsel and his own defence witnesses, soon to be called.

Buddha denied ever having slept at Hazari Mal's house. He had his own house, and lived in it. In spite of not being known at the coffee-shop, he still insisted that he went to Delhi with the regiment on 6th November, reaching there on the 16th or 17th, when they arrived near the camp of the Viceroy. Unfortunately for him, he could not produce any witnesses. He, too, alleged police brutality, and the Chief Justice told the jury that the Magistrate had made a note to the effect that he had examined Buddha after he had made allegations, and that he had not found the slightest signs of injury upon him.

Mohan had never put up any sort of defence, since his alibi was still-born. The best he could do was to declare that Budhu had pointed him out at the instigation of Superintendent Williamson.

Mahomed Ishaq Khan then called Ram Lal's two witnesses. Ram Lal's brother, named Dalchand, a *kachi*, or corn-contractor, said that he and Ram Lal lived with their father at Kirauli. Dalchand's sizeable annual income, he boasted with more than a vain purpose, was between 1,500 and 2,000 rupees. He had a Brahmin servant, who went away, leaving him in difficulties about preparing his food, and therefore he summoned Ram Lal (*not*, after all, living at Kirauli) to help him.

Ram Lal went to him two days before *Diwali** and remained with him until 19th December. Their father was a cultivator, who paid 62 and 9-8 rupees respectively for the rents of his two plots of land. Dalchand kept 200 rupees out of his earnings, and gave the rest to his father.

Ross Alston chose to cross-examine about the annual income, and it turned out that Dalchand was only a sub-contractor to another contractor, and the 1,500 to 2,000 rupees were the profits of his master, not his own. Nor had he paid income tax last year! Fainting seems to have run in the family, because, after a few more questions of this nature, Dalchand, too, passed out, and was assisted from the court. The Brahmin servant took his place, to say that he remembered that Ram Lal was at Kirauli around the time of the murder.

Thursday, 13th March, 1913, was the concluding day of a short, tight trial, and Mahomed Ishaq Khan, for Ram Lal, went straight into his closing speech, since all the evidence had been completed. His comments about the evidence of the vegetables did not, in fact, chime with his client's own alibi defence, but no matter. Nanak Chand's testimony, he contended, did not prove anything against his client. It went to show that it was not likely that he had engaged in such a terrible murder. After such a crime, it would hardly be probable that he would go about in the ordinary business of selling vegetables. A man in such circumstances would be more likely to clear off.

* Hindu festival of lights.

235

Rightly, indeed, Counsel pointed out that Hazari Mal's evidence, on cross-examination, had proved unsatisfactory. The night was dark. And as for the character of Budhu, the approver, a man who, on his own confession, took part in so foul a murder was not worthy of credence. Budhu's life was in danger, and, even up to the present time, his lordship could withdraw the pardon tendered to him on condition that he told the whole truth and suppressed nothing. How far could they rely on the testimony of such a man which was not corroborated in any way? Surely the evidence of the defence witnesses was more to be relied upon than that of Budhu—that blackguard?

Moreover, it was absurd to suggest that Ram Lal, a member of a fairly well-to-do family, would take part in such an atrocious crime merely for his share of 100 rupees—if any such sum *were* offered and accepted. The story of the murder was, in itself, a most unlikely one, for why should five men be employed to kill one helpless lady in her sleep at night? Lieutenant Clark was a clever and educated man, and he would know that the larger the number of murderers employed, the greater the chance of detection. Budhu had not told the whole of the circumstances or there was something that they could not understand.

Ahmed Karim took over for his three clients. In the stress and excitement of the moment, he proceeded to overstate the law regarding the (frankly rotten and dubious matter of) corroboration of an approver's evidence. He stated that it was not the practice, unless an accomplice's evidence was corroborated on every material point, to convict on such evidence. He was quite wrong. Had that, in fact, been the law, there would have been scarcely any convictions. The law relating to corroboration of an approver had been so thoroughly thrashed out, because it was a vital component of the Indian criminal law, that there was no space left for manipulation of this sort.

On sounder ground, Ahmed Karim asked the jury if it was likely that Budhu, when his master told him that he wanted *badmashes*—and Budhu had reason to know what they were wanted for—would go to a man—Sukkha—with whom he had only slight acquaintance. (Probably, though, Budhu knew him well enough.) It was Ahmed Karim, too, who exploited the glaring discrepancy as to who it was who held the *lathi* in the bedroom—Sukkha or Ram Lal. Sukkha, however, cannot have been pleased, if he even understood the concept, by his counsel's comment that, if there *was* any corroboration of the approver's statement, it was against Sukkha alone. (Sukkha, then, should have had separate counsel.)

In the face of the coffee-shop manager's evidence, Ahmed Karim contended that there was no evidence to show that Buddha's story about going with the regiment to the manoeuvres was not true. (Indeed, various *wallahs* used to follow the troops on a more informal basis than direct supply to the coffee-shop, but Buddha failed to put forward his defence with any real enthusiasm.)

As for Mohan, the only corroboration was the spots of blood on his *dhoti*. He was not arrested until 18th January. Was it feasible that he would have carried blood-evidence on his own body for two whole months?

Ross Alston's final speech was stylish and deadly. He entirely agreed with his learned friend that Budhu was not yet out of the wood. It was possible, up to the very end of the trial, for his lordship to withdraw Budhu's pardon, if he thought that he had not told the truth. His learned friend advised them to remember, therefore, that Budhu was not yet free. He asked the jury to bear in mind that the only thing which would stand in the way of Budhu's release would be his not telling the truth.

The observation which was made by his learned friend was one which went to the root of the case, but it was in a manner very different from that which he suggested. If Budhu's only hope was that he should tell successful *lies*, it would be a different matter. In considering Budhu's evidence, they must ask themselves whether anything had been put before them calculated to justify them in the belief that Budhu had any private object to gain in telling untruths with reference to the persons who assisted in the murder.

He could not help thinking that it must have struck the jury as forcibly as it had struck him that the most singular thing about the cross-examination and the statements of the accused was that it had never once been suggested that any of the four men were at enmity with Budhu, nor that Budhu bore them any private grudge for something that had happened in the past. So they approached the approver's evidence with nothing more than an empty suggestion flung into the air that Budhu might be incriminating persons who had nothing whatever to do with the crime.

The defence had been confined, Alston continued, of necessity, it seemed to him, to the narrow question of whether Budhu's evidence had been sufficiently corroborated. Now and then, the remark was made that there was no corroboration, and the jury were told that they ought not to convict for that reason. However, they were not being *asked* to convict the men on the uncorroborated evidence of the approver. That was not the case for the prosecution at all. Rather, it was that Budhu's evidence had been corroborated *so far as it was possible* in the special circumstances of the case to have corroboration.

The Chief Justice summed up carefully: 'You will of course all be aware that Mrs Fullam and Clark were convicted of a very cruel and brutal murder that will stand out in the annals of crime. These men had nothing to do with that. The object was to enable Clark and Mrs Fullam to get married. They have pleaded guilty and they have been sentenced. Their plea of guilty has greatly shortened the present trial, and you begin the consideration of this case with what I may call the previous knowledge that Mrs Clark was most foully done to death by assassins paid by Clark and Mrs Fullam.

'One can hardly speak calmly on the foulness of that crime and the manner in which it was carried out, but we must remember we must not be led astray by the fearful and horrible and odious fashion in which these two murders were perpetrated, when trying these men. They are entitled to their proper trial.'

Ahmed Karim could only bow, as the Judge corrected him, saying that he was greatly indebted to Counsel for taking up the defence of three of the accused, which he had carried out with great ability. However, he thought that it would be extremely unfortunate if it were ever laid down that corroboration in all particulars was necessary.* He was afraid that, in

---

* Section 133 of the Evidence Act expressly provided that an accomplice could be a competent witness against an accused person, and a conviction was not illegal merely because it rested upon the uncorroborated testimony of an accomplice.

the time he had been in India, he had often been perfectly satisfied of the truth of the evidence of an accomplice and perhaps the statement and confession of a co-accused, *where he had the gravest doubts about the independent corroboration.*

The jury would have to watch and scrutinise the evidence of Budhu, the approver, from start to finish. They must approach it with caution. Budhu wanted them to believe that he was very much against the crime, and there was evidence which went to show that he hesitated about it. It was only after his master had spoken to him over and over again that he at last went to Sukkha. Evidently Clark, wicked man though he was, did not look upon himself as coming under the term *badmash*—when he sought *badmashes*—nor did he consider that Budhu was one himself.

Budhu's story of the murder, the Judge continued, was corroborated in a most remarkable way by the fact that Clark and Mrs Fullam had pleaded guilty, by Maud Clark's finding the bed-sheet in the box-room, and by her seeing her father bringing the dog back into the bungalow.

He knew no reason why the jury should not believe the evidence of the little girl, and what she said about someone's coming to the house with Budhu on the night of the murder showed that there was more than one man engaged in the crime. It was perfectly clear that Kathleen Fullam had had grave suspicions when she told the man later, 'You are not a *darzi*. Perhaps I will speak.' She knew then of the death of Mrs Clark and a good deal of what had gone on at her father's house. She had every reason to look at this man. On the whole, the Judge considered that her identification of Sukkha was the most satisfactory and complete corroboration of the evidence of the approver that it was possible to have.

The jury retired to deliberations which were much more contentious than in the Fullam trial. At one stage, they returned to ask a question about Mohan, clearly worried by the lack of independent evidence, but Budhu had identified him at a parade, and the Judge had indicated that, subject to their own consciences, of course, they could rely on his evidence.

Finally, they returned a unanimous verdict of guilty against Buddha, who had not been seen at the coffee-shop, and also against Sukkha, the cyclist, who had never really had a defence.

Mohan, the *bharboonja*, was found guilty by a majority of seven votes to two.

Mahomed Ishaq Khan, however, had done his work well for Ram Lal, the greengrocer who fainted. The alibi was believed above Budhu's evidence, and he was found not guilty by the remarkable majority of eight votes to one. Interestingly, the High Court Judge in India had a special discretion: by Section 305 of the Criminal Procedure Code, when as many as six are of one opinion, and the Judge agrees with them, the Judge shall give judgment in accordance with such opinion. *But* if the Judge disagrees with the majority, he shall at once discharge the jury.

The Chief Justice let the verdict stand, and it was generally thought to be a tactful decision. No one really wanted a new trial just for Ram Lal, and British India congratulated itself that justice had been seen to be done, with leniency towards an Indian defendant.

Buddha, Sukkha, and Mohan were sentenced to be hanged by the neck till they were dead. Amateur assassins, *badmashes* of the bazaar, they were only twenty-year-olds, beguiled by the promise of a handful of rupees and the spurious glamour of a group-slaying.

Ram Lal was set free to sell vegetables again, the luckiest person in the case, but a man marked by the police for ever. As for Budhu, the survivor, he, too, slipped out of the court, but his life-expectancy was not high.

## Chapter Seventeen

# The Pilot's Grandson

There was little British interest in the hanging of the tailor, the pedlar, and the corn-parcher. It was probably a ghastly scene. But it became known that Lieutenant Clark died bravely, without a murmur, an officer and a pedigree gentleman.

After he was condemned, he asked that his sword should be handed over to a member of his family—probably his brother—and this was done. His last request in gaol* was to be allowed to say his farewell to Augusta, and, by the rules, a meeting could have been arranged, but she refused to see him.

On Wednesday, 26th March, 1913, in the morning, Clark was hanged in the Naini district gaol at Allahabad. Tall and straight, he marched to the awesome end—the trussed figure, the thick rope, the canvas hood, the long moment. Had Augusta been quite sufficient to atone, all the remainder of their lives?

Afterwards, on the same day, his brother, his three children, and a handful of his friends waited for his coffin to be brought by carriage to Allahabad Cantonment Cemetery, and followed him to the grave. He was allowed a decent burial. The service was read by the Garrison Chaplain, Ronald Irwin. The Burial Register gives the cause of death as 'Executed by order of the High Court, United Provinces'.†

An appeal for clemency from a conviction for murder lay

---

* The sole authority for this is Walsh.
† All the sadness and violence that beset the British in India are epitomised in the two preceding entries. On January 14th, Elizabeth May Wager, aged eight months, had died of 'pneumonia and convulsions'. On January 15th, James Bourne, aged 31, Private, 1st Battalion Northumberland Fusiliers, had died of 'suffocation from strangulation'.

first to the Provincial Governor, and then to the Viceroy. In a somewhat inaccurate account,* Clark is said to have lodged an appeal with the Viceroy for a stay of execution pending an appeal to the Privy Council, but it was refused, and a telegram direct to the King was also futile.

Augusta, too, and she had time on her side, contemplated an appeal to His Majesty in Council—a rare procedure then, as now. A brief was, in fact, delivered to London chambers for counsel's opinion, but there were no extraordinary circumstances, such as a flagrant violation of the law, which would have led the Privy Council to intervene, and the matter was not proceeded with.

Memsahibs were not supposed to commit murder, and Augusta could not expect leniency: it would have been inappropriate. As a member of the ruling class, she had dented the reputation of the Raj in a manner that was unforgivable. She had offended by her flagrant adultery, by her choice of lover, by being found out, by associating with *badmashes*, and by making a mockery of marriage and family life. In Edward Fullam, she had eliminated the very paradigm of the hard-working, dedicated official. She had betrayed the image of British femininity by abdicating from her post as helpmeet, and by letting sex be her master.

Naturally, then, they treated her harshly. There were prisons for Europeans up in the Hills, but they incarcerated her, instead, in Naini Prison, where Clark also was confined and executed. The gaols were all run by British officers, and the Governor here was a Colonel Hudson, of the Indian Medical Service. He was soon charmed by his new prisoner, who showed him that aspect of herself which he most liked to discern. She seemed to him to be truly contrite, and he often said that he could not understand how a woman of so sweet and attractive a nature, and apparently tender conscience, could have been guilty of such conduct.

The European custodial staff, too, were completely won over. Miss D. Smidt, Assistant Matron, who, under her mother, Mrs M. Smidt, Senior Matron of the female ward, was in charge of Augusta, described her as 'a good lady and gentle... an

* *Memories of a K.C.'s Clerk*, Francis Pearson. (Sampson Low, n.d.)

English lady and not an Anglo-Indian and by no means a wicked woman'.

The Indian and Eurasian wardresses, however, saw another side of her; they regarded her as a 'narty' or flighty woman, because she did not lose her natural high spirits, and used to sing and joke with the other female prisoners. The world was lost, and so was her lover, but she was still alive, and she carried within her a tender new life.

On 28th July, 1913, in the prison infirmary, Augusta gave birth to a healthy male child, and, on 12th August, by a compassionate ruling, he was allowed to be baptised at St David's Church, Allahabad Cantonment. The new Garrison Chaplain, Sydney A. Bill, performed the ceremony.

The father's name does not appear on the certificate of baptism; only Augusta Fairfield Fullam is designated as parent, with her abode given as Allahabad. The baby's Christian names were Lovell Harry William Goodwyn, and, set against Clark's Christian names—Henry Lovell William— Augusta is proclaiming, if not even celebrating, his fatherhood. There is something both defiant and wistful here, and for the first name she has chosen the most romantic: Lovell.

She nursed her baby devotedly through the hot summer, and he was a comfort to her, but the second summer, in 1914, was too much for her. The only relief from the baking heat that built up within the walls of a prison in the Plains was the portable hand-fan which was supplied to prisoners at that time. There was no servant to pull the swishing *punkah* that she was used to, no escape to the Hills, no evening airing in a phaeton.

On 28th May, 1914, Augusta Fairfield Fullam, aged 38, died of heat-stroke in the prison infirmary. It will have been thought a pretty poor show to lose her (the author is reliably informed), and Colonel Hudson will have been chagrined, but he was restricted by the conditions that prevailed.* The poetic justice

---

* Imprisonment in an Indian gaol was always an ordeal for a European woman. In 1931, a young Englishwoman, daughter of a missionary, and graduate of the University of London, who had married an Indian barrister but subsequently left him, harboured a terrorist involved in .n attempt to murder the Viceroy on 29th December, 1929, by blowing up the train which was taking him from

of the fatal illness which she herself had designed for her own husband was well remarked by the British community.

The following day, she was buried at Morris or Muir Road Cemetery, Allahabad (*not* with Clark in the military cemetery) by A. W. Douglas, Officiating Garrison Chaplain. And there, described as widow of the late E. M. Fullam, she lay with other, stranded widows and retired tradesmen.

Broken, no doubt, by the shame and the grief, Augusta's mother, Mary Augusta Goodwyn, lived on to die of heart-failure on 29th January, 1920, at the age of 79. She was buried the next day at the Lower Circular Road Cemetery, Calcutta, according to the rites of the Methodist Church, by George Henderson, Minister. In the same ground, her baby grand-daughter, Doris Goodwyn Fullam, had lain for twenty years before her.

It is pleasant to know that Kathleen overcame her lonely ordeal. A small heroine of the past, she emerged from the tunnel, and was, ever afterwards, a seeker of normality. Prosecuting counsel provides the link. Ross Alston had a daughter, who married a surgeon named Strother Smith. In 1970, she, the daughter, remembered that Kathleen 'married an Englishman in India and we came across her some fifteen years later when she came to see my husband to ask him to operate on a squint she had, which he did.' Augusta had tried to make use of Kathleen's 'very weak eyesight' during the trials...

Myrtle became a nurse. By 1935, she was Home, beseeching a firm of London solicitors to obtain proof of her birth and adoption, in order to satisfy the formalities before taking English examinations.

Calcutta to New Delhi. She was known to the C.I.D. in Allahabad, where she was then living, as 'The Mysterious Lady of the Flat'. When she was sentenced to two years' imprisonment, her previous husband, who had divorced her when she left him, but still loved her, could not bear the thought of her languishing in an Indian gaol, associating with criminal women. He wept when he was promised that she would be repatriated on her release, but, after only one year in prison, she died. This story is told in S. T. Hollins' *No Ten Commandments*.

Edward's name endured in Meerut. A namesake, Edward McKeon Fullam, son of William Arnold, was employed in the Military Accounts Department there—*the same office*—in the 1920s. This Edward is the nephew whose wedding Augusta probably attended in 1911. The information to support this assertion is shown on records for the death of his son, William Fullam, who succumbed to diphtheria on 29th October, 1927, at the age of seven and a half, and was buried the following day by the Catholic Chaplain, Monsignor Henry Norman.

Notorious criminal cases, in their aftermath, are often attended by the wildest fantasies. It was whispered that Clark had killed before. A tale even found its way into print that Augusta was released after eighteen months, married an official attached to one of the Romanian consulates in India, and took up residence in Bucharest.* How Augusta would have liked that!

Although the baby boy born in prison was said to have been 'adopted by some kind people',† his subsequent life was a well-kept secret. Indeed, the boy, and then the man, himself lived his whole life not knowing his origins. He wanted to know, but they would not tell him. What actually happened was that on 5th June, 1914, one week after Augusta's death, S. H. Fremantle, Collector‡ of Allahabad, arranged for the child to be taken by Miss D. Smidt, Assistant Matron, to an orphanage set high in the foothills of the Himalayas. Spurned by the relatives on all sides, he was to depend on the charity of strangers.

St Andrew's Colonial Homes, now Dr Graham's Homes, at Kalimpong, in Bengal, were founded in 1900 by John Anderson Graham (1861–1942), a Church of Scotland missionary. They began with six children in a rented cottage on a bare hillside, and have expanded to an impressive 'children's city'. Originally taking only destitute and underprivileged children of British descent, they now admit any child in need for whom they have room. Their ideals and achievements are outstanding.

* *Memories of a K.C.'s Clerk*, Francis Pearson.
† Walsh.
‡ An exalted member of the Indian Civil Service—chief administrator of a district.

Here, for his own sake, and most unusually, Lovell was baptised a second time, and his name was changed to Henry William Hope. Hope was the family name of Lord Linlithgow, Vice-Patron of the Homes. The baptism into the Church of Scotland was performed by Dr Graham himself, and all details of parentage on the certificate of baptism are marked 'unknown'.

Henry Hope did well at the Homes. He became fond of those who cared for him, and developed the strong drive to excel which is characteristic of the children of Kalimpong. Bravely, in 1927, at the age of fourteen, he travelled to England to join the training ship *Indefatigable*, to equip him for a career in the Merchant Navy. Although he could not have known that he was a pilot's grandson, the sea was evidently in his blood, because, in a homesick letter written *en route*, he announced, 'I am quite happy and I seem to have a liking for the sea.'

The boy from the Indian orphanage studied for his tickets and became a captain. During the Second World War, he served in the Australian, British, and American Merchant Services, carrying troops and supplies to England, New Guinea, and the Philippines. On the *Aorangi*, he evacuated women, children, and others, just before Singapore fell. On the *William Channing*, he was torpedoed by a Japanese submarine off the northern Australian coast. The ship went down, and, with it, the treasured telescope awarded to him for signalling when he was on the *Indefatigable*.

By a remarkable correspondence, if only he could have appreciated it, in March 1945, he, too, as his grandfather had done, survived a cyclone:

> With less than a day's oil left in her tanks, an Allied merchantman reached a North Queensland port on Thursday after a nightmarish experience in the Coral Sea. It required a stout ship and a stout-hearted crew to withstand the ordeal they had experienced, and the ship's master, Captain H. W. Hope, paid tribute to both his ship and his crew.'*

* A cutting from an Australian newspaper, probably printed in Townsville, northern Queensland, in the possession of the family.

In 1938, in Sydney, he had married, and in 1946 he settled in Australia and built up a successful and pioneering paint-manufacturing business. He had two sons and one daughter. Over the years, he wrote several times to the orphanage asking about his family history. In 1940, his old house-father, James Purdie, wrote to him:

> The Collector of Allahabad wrote to Dr Francis who was then acting for Dr Graham asking if you could be received at once as your mother had died suddenly, and that it was important that no information should be given. So far as I can gather one parent was Anglo-Indian and the other European, but of this I cannot be perfectly sure. I remember clearly your arrival at the Mission House and my lifting you out of the basket and carrying you into the house to show you off, for you were a lovely baby.

Henry William Hope died of a heart attack in 1975, at the age of 62, not displeased with what he had made of his life, but, in the words of James Purdie, 'still hankering after the knowledge sought'. If he had known, would he have lived differently? Would he still have chosen a life of adventure, or would he have denied his own active character in a neurotic seeking to understand, atone, and transcend? Perhaps it *was* better that he never realised the origins of the call of the restless sea that led him onwards. His children in Australia, adults now, with children of their own, distanced from the old tragedy, extremely proud of their father's achievements, are intrigued by all that they have learned of their own accord.

Wide-ranging genealogical research, together with a series of imaginative individual enquiries, followed by chance readings about the trials in contemporary Australian newspapers and then in Jonathan Goodman's *Posts-Mortem*, together with contact with J. H. H. Gaute (author, with Robin Odell, of *The Murderers' Who's Who*) and Jonathan Goodman himself, alerted them to their true background. It was a shock at first, naturally, but there were compensations. They were content to share a feeling of history, and a sense of belonging to a family.

It was Henry Hope's daughter who was especially affected by the discovery of her Indian heritage. Upon being told by her

brother, over the telephone, about his findings, she immediately had a 'past-life experience', in which she could, as it
were, inwardly see dusty streets, stone fort walls, flags, and a
large, official building. Under three sessions of regression,
later, she 'became' Augusta, and, it seemed to her, felt the pain,
and a peace at the end.

As part of the process of coming to terms with the
recognition that Augusta was her grandmother, and Clark her
grandfather, in October 1987, with her husband, she travelled
to India and visited Agra. There, at once, she recognised the
architectural styles and colours of the buildings and walls—
and the flags—materialised images which had crowded into
her mind many months before.

An Indian historian helped them to trace 9 Metcalfe
Road—now, since Independence, renamed General Cariappa
Road. Right at the end of the road in the cantonments, within
sight of the Taj Mahal, they found the old Agra Fort, its red
sandstone walls stretching into the distance. As they stood on
the bridge over the moat, they suddenly saw, engraved in the
stone, *Metcalfe Road*.

Houses decay rapidly in India, and the original building was
remodelled in 1956. In a corner, some yellowing outhouses
remained—probably the servants' quarters and cook-house
from which Augusta fetched Edward's last dinner. The owner
knew that a murder had been committed on the site, but he did
not know any details. He said that in one particular area,
people had a strange feeling. Every time that a woman lived
there, she fell gravely ill, and did not recover until she
moved away. An exorcism was planned.

The daughter and her husband wandered around the Agra
Cantonment Cemetery, where Edward and Louisa lay hidden.
The plots were laid out in a semblance of Home, but it was a
dry soil and these were alien plants. A pale cow blundered
along one of the hedged pathways.

On explaining their interest, they were allowed to look
around the Agra Club, now strictly for Indians only, a carefully
preserved time capsule with its billiards-room, stuffed tiger in a
glass case, and hunting trophies on the panelled walls.

In Allahabad, they located Naini Prison, a couple of miles
from the city, big and looming, set by yellow mustard-seed

crops, with its gloomy walls perhaps half a mile square. This, then, was the birthplace of Henry William Hope.

Finally, they made the difficult expedition up to the village near the small town of Kalimpong, where the Darjeeling tea grows all around on precipitous slopes. Her father had often spoken to her of the view of the snow-capped mountains, and, as the daughter stood where he had stood, she felt that she had found a place of perfect tranquillity, untouched by the world elsewhere.

# Bibliography

There is only one volume devoted to the case:

*The Agra Double Murder*, Sir Cecil Walsh, K.C. (Ernest Benn Ltd, 1929). Out of print, and virtually unobtainable. Naturally a dated account, with intrusive passages of moralising. Incomplete and fragmentary. But Walsh was a near-contemporary, he knew the Anglo-Indian community, he knew the devices of the Indian criminal, and his solitary book, with its shorter offshoots from other hands, has kept the affair alive. He himself was born in 1869 and died in 1946. Called to the English Bar, 1895. Puisne Judge, India, 1915–28. Other English publications: *Indian Village Crimes* (Benn, 1929) and *Crime in India* (Benn, 1930).

Short accounts appear in:

*The Stroke of Murder*, Winifred Duke (Robert Hale, 1937)
*Posts-Mortem*, Jonathan Goodman (David and Charles, 1971)
*Such Women are Deadly*, Leonard Gribble (John Long, 1965)
*Extraordinary Crimes*, John Laurence (Sampson Low, 1929)
*Memories of a K.C.'s Clerk*, Francis Pearson (Sampson Low, no date)
*Guilty or Not Guilty?* Guy Russell (Hutchinson, 1931)
*Poison Mysteries in History, Romance and Crime*, C. J. S. Thompson (The Scientific Press, 1923–5)

There is rumoured to exist, perhaps privately printed in India, an account entitled *The Fullam–Clark Murder Case*. The authorship of this volume is nowhere specified, and the most exhaustive enquiries both in Britain and in India have failed to turn up any record of such a work.

# Index

251